ART OF VERSIFICATION AND
TECHNICALITIES OF POETRY

ORTHOMETRY

THE ART OF VERSIFICATION AND THE TECHNICALITIES OF POETRY

WITH A NEW AND COMPLETE

RHYMING DICTIONARY

BY R. F. BREWER, B.A.

JOHN GRANT BOOKSELLERS LTD.
EDINBURGH: 31 GEORGE IV BRIDGE
LONDON: 39A WELBECK STREET, W.1
1962

EIGHTH REPRINT . . 1962

PRINTED IN GREAT BRITAIN BY
OLIVER AND BOYD LTD., EDINBURGH

PREFACE

THE chief aim of this book is to instruct. Those for whose use it is primarily designed, form that large and increasing number of the youth of both sexes, whose cultivated taste leads them to the study of our poets, and often, by original verse-making, to their imitation.

Although numerous works on Versification have been published of late years, the subject is treated in them, for the most part, in fragmentary fashion, rather than as a complete whole. Canons are laid down without adequate illustration, and generally with no discussion of principles. Other works, again, are too scholarly for general use, and are, in some cases, devoted to the elaboration of a pet theory. No one work, as far as I am aware, has yet been issued which embraces full and accurate information respecting the technicalities of poetry and verse-making, such as the student requires ; and to obtain which he has hitherto had to search through a number of separate authors.

In the preparation of this book, to impart sound and useful knowledge has been the aim rather than to parade originality, and therefore I have not scrupled, in some cases, to avail myself of the views, and even the expressions, of previous writers on the subject, whenever they seemed best suited to the purpose. Clear and simple exposition, logical arrangement, and copious illustration have been used throughout, while the student's interest in the subject is stimulated and increased by the intrinsic beauty of the selected examples.

Publishers of books and editors of serial literature have just cause of complaint at the onerous labour imposed upon them by the perusal of the mass of poetical composition continually submitted to them. The general public has no conception of the enormous quantity of material of this kind which is sentenced to oblivion every year by the high priests and princes of the Fourth Estate of the Realm, largely on account of the ignorance of the first principles of Orthometry displayed by the writers. If it were fully realised that *the only sure passport to success is good work,* this common dream of struggling into print by clinging to those whose very position compels them to sift the golden grain from the chaff, would cease to cause bitter disappointment. Indeed, the various agencies which profess to introduce amateur writers to the notice of editors and publishers can exist only by reason of an almost incredible amount of ignorance, in this respect, on the part of the public.

It can hardly be doubted that a correct knowledge of metrical laws, and the relative bearings and soundings of poetic breadth and depth, such as a careful perusal of a work of this kind affords, would tend to minimise this waste of effort, by diminishing the output, and improving the quality. It would, at least, accustom the beginner to the proper use of his *feet* before trusting himself to untried *wings*. As many an amateur actor has aspired to the rôle of Hamlet as his maiden effort, so the youthful poet oft dashes into the composition of an epic at the first motive impulse of the Muses. A preliminary course of Orthometry would doubtless save him a world of disappointment, by inducing him to try his 'prentice hand upon a ballad, say, a rondeau, or a sonnet. While it is not given to more than a dozen men in a century to create a poem that will live ages after them, pleasing and graceful verses may be produced by anyone who has the requisite taste, knowledge, and patience.

Again, I venture to look forward with expectancy to a more widespread appreciation of literary excellence in the near future. Culture is no longer the privilege of the wealthy. The study of our poets has now happily obtained a footing in the curriculum of nearly all our public schools and colleges; while the millions who attend our elementary schools have suitable poetic passages indelibly impressed upon their memory in youth. All but pessimists anticipate the good results of this early training upon the tastes and recreative pleasures of young England of the twentieth century. The horizon is already aglow, here and there, with promising indications of a brighter day. I fully trust and believe that this universal acquaintance in early life, be it ever so superficial, with noble thoughts and generous sentiments, clothed in choice language, will contribute in no small degree to the moral and intellectual development of the young democracy.

If by this treatise I have assisted, even to a slight degree, in the formation of a truer conception of good verse, fostered a liking for poetry generally, and enabled those who possess natural gifts for poetical composition to overcome the initial difficulties presented by the technicalities of their art, this 'labour of love' will not have been in vain.

I have now only to express my indebtedness to Mr. Robert D. Blackman for his many valuable suggestions embodied in the work.

R. F. B.

TABLE OF CONTENTS.

——◆——

ORTHOMETRY.

POETRY AND PROSE

POETRY differs from prose mainly in the fact that the words of the former are arranged upon a definite principle of order as to their sound. This principle has not been the same at all times and in all languages. Amongst the Greeks and Romans it was based upon *quantity*, *i.e.* the time occupied in pronouncing the syllables, those that are long taking up twice as much time as those that are short. In our own poetry the principle of arrangement is the regular recurrence of *accented and unaccented syllables;* the stress of the voice in uttering the accented ones occurring as regularly as the beats of the pulse or the ticks of a watch. The undulation of sound produced by this continuous flow of accents and non-accents is known as *rhythm*, and this it is which constitutes the essential difference between poetry and prose. Other elements, such as rhyme and alliteration, are employed, in some kinds of poetry, in the way of embellishment and aid to the rhythm, but they are not of its essence, for the larger part and the highest achievements of our poets are constructed without them.

The words of Dr. Guest may appropriately be quoted here.* He says : " Rhythm in its widest sense may be defined as the law of succession. It is the regulating principle of every *whole* that is made up of proportionate parts, and is as necessary to the regulation of motion, or to the arrangement of matter, as to the orderly succession of sounds. By applying it to the first of these purposes we have obtained the dance, and sculpture and architecture are the results of its application to the second. The rhythmical arrangement of sounds not articulated produces music, while from the like arrangement of articulate sounds we get the cadences of prose and the measures of verse. Verse may be defined as the succession of articulate sounds, regulated by a rhythm so definite that we can readily form the results which flow from its application. Rhythm is also met with in prose, but in the latter its range is so wide that we rarely can anticipate its flow, while the pleasure we derive from verse is founded on this very anticipation. As verse consists mainly of the arrangement of certain sounds according to a certain rhythm, it is obvious that neither poetry nor even *sense* can be essential to it. We may be alive to the beauty of a foreign rhythm though we do not understand the language, and the burden of many an English song has long yielded a certain plea-

* Dr. Guest's " History of English Rhythms."

sure though every whit as unmeaning as the non-sense verses of the schoolboy."

Besides this fundamental distinction between poetry and prose, which is all we are concerned with in dealing with versification, it seems desirable to trace briefly the lines that separate them still further. Without attempting the hazardous task of formulating a definition of poetry, we may say that, in its widest sense, poetry is creation or invention of ideal beauty.* Macaulay says of it : " By poetry we mean the art of employing words in such a manner as to produce illusion on the imagination—the art of doing by words what the painter does by means of colours."

Poetry is one of the Fine Arts ; it is indeed the queen of the Nine Sisters of the fabled family of the Muses ; her children are the myriad forms of the beautiful in sentiment and emotion which are scattered through the world's literature. It is the result " of a divinely bestowed faculty operating upon the infinite resources of nature, creating new forms of the beautiful by combinations of existing materials, through the aid of the imagination."

> The poet's eye, in fine frenzy rolling,
> Doth glance from heaven to earth, from earth to heaven ;
> And, as imagination bodies forth
> The forms of things unknown, the poet's pen
> Turns them to shapes, and gives to airy nothing
> A local habitation and a name.

* The Greek word for it is derived from the verb *to make*, as the French equivalent is from *to find ;* and in Lowland Scotch the poet is still *a maker.*

In this broad signification poetry is to be found embodied in the higher forms of prose quite as much as in verse. Creations of ideal grace and loveliness abound in amorphous prose, but as in that shape their dress lacks the wavy flow of rhythm, the designation of poetry is denied them. Frequently in impassioned prose there is, indeed, a perceptible rhythm which approaches very nearly the measured movement of verse. Many passages from George Eliot, Dickens, and Ruskin, for instance, not to mention others of the skilled masters in word-painting, might well be arranged as poetic lines. Yet, as metrical rules have not been observed in them throughout, as the cadences cease abruptly, they cannot be dignified by the name of poetry. The poet must always conform to metrical laws, while his brother artist only occasionally falls under their seductive influence.

Again, the two forms of literary composition differ with respect to their object; prose seeks for the most part to instruct, whereas the aim of the poet is to give pleasure. And here again we find the two frequently running upon parallel lines, the fictions of romance and the creations of the poet showing a marked family likeness which the presence or absence of rhythmical arrangement alone can differentiate.

In addition to these distinctions of form, matter, and aim, the style and *diction* of poetry differs in many respects from that of prose. Poetry should be " simple, sensuous, and passionate," said Milton; hence it chooses picturesque images and quaint words and epithets that would be out of place in prosaic description. Metaphors, similes, and indeed all the rhetorical figures of speech are freely used to variegate the conventionalities of everyday expressions, as the many-coloured blossoms of spring do the all-pervading sombre tints of winter. There are many words protected by poetic association from vulgar use, such as : *woe, ire, blissful, a-weary, haply, list, ken, methinks, morn* and *eve, thou* and *ye* for you. Striking epithets and picturesque compounds such as those that follow would disfigure good prose, while in verse they are pleasing and natural : *sea-girt* isle, *vasty deep,* the *breezy blue, air-built* castles, *rosy-fingered* dawn, the *iron tongue* of midnight. The poetic sentence is nervous, terse, and euphonious, and every kind of inversion, elision, and departure from ordinary rule is tolerated in order to make it so. Though bound to be musical, and to excite pleasure, the poet is a chartered libertine in most other respects.

In spite of the freedom of treatment necessary in dramatic composition, Shakspere maintains a clear distinction between poetry and prose. His servants and jesters always speak prose, and others also in light conversation, but the language of emotion and passion is invariably metrical. Brutus commences his famous speech to the populace after the murder of Cæsar in plain, direct prose ; but as soon as he begins to declaim and appeal to the feelings of his hearers, his words run into verse. The eloquent art of Antony's speech is metrical throughout.

KINDS OF POETRY.

THE earliest compositions in all languages were metrical. Long before the art of writing was invented, rude songs of war and love and hymns to the gods were composed in some rude form of measure or jingle that was catching to the ear, and handed down by tradition. We find bards or poets amongst all nations when emerging from a state of barbarism, whose duty it was to sing those traditional odes on great national, religious and athletic festivals, and to celebrate the achievements of their own heroes and the stirring events of the day in original compositions. In course of time these rude *lyrical* pieces were collected and committed to writing, with narrative verses interspersed, in order to give a unity to the collection; hence, in broad outline, the origin of the *Epic* poem. On national annual holidays the celebration of the deeds of past heroes in song, as well as the chanting of hymns to the gods, formed the chief feature of public gatherings. A rude stage was erected, and performers, fantastically dressed, and made up in some cases to heroic proportions, chanted these national odes in chorus. Gradually, in order to vary the entertainments, soliloquies and dialogues were introduced; here we have the dawn of the *drama*.

The different kinds of poetry may be briefly considered under the following heads :—

i.—LYRIC POETRY.

This is so called, because it was originally intended to be sung and accompanied on the lyre. We find some early specimens of it in the Old Testament, such as Miriam and Deborah's songs, and David's elegy on Saul and Jonathan. Lyric poetry comprehends several different kinds.

(a). THE ODE.

Ode is from a Greek word meaning song. The term ode, though generic, is restricted to lyrical compositions of some length and generally of complexity of structure, corresponding in some degree to the typical form of the Greek choral odes. These consisted of irregular stanzas, arranged in groups of three; the *strophe* to be chanted by one half of the singers, the *antistrophe* by the other half, and the *epode* by the whole. In our own language we have odes written upon a variety of subjects, heroic, sacred, moral, and amorous. Gray has composed some fine examples, adhering in one case strictly to the Greek model; but perhaps the finest specimen we have is Dryden's *Alexander's Feast*. Collins, Campbell, Shelley, Wordsworth, and Tennyson have produced almost equally noted poems of this class, but modern poets rarely adopt this form.

(*b*). THE BALLAD.

Ballads are distinguished from songs proper by the fact of their containing a narrative. Love and war are the two chief topics of our ballad literature, while pathos and humour also furnish abundant material for these stories in verse. *Chevy Chase*, the *Robin Hood* ballads, *John Gilpin*, *Lord Ullin's Daughter*, *Lucy Gray*, *Ben Battle*, *Nancy Bell*, may be mentioned as typical specimens.

(*c*). THE HYMN AND SONG.

The only difference between these is that the former is always upon some sacred subject. Each is generally nothing more than the expression of some single sentiment, or the elaboration of some one feeling. Ken, Heber, Watts, Cowper, Wesley, and Keble are the authors of some of our most beautiful hymns, while to enumerate our song-writers would be to name nearly every one of our poets. Nothing has surpassed the sweet melodic charm of the lyrics of the Shakspere—Milton period of our literature, though perhaps *Burns* and *Moore*, as song-writers, may be mentioned as approaching very nearly the same excellence.*

(*d*). THE ELEGY.

This differs from other odes in that its subject is always mournful and its construction generally

---

* For fuller particulars on this subject, see p. 217.

more regular. Milton's *Lycidas*, Gray's *Elegy written in a Country Churchyard*, Collins's *Dirge in Cymbeline*, Burns's *Man was made to Mourn*, and Tennyson's *In Memoriam* are the finest specimens we have.*

2.—EPIC OR HEROIC POETRY.

This term is applied only to great and lengthy narrative poems, in which the dramatic element is also introduced in the form of impassioned harangues, detailing some important national enterprise or the adventures of a distinguished hero. Homer's *Iliad* and *Odyssey*, Virgil's *Æneid*, Dante's *Inferno* and *Paradiso*, Tasso's *Jerusalem Delivered*, Camoens's *Lusiad*, and Milton's *Paradise Lost* and *Regained*, stand at the head of this species of poetry as the *Classical Epics*.

Scarcely inferior to these, and differing from them only in the fact that they depict less dignified undertakings, and which are fictitious, come such poems as Ariosto's *Orlando Furioso*, Spenser's *Faerie Queene*, and Tennyson's *Idylls of the King*. These may be classed under this head as *Romantic Epics*. Byron's *Childe Harold* may be included in the same category preferably to being considered a purely descriptive poem.

Another subdivision of poems of this class, but with still less of the heroic element in them, may, for want of a more suitable name, be grouped

* The reader is referred to Palgrave's " Golden Treasury of the Best Songs and Lyrical Poems in the English Language."

together as *Poetical Romances.* Scott's *Marmion* and *Lady of the Lake,* Moore's *Lalla Rookh,* Byron's *Don Juan,* Coleridge's *Christabel,* and Tennyson's *Enoch Arden* are of this kind; and if we allow the burlesque element to be added, such poems as Butler's *Hudibras* and Burns's *Tam O'Shanter* would be included.

3.—DRAMATIC POETRY.

" The very purpose of playing, both at the first and now, was, and is, to hold, as 'twere, the mirror up to nature; to show virtue her own feature, scorn her own image, and the very age and body of the time his form and pressure."

Shakspere.

The word drama means action, and the term dramatic poetry is applied to that species of composition which is made up of dialogue, and which is, for the most part, intended to be acted. All poems, however, which are thrown into the dramatic form, are not intended, or are not suited, to dramatic representation—*e.g.* Bailey's *Festus,* Taylor's *Philip Van Artevelde,* Byron's *Manfred,* could not be so produced intact ; and many of the plays of Shakspere are more suited to study than the stage, and require grievous hacking before they can be adapted to the requirements of the stage carpenter.

For the origin of the drama we must look to ancient Greece ; there, we have seen above, the germ of the theatre arose out of the national custom of singing odes in praise of gods and heroes on festive occasions, speech and action being gradually

introduced for variety and broadened requirements.

The word *Tragedy* (literally the goat-song) takes
its name from the fact that the actors who sang and
danced at these entertainments were dressed as
satyrs. *Comedy* (a festive or rural song) was originally applied to the coarse, comic verses, mixed
with extempore witticisms, which were indulged in
by bands of revellers at harvest homes and vintage
festivities. In course of time men of genius began
to avail themselves of the opportunities which the
recital of these crude verses afforded, and which no
other species of composition then presented for
national instruction, and we soon find plays more
regularly constructed and based upon an organised
plot. Under Æschylus, Sophocles, Euripides, and
Aristophanes, the drama was rapidly developed
and elaborated to its utmost perfection. Tragedy
was intended to excite the patriotic and heroic feelings of the audience, and to arouse its sympathy
and pity for devotion and suffering virtue. Comedy,
by its ridicule, turned the laugh of the hearers
against the foibles and vices of the time. The
difference between a Greek play and a modern one
will be clearly seen by comparing Milton's *Samson
Agonistes*, which is constructed upon the classic
model, with any of Shakspere's plays.

The *English Drama*, or, as it is called, the *Gothic*,
to distinguish it from the classic drama, came into
existence about the latter half of the sixteenth century. It grew out of the crude *Mysteries*, or miracle
plays, and *Moralities*, or moral plays, which we find

regularly represented at holiday times throughout Christendom about the end of the Middle Ages. They were produced all over Europe under the direction of the clergy as aids to religious and moral instruction. We see their survival down to the present day in the triennial representation of the *Passion Play* in the Bavarian village of Ober Ammergau. The former were coarse, and, to us, profane burlesques of Scripture narratives, the Deity Himself being frequently introduced; the latter consisted of quaint, comical dialogues, and frequently of furious disputes between characters personating abstract virtues and vices, the devil being the most important personage, as he always overcame the vices, and carried them off in triumph on his back or in a wheel-barrow at the finish.

Interludes occupy an intermediate place between the Moralities and the regular Comedy, as characters drawn from life were introduced. Heywood's *Four P's*, which we should consider a broad farce at the present day, may be taken as a fair specimen. The first comedy was *Ralph Roister Doister*, written by Nicholas Udall, master of Eton, about 1550, which was modelled after the Comedies of Terence; and this was followed a year or two later by *Gammer Gurton's Needle*, the work of John Still, bishop of Bath and Wells. The earliest known tragedy in English was *Gorbudoc, or Ferrex and Porrex*, the joint composition of Norton and Lord Buckhurst, which was represented in 1562, before Queen Elizabeth, at Whitehall. Within an amazing short time after this, Peele, Greene, Marlowe, and others, produced a large number of dramas, the tragedies of the last-named, in particular, being hardly inferior to his great successor's early efforts; and by 1590 Shakspere himself was at work as a playwright, and by him the drama was raised to the highest excellence ever attained.

In the Classic Drama (and the French theatre is constructed upon that model) what are called the *Unities* are preserved, *i.e.* a unity in time and place and dramatic action. This means that the scenes portrayed should occur in about the same time that is occupied in acting them on the stage, and in the same immediate neighbourhood, and that the tragic and comic elements be kept quite distinct. A tragedy must be tragic throughout, and a comedy more or less amusing throughout. These arbitrary and artificial limitations our great master of dramatic art declined to conform to; he depicted human nature as it is, and drew his characters with realistic truth from the living world around him, in which the sad and the joyous are ever found inextricably blended. The *Tempest* and the *Comedy of Errors* are the only plays in which the unity of time and place is preserved. Several of his comedies present a continuous panorama of happy, buoyant life; but in all his great tragedies the humorous is constantly found mingled with the dark and suffering side of humanity. The only distinction that can be drawn between his tragedies and comedies is that the former have mournful terminations, while the latter end happily.

4.—DESCRIPTIVE POETRY.

Description enters into every kind of poetical composition, but there are some poems almost wholly of that kind. To this class belong Drayton's *Polyolbion*, Pope's *Windsor Forest*, Denham's *Cooper's Hill*, Thomson's *Seasons*, Goldsmith's *Traveller* and *Deserted Village*, &c. Perhaps the choicest speci mens in the language are Milton's *L'Allegro* and *Il Penseroso*.

Pastoral is a species of descriptive poetry. It consists of descriptions of rural life and scenery, of the simplicity and loves of shepherd swains and village maids. It is rarely attempted by modern poets, perhaps because much of the charm and simplicity of country life has disappeared before the manifold invasions of commercial enterprise. Shenstone's *Pastoral Ballad* and Allan Ramsay's *Gentle Shepherd* are typical examples.

5.—DIDACTIC POETRY.

Under this head are included all poems the prime object of which, distinct from the conveyance of pleasure, is to instruct, whether in arts, morals, or philosophy. Tusser's *Hundred Points of Good Hus-bandrie*, Armstrong's *Art of Preserving Health*, Pope's *Essay on Criticism* and *Essay on Man*, Young's *Night Thoughts*, Blair's *Grave*, Akenside's *Pleasures of the Imagination*, and most of Cowper's poems are of this class. The finest didactic poem in English is Wordsworth's *Excursion*.

Satirical poetry is a species of didactic, as its

object is to improve manners and promote virtue
by depicting vice in its true colours, and by holding
up to ridicule hypocrisy and cant. Dryden, Pope,
Butler, Dean Swift, Burns, Byron, Tom Hood, and
Robert Buchanan are our most famous satirists in
verse.

6.—THE SONNET.
(See page 203.*)*

7.—THE EPIGRAM.

This is a short poem on some single thought,
brevity and wit being its essentials, the point
generally coming at the end, *e.g. :*

On an M.P. who wrote a severe critique on " The Pleasures
of Memory.'

> They say he has no heart, but I deny it ;
> He has a heart—and gets his speeches by it.

On a Curate's Eyes.

> My daughters praise our curate's eyes—
> I know not if their light's divine,
> For when he prays he closes his,
> And when he preaches I shut mine.

The *Epitaph* is a species of epigram, designed
to eulogise or satirise some defunct individual, and
as the name implies is supposed to be inscribed on
his tomb, *e.g. :*

> Here lie the bones of Robert Lowe,
> Where he's gone to I don't know ;
> If to the realms of peace and love,
> Farewell to happiness above ;
> If haply to some lower level,
> We can't congratulate the devil

ELEMENTARY PARTS OF ENGLISH VERSE.

ΓHE elements of verse are *syllables*, which grouped together in twos or threes form *feet*, and these in combination form *verses* or lines. As verses are made for articulate utterance, their effect on the ear is of the first importance, and to produce a good effect the smallest parts which enter into their composition should receive attention. The elementary sounds of the language, therefore, claim our first consideration as to whether they are rough or smooth, easy or difficult in utterance, and in combination with other sounds. And thus we are called upon to review in brief the defects and anomalies of our *alphabet.*

1.—SOUNDS.

The spoken alphabet of English consists of forty-five sounds, to represent which we have only twenty-six written characters or letters, and of these three, viz. *c, q,* and *x* are redundant. The deficiency is made up by making one letter stand for several different sounds, and by giving combinations of letters only one sound. Without going into details which are foreign to our purpose here, we will reproduce first

Mr. Morris's list of *Elementary Sounds in the English spoken Alphabet.*

(a) Consonants.					
1	b	9	m	17	y
2	d	10	n	18	z
3	t	11	p	19	ch
4	g	12	r	20	th (bathe)
5	h	13	s	21	th (bath)
6	j	14	t	22	zh (azure)
7	k	15	v	23	sh (sure)
8	l	16	w	24	hw (what)

To these should be added the nasal *ng*

(b) Vowels.					
25	a	in gnat	32	e	in meet
26	a	pair, ware	33	i	,, knit
27	a	fame	34	o	,, not
28	a	father	35	o	,, note
29	a	all	36	oo	,, foot, rule
30	a	want	37	oo	,, wood, put
31	e	met	38	u	,, nut

(c) Diphthongs.		
39	i	in high
40	i	,, aye
41	oi	,, boil
42	ow	,, how, bound
43	eu	,, new

The sounds of the *vowels* and *diphthongs* are produced by the uninterrupted passage of the breath through the open mouth, and the predominance of these sounds renders speech easy and musical. The *consonant* sounds are the result of the more or less complete stoppage of the breath in utterance by the partial or entire closing of the air passage by one or other of the organs of speech, and it is the degree of effort to produce these imperfect sounds that causes that harshness and roughness which renders speech difficult and unmusical. We will next present an arrangement of the consonants which exhibits them in what may be regarded as the order of their discordance.

The *liquids*, *l, m, n, r,* easily combine with other sounds.

The *sibillants*, *s, z, j, x, vp, sh, zh,* have varying degrees of a disagreeable hiss.

The *mutes* are the most difficult of all in utterance, as they completely close the air passage. They are classed according to the organ of speech by which they are produced into—

> *Labials* (lip sounds) *p, b, f, v.*
> *Dentals* (tooth sounds) *t, d, th, dh.*
> *Gutturals* (throat sounds) *k, g.*

It may here be pointed out that the rules of English prosody and rhyme are not applicable to the language as it appears in writing, but as it is heard in pronunciation. Our language so considered is not inferior to others ; its elementary sounds, both in variety and number, are adequate to all our occasions.

All the elements enumerated above have their distinguishing qualities of smooth, rough, soft, strong, close, open, clear, obscure, and others, by which they give a corresponding character to the sound of a verse, and furnish opportunities of assimilating sound to sense of which our poets have freely availed themselves.* The comparison between the English tongue and others, as to metrical elements, given in the following passage, will, perhaps, entertain the reader. It is taken from Steele's "Prosodia Rationalis," page 168. "In English the proportion of monosyllables to polysyllables is more than as five to two ; in French, something less than as three to two ; but in Italian, which, having more vowels, has less occasion for monosyllables, their proportion to polysyllables is not quite three to four, or one and a half to two. The superior melody of one language over another will be nearly in proportion as one exceeds the other in the number of vowel sounds. The number of vowel and consonantal sounds in Italian is nearly equal ; in Latin, five consonants to four vowels; in French, supposing the orthography not as written, but as sounded in pronunciation, the consonantal to the vocal sounds are as four to three ; and in English, in the like manner, the proportion is three to two. Therefore, in this view, the French has an advantage over the English in the proportion of nine to eight; but this is overbalanced by the English

* See " Imitative Harmony," p. 269.

advantage in its monosyllables, which it has more than the French in the proportion of five to three."

No single element in a man's native tongue is of difficult pronunciation to him whose organs of speech are naturally perfect ; in a foreign language there may be such, as the Welsh and German gutturals, and the French *u*, to an Englishman. But there are various combinations, either difficult to utter, or unpleasant to hear, and others again of an opposite character, with all of which it is useful for every writer to be acquainted. The maker of verse, who has command of his language, will not feel himself much cramped by these combinations ; some few there may be which are unmanageable : such is that made by the second person singular of the past tense, in verbs ending with a double consonant : as touch, touchedst.*

Let it not be thought degrading to any composer of English verse to attend to the power and effect of these elementary sounds, since Bacon has recommended an inquiry into the nature of language for purposes of the same kind, nor accounted it beneath him to record in his works that we cannot pronounce the letter *t* after *m*, without inserting *p*, as a circumstance worthy of notice. Ex. empty, Hampton.

2.—SYLLABLES.

A syllable is a word, or a part of a word, uttered by one effort of some of the organs of speech. It may be one elementary sound, or a combination

* See " Poetic Licenses," p. 108.

of several. Like its elements, it is rough, smooth,
harsh, easy, or difficult in utterance. But there
are other qualities of syllables which claim our
special attention and demand clear elucidation,
inasmuch as they constitute the very essence of
verse; these are *accent* and *quantity*.

(*a*). ACCENT.

is a certain *stress* of the voice upon a syllable in
pronouncing it. Every word of more than one
syllable has an accent invariably attached to one
of its syllables which is called the *tonic accent*, and
no word, however long, has more than one accent,
e.g. deplóre, térrible, eleméntary. Monosyllables
are accented or not according to their grammatical
importance; thus all nouns, verbs, adjectives, and
adverbs are accented, while the articles, prepositions, pronouns (when not emphatic), and particles
are unaccented. We shall see as we proceed that
the exigencies of metre require that *metrical accents*
be attached to syllables in verse in addition to the
tonic accent, and that the stress occasionally varies
in degree, *e.g.* :

Swéét are the úses of advérsity.

The precise nature of accent has given rise to
diversity of opinion; some maintaining that it is an
alteration in the *pitch* of the voice, others an increase
in *loudness* of tone; we will content ourselves, however, with regarding it as *stress* merely, as is now
generally accepted

(*b*). QUANTITY.

is the time occupied in pronouncing a syllable, one *long* syllable being considered equivalent to two *short* ones. This division into two classes has been deemed sufficient for all the purposes of prosody; though it is certain that in neither class are the syllables all equal among themselves, as will appear when we have stated what is allowed to constitute a short and a long syllable.

(i) A short vowel when alone, or when no consonant follows it, is taken for a short syllable, as the articles a, the.

(ii) A short vowel, when followed by a single consonant, is a short syllable, as, man, pen; or by the same consonant doubled, as, manner, penny.

(iii) A short vowel, in some cases, when followed by two consonants, makes a short syllable, as, decline, reprove, at last. For this we have the example of the ancients both in Greek and Latin, who permitted a short vowel to stand for a short syllable, though followed by two consonants, if the first was a mute and the second a liquid. The cause is founded in nature; and therefore holds with us; it is, that such a combination of consonants is more readily pronounced than others are.

A syllable is long—

(i) When it contains a long vowel, or a diphthong, as, see, go, loud, joy.

(ii) When it consists of a short vowel followed by two different consonants, if they be not a mute and a liquid; as, into, number. Such a syllable is called long by position.

The ancients, by whose authority we are guided
in this arrangement of syllables, allowed a short
vowel before a mute and liquid, to make the syllable
either short or long : in that point, therefore, they
fixed the boundary between them. The reason why
such a syllable might be accounted short, was because the mute and liquid could be pronounced more
readily than two other consonants in their place. It
follows then that the same vowel before two other
consonants would make a syllable requiring more
time in the utterance ; which, of course, must be
ranked together with the long. When it is recollected
that every letter is formed by a particular position
of the organs of speech, and each different letter by
a different position, it is certain that some time is
employed in passing from one to another.

The RHYTHM of English verse, as has been already
pointed out, is based upon *accent*, the measured undulation of accented and unaccented syllables being
its essential feature, without which it becomes
mere prose. On the other hand the rhythm of
classical verse is based upon *quantity*, which in
Latin and Greek poetry is governed by much more
rigid laws than the metrical rules of English verse.
Much learned nonsense has been written upon this
subject, and many attempts have been made to show
that quantity and not accent is of the essence of
English verse, but all recent scholarship and
taste concur in the view stated above ; and we
may regard the controversy as finally settled. It
would be almost equally wrong, however, to hold
the opposite view, and regard quantity as having

no bearing upon our versification. It is an important aid to metrical perfection, and is sedulously cultivated by all our poets as an embellishment, though not as the foundation of rhythm. Verses in which the proportion of long syllables in the accented parts of the feet predominate, produce quite a different melody from others in which short syllables obtain. The following extracts from Milton's *L'Allegro* and *Il Penseroso* admirably illustrate this.

(i) Long quantity predominant—

> Come, pensive Nun, devout and pure.
> Sober, steadfast, and demure ;
> All in a robe of darkest grain,
> Flowing with majestic train,
> And sable stole of Cyprus lawn
> Over thy decent shoulders drawn

(ii) Short quantity predominant—

> Hast thee, nymph, and bring with thee
> Jest and youthful jollity.
>   *   *   *   *
> Sport that wrinkled Care derides,
> And laughter, holding both his sides.
> Come and trip it as you go
> On the light fantastic toe.
> And in thy right hand lead with thee
> The mountain nymph, sweet Liberty.

We see then that syllables have a fourfold difference ; some are long, either accented, as, *holy*, or unaccented, as, *consent ;* others are short, either accented, as, *refer*, or unaccented, as, *habit*.

There are some who will think these observations on quantity might have been spared, because they maintain that quantity has no concern whatever with English versification, but that it depends entirely upon accent. Rather let it be said that quantity cannot be altogether neglected without manifest and great injury to the verse. But if the question be put, whether verse cannot be composed without any regard to the quantity of syllables, so that the accents be set in their due places, it is to be acknowledged that it may. Still the verse would have juster measure, would sound better to the ear, and be much nearer to perfect, if the accented syllables were long and others short ; so that the quantity and accent should coincide. Let us make this still clearer by an example—

The busy world and what you see,
It is a silly vanity.

Of this couplet the first line has its accents regular in place and number, together with three long syllables. The second line is accented regularly as to place, but it contains only two accented syllables, and not one long. It cannot be denied that these verses are in true and exact measure ; and, if accent alone be requisite, they are in nothing defective. But now let them be altered, so as to observe quantity as well as accent, in this manner—

> The gaudy world, whate'er you see,
> Is all an empty show to me.

It does not require a nice ear to perceive the difference of these lines from the former, nor any
great skill to form a right judgment between them
in respect of their structure, which is the only
point, at this time, under consideration.

Regard to quantity is not indeed essential to
English verse; neither is symmetry nor proportion
essential to a dwelling-house: but to a good dwelling-house they are essential, and so is regard to
quantity to good English verse.

This, however, was a matter to which Pope, at
least in his early life, appears to have been insen-
sible or inattentive, if the following anecdote be
true. The second line of his first pastoral stood
originally thus—

> Nor blush to sport on Windsor's *peaceful* plains.

He would have altered it to *happy ;* but Walsh
objected to that correction, saying the quantity
would not then be the same ; for the first syllable
of *happy* was short; Pope therefore put *blissful.**
Here are other examples of the effect of long syllables worthy of quotation—

> The waves behind impel the waves before,
> Wide-rolling, foaming high, and tumbling on the shore.
> > *Pope.*

* Boswell on Shakspere's Metre.

Thou dost preserve the stars from wrong ;
And the most ancient heavens through thee are fresh and
    strong.

Wordsworth.

3.—FEET.

The unit of measurement in verse is a foot and
not a syllable. A *foot* is a group of two or three
syllables, hence the division into *Dissyllabic* and
Trisyllabic verse. The names given to the different
kinds of feet in English poetry are usually those of
the classic metres, and the method of marking the
accented and unaccented syllables is from the same
source. Many writers have objected to this
system of nomenclature as liable to mislead,
and have invented other fanciful names in their
stead, but none of these have met with general ac-
ceptance. Throughout this treatise, therefore, we
shall adhere to the old lines in this respect, with
every confidence that no confusion can arise, since
the distinction between accent and quantity has
been clearly pointed out ; thus the usual marks for
long and short (- ‿) must be taken to indicate
accented and unaccented syllables.

(*a*). DISSYLLABIC.

There are two kinds of *Dissyllabic* feet of which
verse is constructed, viz.: *Iambus* ‿ -, as děspaīr,
and *Trochee*, - ‿, as tēmplě. In addition to these
there are two other kinds in frequent use intermixed
with the above, but of which it is impossible to construct verses entirely: viz. *Spondee* - -, and
Pyrrhic ‿ ‿.

(*b*). TRISYLLABIC.

Of *Trisyllabic* feet there are also only two kinds
of which whole poems are composed : *Anapest*,
⌣ ⌣ -, as sĕrĕnāde, and *Dactyl*, - ⌣ ⌣, as
trēmŭloŭs. Another kind occasionally met with is
called *Amphibrach*, ⌣ - ⌣.

We might have omitted all mention of the *Amphibrach* but for the mistake of certain prosodians
who, finding such a foot at the end of a verse, have
asserted that the same kind of foot properly constituted the whole verse, and was the legitimate
measure by which it was to be scanned.

The following line from Swift is an example of
the measure in question :—

Bĕcāuse | hĕ hăs nēv | ĕr ă hānd | thăt ĭs ĭ | dlĕ.

Here, it is true, the three last syllables make the
foot termed *Amphibrach*, and the whole line may
be divided into such feet as shown below—

Bĕcaûse hĕ | hăs nevĕr | ă hand thăt | ĭs īdlĕ |

It is nevertheless certain that the line belongs
to verses of another class, and is measurable by
anapests, only taking such a licence as is always
allowed to anapestic verses, viz. that the first foot
may be truncated or curtailed of its first syllable.
The next line in the poem, to describe it accurately,
is an anapestic verse of four feet, with a redundant
syllable :—

Fŏr thĕ rīght | hŏlds thĕ swōrd, | ănd thĕ lĕft | hŏlds thĕ brĭ | dle.

So likewise is the former, notwithstanding the difference in the first foot. If the *Amphibrach* had been a foot by which any English verse ought to be measured, there would have been entire poems in that measure, or, at least, poems wherein verses of that measure predominate ; but there are none such, nor does a line, measurable by that foot, ever occur, except accidentally among a much greater number of anapestic ones.

The following table exhibits at a glance the various feet of which English verse is composed, and also those which enter occasionally of necessity and for variety into its construction.

Name of Foot.	Accents.	Name of Metre.
Iambus	⌣ –	Iambic.
Trochee	– ⌣	Trochaic.
Anapest	⌣ ⌣ –	Anapestic.
Dactyl	– ⌣ ⌣	Dactylic.

OCCASIONAL FEET

Spondee	– –	
Pyrrhic	⌣ ⌣	
Amphibrach	⌣ – ⌣	*

* Some metrists recognise another trisyllabic foot occasionally in scanning blank verse, the *Tribrach,* ⌣ ⌣ ⌣, but this is vigorously contested by others.

MEASURES OF VERSE.

EACH of the four kinds of feet enumerated above may be combined in varying numbers according to the taste and fancy of the 'maker,' and the requirements of the metrical effects sought to be produced. The number of feet in each verse may vary from one to eight, and they are generally known as Monometer, Dimeter, &c., as enumerated in the following table:

(1)	Monometer	verse of one foot.
(2)	Dimeter	verse of two feet.
(3)	Trimeter	verse of three feet.
(4)	Tetrameter	verse of four feet.
(5)	Pentameter	verse of five feet.
(6)	Hexameter	verse of six feet.
(7)	Heptameter	verse of seven feet.
(8)	Octameter	verse of eight feet.

1.—IAMBIC MEASURE.

Most English poetry, probably as much as five-sixths of the whole, is in Iambic measure. All our Heroic, Blank and Dramatic verse, in fact all the lengthy poems of our tongue are of this order. This is no doubt due to the structural peculiarities of our language. English, as compared with other tongues, is non-inflectional; there are no case endings to its nouns, nor elaborate terminations to the moods and tenses of its verbs. And although the great majority of words of more than two syllables have their accent to the fore, the very frequent recurrence of unaccented articles, prepositions, and auxiliaries preceding the emphatic nouns and verbs tends to impart an Iambic measure to English speech.

(*a*). IAMBIC MONOMETER.

Normal line, Two Syllables ⌣ – .

This measure is seldom used except as furnishing refrains in lyric poems. The example quoted below from Herrick can only be regarded as a literary curiosity.

> She has a bosom white as snow ;
> > *Take care !*
> She knows how much it is best to show ;
> > *Beware !*
> Trust her not, she is fooling thee.
> > > > *Longfellow.*

> Thus I
> Pass by,
> And die
> As one
> Unknown
> And gone.

I'm made
A shade,
And laid
I' th' grave ;
There have
My cave,
Where tell
I dwell.
Farewell.

Herrick.

All regular measures of verse, as will be more fully explained in dealing with poetical licence, have occasionally an additional unaccented syllable added. This is usually called a *feminine ending,* and the verse is said to be *hypermetrical,* *e.g.* :

Heărts bĕat | ĭng
At meet | ing.
Tears start | ing
At part | ing.

(*b*). IAMBIC DIMETER.

Normal line, Four Syllables ⌣ – | ⌣ –.

This verse is also too short for whole poems, but is freely introduced in odes, songs, &c., *e.g.* :

Wĭth răv | ĭshed eărs
The mon | arch hears,
Assumes | the god,
Affects | the nod.

Dryden.

If thou | hadst not
Been true | to me,
But left | me free,
I had | forgot
Myself | and thee.

Jonson.

> I feel | like one
> Who treads | alone
> Some banquet hall deserted,
> Whose lights | are fled,
> Whose gar | lands dead,
> And all but he departed.
>
> *Moore.*

> The rag | ing rocks
> And shiv | 'ring shocks
> Shall break | the locks
> Of pri | son gates,
> And Phib | bus' car
> Shall shine | from far,
> And make | and mar
> The fool | ish fates.
>
> *Shakspere.*
> " Mid-Night's Dream.'

> The poet in a golden clime was born,
> With gold | en stars | above,
> Dowered with the hate of hate, the scorn of scorn,
> The love | of love.
>
> *Tennyson.*

In the last example, from Tennyson's *The Poet*, the second verse is Iambic trimeter, the fourth dimeter.

(c). IAMBIC TRIMETER.

Normal line, Six Syllables ⌣ – | ⌣ – | ⌣ – .

This measure is greatly used by our poets in the composition of ballads and hymns ; when it is attended with Iambic tetrameter it constitutes our *Ballad metre* and the *Common metre* of hymns.

> Have mer | cy, Lord, | on me,
> As thou | wert ev | er kind ;
> Let me opprest with loads of guilt
> Thy wont | ed mer | cy find.

D

Aloft | in aw | ful state
The god | like he | ro sate
On his | imper | ial throne.

Dryden.

The mon | arch saw | and shook,
    And bade | no more | rejoice ;
All blood | less waxed | his look,
    And trem | ulous | his voice.

Byron.

Shakspere seems to have used this measure
mostly for rapid dialogue and retort, as in the
Ghost-scene in Hamlet :—

> *Ghost.* To what I shall unfold.
> *Hamlet.*   Speak, I am bound to hear.[*]

(*d*). IAMBIC TETRAMETER.

Normal line, Eigh Syllables ⌣ – | ⌣ – | – | ⌣ – .

This octosyllabic measure, which is of dangerously easy construction, and very apt to degenerate
into sing-song, has been largely used by our poets
of later times.   In it are composed Butler's *Hudibras*, Scott's *Marmion*, &c., Burns's *Tam O'Shanter*,
Tennyson's *In Memoriam*, and numerous poems
by Shelley, Byron, Wordsworth, Coleridge, &c.

O la | dy, twine | no wreath | for me,
Or twine | it of | the cy | press tree.

Scott.

By fairy hands their knell is rung,
By forms unseen their dirge is sung ;

---

[*] Abbott's " Shaksperian Grammar," p. 405.

There Honour comes, a pilgrim grey,
To bless the turf that wraps their clay ;
And Freedom shall a while repair,
And dwell, a weeping hermit there.
Collins

Some have been beaten till they know
What wood a cudgel's of by th' blow,
Some kicked until they can feel wheth | er
A shoe be Spanish or neat's leath | er.
Butler.

So find I every pleasant spot
   In which we two were wont to meet,
   The field, the chamber, and the street,
For all is dark where thou art not.
      *   *   *
Ring out the old, ring in the new,
   Ring happy bells across the snow ;
   The year is going, let him go ;
Ring out the false, ring in the true.
Tennyson.
" In Memoriam."

Of the *Ballad metre*, the following examples will
suffice :

They followed from the snowy bank
   Those footmarks one by one,
Into the middle of the plank—
   And further there was none.
Wordsworth.

I am the Rider of the wind,
   The Stirrer of the storm ;
The hurricane I left behind
   Is yet with lightning warm.
Byron.

(*e*). IAMBIC PENTAMETER.

Normal line, Ten Syllables

$$\smile - \mid \smile - \mid \smile - \mid \smile - \mid \smile - .$$

This when rhymed is known as the *Herou Measure* of English poetry. It was much used by Chaucer, Dryden, Pope, Goldsmith, Keats, and Southey, and is perhaps the most frequently used of any English metre. Pope rendered it somewhat monotonous by over-refinement, and by making his pauses occur too frequently in the middle of the verse and his sentences terminate at the end of the line. It is, however, a noble metre, and its rhythm is capable of infinite variation.

> Great wits | are sure | to mad | ness near | allied,
> And thin | parti | tions do | their bounds | divide.
> > *Dryden.*

> All nature is but art unknown to thee ;
> All chance, direction which thou canst not see ;
> All discord, harmony not understood ;
> All partial evil, universal good.
> > *Pope.*

> How commentators each dark passage shun,
> And hold their farthing candle to the sun.
> > *Young.*

> And as a child, when scaring sounds molest,
> Clings close and closer to his mother's breast,
> So the loud torrent and the whirlwind's roar
> But bind him to his native mountains more.
> > *Goldsmith.*

Four heroics rhyming alternately form the *Elegiac stanza, e.g.:*

Full many a gem of purest ray serene
The dark unfathomed caves of ocean bear;
Full many a flower is born to blush unseen,
And waste its sweetness on the desert air.

Gray.

Iambic pentameter unrhymed is the famous *Blank verse* of literature (*see page* 184).

(*f.*) IAMBIC HEXAMETER.

Normal line, Twelve Syllables

◡ – | ◡ – | ◡ – | ◡ – | ◡ – | ◡ –.

This measure has been seldom used by our poets since Drayton composed his *Polyolbion* in it in 1610. From an old French poem written in this measure detailing the deeds of Alexander the Great, verses of this dimension are known as *Alexandrines*, and are seldom used except with pentameters to vary the monotony of their rhythm. A notable instance of this is in the use of an Alexandrine to form the ninth line of the *Spenserian stanza.*

A needless Alexandrine ends the song,
Which like | a wound | ed snake | drags its | slow length | along. *Pope.*

An hundred valiant men had this brave Robin Hood,
Still ready at his call, that bowmen were right good,
All clad in Lincoln green, with caps of red and blue,
His fellow's winded horn, not one of them but knew.

Drayton.

When spring unlocks the flowers to paint the laughing soil,
When summer's balmy showers refresh the mower's toil.

Heber.

Thou glorious mirror, where the Almighty's form
   Glasses itself in tempests ; in all time,
Calm or convulsed, in breeze, or gale, or storm,
   Icing the pole, or in the torrid clime ;
Dark, heaving, boundless, endless, and sublime,
The image of eternity, the throne
   Of the Invisible ; even from out thy slime
The monsters of the deep are made ; each zone
O | beys thee ; | thou go | est forth, | dread, fath | omless, |
   alone.

                                 Byron.

  Note the additional syllable at the beginning of
this last Alexandrine.

(*g*). IAMBIC HEPTAMETER.

Normal line, Fourteen Syllables

⌣ – | ⌣ – | ⌣ – | ⌣ – | ⌣ – | ⌣ – | ⌣ – .

  The longest poems in this measure is Chapman's
translation of the *Iliad ;* Macaulay's *Lays of Ancient
Rome*, and Tennyson's *May Queen*, furnish recent
specimens. The verses of it are sometimes broken
up and printed in alternate four and three feet
Iambics, thus forming Ballad metre.

And none | will grieve | when I | go forth, | or smile | when I
   return,
Or sit | beside | the old | man's bed, | or weep | upon | his urn.
                               Macaulay.

There's not a flower on all the hills ; the frost is on the pane ;
I only wish to live till the snowdrops come again.
I wish the snow would melt, and the sun come out on high ;
I long to see a flower so before the day I die.
                               Tennyson.

No marvel that the lady wept, it was the land of France,
The chosen home of chivalry, the garden of romance.
                                                  Bell.

(*h*). IAMBIC OCTAMETER.

Normal line, Sixteen Syllables

⏑ – | ⏑ – | ⏑ – | ⏑ – | ⏑ – | ⏑ – | ⏑ – | ⏑ – .

This metre is very rare. Webbe, in his " Discourse of Poetry," says, " The longest verse which
I have seen used in English consisteth of sixteen
syllables, each two verses rhyming together ; thus—

' Where virtue wants and vice abounds, there wealth is but a
    baited hook,
To make men swallow down their bane, before on danger deep
    they look.' "

This species, therefore, did once exist, in form and
show, as a single verse ; but, in fact, it was two ;
" for," says he, " it is commonly divided each verse
into two, whereof each shall contain eight syllables,
and rhyme crosswise, the first to the third, and
the second to the fourth," forming the *Long metre*
of our psalms.

        When in the night I sleepless lie,
        My soul with heavenly thoughts supply ;
        Let no ill dreams disturb my rest,
        No powers of darkness me molest.
                                        Ken.

A few modern specimens of it may be seen in
the poems of Owen Meredith.

2.—TROCHAIC MEASURE.

The rhythm of Trochaic verse has a distinctive flow from that of Iambic ; it is more sprightly and lively, and therefore suited for the dress of cheerful themes and the description of quick-moving action. Milton's *L'Allegro*—the cheerful man—is written for the most part in this measure, while the sombre *Il Penseroso* is mostly Iambic. It is often called the Tripping measure.

(*a*). TROCHAIC MONOMETER.

Normal line, Two Syllables $-\smile$.

This one-foot verse is only met with mixed with longer verses, *e.g* :

> Crying,
> Sighing,
> Whining,
> Pining,
> Is the lover's part.

> Through all the mazes of the grove,
> Through all the mingling tracks I rove,
> Turning,
> Burning,
> Changing,
> Ranging,
> Full of grief and full of love.
>
> *Addison.*

(*b*). TROCHAIC DIMETER.

Normal line, Four Syllables $-\smile- \mid \smile$.

> Rĭch thĕ | trēasŭre,
> Swēet thĕ | plēasŭre,
> Sweet is pleasure after pain.
>
> *Dryden.*

> Hope is banished,
> Joys are vanished,
> Damon, my beloved, is gone !
>
> *Dryden.*

It is difficult, if not almost impossible, to find suitable specimens of exact verses in all the trochaic measures, because our poets avail themselves so freely of licences. It has been already pointed out that extra unaccented syllables are frequently used at the end of a verse, making it *hypermetrical ;* it is now necessary to add farther that an additional unaccented syllable is allowed before the first foot of a trochaic line, to which the term *anacrusis* has been applied, *e.g. :*

> Thĕ | Quēen wăs | ĭn thĕ | gārdĕn.

Besides this, *truncated lines*, as they are called, are frequently met with, *i.e.* verses shorn of their last unaccented syllables, *e.g. :*

> Dreadful | gleams,
> Dismal | screams,
> Fires that | glow,
> Shrieks of | woe,
> Sullen | moans,
> Hollow | groans.
>
> *Pope.*

Gray's Liliputian ode is almost entirely in this diminutive metre.

> In a maze,
> Lost, I gaze
> Can our eyes
> Reach thy size ?

May my lays
Swell with praise
Worthy thee,
Worthy me !

(c). TROCHAIC TRIMETER.

Normal line, Six Syllables — ⌣ | — ⌣ | — ⌣.

Nearly all verses in this measure are truncated in the last foot. In the annexed passage from *The Passionate Pilgrim*, only the 2nd, 3rd, and 6th verses are perfectly symmetrical.

Crăbbĕd | āge ănd | yōuth
Cānnŏt | līve tŏ | gēthĕr ;
Youth is | full of | pleasance,
Age is | full of | care ;
Youth like | summer | morn,
Age like | winter | weather ;
Youth like | summer | brave,
Age like | winter | bare ;
Youth is | full of | sport,
Age's | breath is | short.

Shakspere.

Tennyson's *Maud* furnishes an example of twenty· eight consecutive lines of the same measure :—

Go not, happy day,
　From the shining fields ;
Go not, happy day,
　Till the maiden yields
Rosy is the west,
　Rosy is the south,
Rosy are her cheeks,
　And a rose her mouth.

Tennyson.

A beautiful combination of verses of this kind but slightly varying is seen in Shelley's *Prometheus*.

> In the world unknown,
> Sleeps a voice unspoken ;
> By thy stop alone,
> Can its rest be broken,
>   Child of ocean ?
>
> *Shelley.*

Again—

> Now the day is over,
>   Night is drawing nigh ;
> Shadows of the evening
>   Steal across the sky.
>
> *Baring Goula*

> Fill the bumper fair !
>   Every drop we sprinkle
> On the brow of care
>   Smoothes away a wrinkle.
>
> *Moore.*

(*d*). TROCHAIC TETRAMETER.

Normal line, Eight Syllables $- \smile | - \smile | - \smile | - \smile$.

This measure is sufficiently lengthy for continuous composition, and seems to be a favourite with all our modern poets. Longfellow's *Hiawatha*, a poem of upwards of five thousand lines, is composed in it in unrhymed verse. Tennyson and Shelley also furnish numerous examples, chiefly with symmetrical and truncated verses intermingled.

Whȳ sŏ | pāle ănd | wăn, fŏnd | lovĕr,
  Prythee, | why so | pale ?
Will, if | looking | well can't | move her,
  Looking | ill pre | vail ?
  Prythee, | why so | pale ?

Suckling.

Thus it | is our | daughters | leave us,
Those we | love and | those who | love us !
Just when | they have | learned to | help us,
When wĕ ăre | old and | lean up | on them,
Comes a youth with flaunting feathers,
With a flute of reeds, a stranger
Wanders piping through the village.
Beckons to the fairest maiden,
And she follows where he leads her,
Leaving all things for the stranger !

Longfellow.

Though in distant lands we sigh,
Parched beneath a hostile sky ;
Though the deep between us rolls,
Friendship shall unite our souls ;
Still in fancy's rich domain
Oft shall we three meet again.

Wha will be a traitor knave ?
Wha will fill a coward's grave ?
Wha sae base as be a slave ?
  Traitor ! coward ! turn and flee !

Burns.

The following quatrains exhibit the four-foot line in both its complete and truncated forms ; this is the 8,7 measure of our hymns.

Lives of great men all remind us
  We can make our lives sublime,
And, departing, leave behind us
  Footprints on the sands of time.

Longfellow.

In her ear he whispers gaily,
  "If my heart by signs can tell,
Maiden, I have watched thee daily,
  And I think thou lov'st me well."
Tennyson.

Praise the Lord! ye heavens adore Him!
  Praise Him, angels, in the height!
Sun and moon rejoice before Him!
  Praise Him all ye stars of night!

(e). TROCHAIC PENTAMETER.

Normal line, Ten Syllables

$$- \smile \mid - \smile \mid - \smile \mid - \smile \mid - \smile .$$

Composition in this measure is very rare, and even when combined with truncated and hypermetrical verses it has been but little cultivated.

Spăke fŭll | wĕll ĭn | lănguăge | quăint ănd | ōldĕn,
One who | dwelleth | by the | castled | Rhine,
When he | called the | flowers so | blue and | golden
Stars that | in earth's | firma | ment do | shine.
Longfellow.

What is yon so white beside the greenwood?
Is it snow or flight of cygnets resting?
Were it snow, ere now it had been melted;
Were it swans, ere now the flock had left us.
Aytoun.

Then methought I heard a hollow sound,
Gathering up from all the lower ground;
Narrowing in to where they sat assembled,
Low voluptuous music, winding, trembled.
Tennyson.

(*f*). Trochaic Hexameter.

Normal line, Twelve Syllables

$$- \smile | - \smile | - \smile | - \smile | - \smile | - \smile.$$

There are but few examples of this measure.

Holy, | holy, | holy, | all the | saints a | dore Thee,
Casting | down their | golden | crowns a | round the | glassy |
  sea.   *Heber.*

Here is a specimen of this verse truncated.

Love with | rosy | fetter | held us | firmly | bound ;
Pure un | mixed en | joyment | grateful | here we | found.
Bosom | bosom | meeting | 'gainst our | youths we | pressed;
Bright the | morn a | rose then | glad to | see us | blessed
         G. Borrow

(*g* and *h*). Trochaic Heptameter and Octameter.

Normal lines Fourteen and Sixteen Syllables.

There are but few symmetrical poems in these measures, although they have been freely used by Longfellow, Lord Lytton, Aytoun, and Tennyson in irregular combinations. Tennyson's *Locksley Hall* and Poe's *Raven* supply good examples.

Cursed | be the | social | wants that | sin a | 'gainst the |
  strength of | youth !
Cursed | be the | social | lies that | warp us | from the | living
  | truth !
Cursed | be the | sickly | forms that | err from | honest | na-
  ture's rule !
Cursed | be the | gold that | gilds the | straitened | fore-
  head | of the | fool !
         Tennyson.

Ah! distinctly I remember, it was in the bleak December,
And each separate dying ember wrought its ghost upon the
    floor.
Eagerly I wished the morrow; vainly I had sought to borrow
From my books surcease of sorrow—sorrow for the lost Lenore—
For the rare and radiant maiden whom the angels name
    Lenore—
      Nameless here for evermore.

                        Poe.

In the market-place of Bruges stands the belfry old and brown:
Thrice consumed and thrice rebuilded, still it watches o'er the
    town.
As the summer morn was breaking on that lofty tower I stood,
And the world threw off the darkness like the weeds of widow-
    hood.   *Longfellow.*

Then we bounded from our covert. Judge how looked the
    Saxons then,
When they saw the rugged mountain start to life with armed
    men.   *Aytoun.*

Come, my lad, and sit beside me; we have often talked before
Of the hurricane and tempest, and the storms on sea and
    shore:
When we read of deed and daring done for dear old England's
    sake,
We have cited Nelson's duty and the enterprise of Drake.
                      Clement Scott.

3.—ANAPESTIC MEASURE.

Trisyllabic measures have not been much used
by our poets for reasons that are not far to seek.
They require the constant recurrence of two syllables both unaccented and short to one syllable
accented, and our language does not afford that
proportion. Their construction being thus rendered

more complex and artificial than dissyllabic verse, and their rhythmical ring being more pronounced and therefore liable to become monotonous, it need not surprise us that no lengthy poem has been attempted in the three-syllable metre. The licences made use of in verse of this kind are many and varied, the interchange of feet, the omission and addition of syllables being almost the rule instead of the exception. Pure symmetrical lines are rarely met with consecutively unless the rhyme demands it.

It is unnecessary, we think, to preserve further the detailed classification of dimeter, trimeter verse, as has been done in the dissyllabic measures; numerous and varied examples are, however, given, adequate for all the purposes of illustration and explanation, and the reader will find abundant material for the exercise of the critical faculty and skill in scanning in the works of all our modern poets, especially in Shelley, Longfellow, and Tennyson.

Normal Measure ⌣ ⌣ – | ⌣ ⌣ –.

Ī ăm ōut | ŏf hŭmān | Ĭtў's rĕach,
　I must fin | ish my jour | ney alone,
Never hear | the sweet mu | sic of speech.
　I start | at the sound | of my own.

Cowper.

Tĭs thĕ lāst | rŏse ŏf sūm | mĕr,
　Lĕft blōom | ĭng ălōne ;
All her lovely companions
　Are faded and gone.

Hĕ ĭs gōne | ŏn thĕ mōun | tăin,
He is lost | to the fo | rest,
Like a summer-dried fountain,
When our need was the sorest.

Scott.

She is far | from the land | where her young | hero sleeps,
And lov | ers around | her are sigh | ing ;
But coldly she turns from their gaze and weeps ;
For her heart in his grave is lying.

Moore.

Note here that the first verse is the only symmetrical one in the stanza, yet the melody throughout is perfect.

There the war | rior lay stretched | in the midst | of his pride,
And the bride | groom fell dead | by the corpse | of his bride
Unwept was the lyre, and forsaken the lute,
And the lips of the minstrel for ever was mute.

Anon.
" Pompeii."

And the rose | like a nymph | to the bath | addrest,
Which unveil | èd the depth | of her glow | ing breast,
Till fold | after fold | to the faint | ing air
The soul | of her beau | ty and love | lay bare.

Shelley.

Not a drum | was heard, | not a fun | eral note,
As his corse | to the ram | part we hur | ried ;
Not a sol | dier discharg | èd his fare | well shot
O'er the grave | where our he | ro we bur | ied.

Wolfe.

I come, | I come, | ye have call | èd me long,
I come | o'er the mount | ain with light | and song ;

E

You may trace | my step | o'er the wak | ening earth,
By the winds | which tell | of the vi | olets' birth,
By the prim | rose stars | in the shad | owy grass,
By the green | leaves op | ening as | I pass.

In the last example the rhythm demands that there shall be no elision in *callèd, wakèning, vïolet, opèning*. The concluding specimens exhibit still greater irregularities, though in every case the flow is distinctly anapestic, and the melody runs smoothly.

I arise | from dreams | of thee,
  In the first | sweet sleep | of night,
When the winds are breathing low,
  And the stars are shining bright.
I arise from dreams of thee,
  And a spirit in my feet
Has led me—who knows how ?—
  To thy chamber-window, sweet.

Shelley.

I have laid him down in the cot that each night used I rock, and spread
All the tender flowers I could gather about his head ;
Early springtime it is, so I could only find
Delicate violet-bloom that shrank from the bitter wind.

E. Hickey.

For the lawyer is born but to murder—
  The Saviour lives but to bless.
And the first may be last—I have heard it in church —
  And the last may be first.

Tennyson.
"Rizpah."

4.—DACTYLIC MEASURE

Normal Measure | – ᴗ ᴗ | – ᴗ ᴗ |

The rhythm of this measure presents the same
antithesis to Anapestic that Trochaic does to
Iambic: it has a bounding, martial ring about it
which renders it suitable for gay and sprightly
lyrics.

> Shădŏws ŏf | beāutў!
>   Shādŏws ŏf | pōwĕr!
> Risē tŏ yoŭr | dūtў—
>   Thīs ĭs thĕ | hōŭr.
>
> *Byron.*

> Make no deep | scrutiny
> Into her | mutiny,
>   Rash and un | dutiful:
> Past all dis | honour,
> Death has left | on her
>   Only the | beautiful.*
>
> *Hood.*

> Bird of the | wilderness,
> Blithesome and | cumberless,
> Light be thy | matin o'er | mountain and | lea ;
> Emblem of | happiness,
> Blest be thy | dwelling-place ;
> O to a | bide in the | desert with | thee.
>
> *Hogg.*

> Come, let us | sit and be | merry, lads.
>   Here we se | curely can | hide ;
> Here we have | claret and | sherry, lads.
>   Port and Ma | deira be | side.

* Mr. Ruskin, in his " Elements of English Prosody," p. 24,
remarks upon this poem, " the emotion is entirely continuous, and
the accent equal on every syllable " (*sic*).

Cannon to | right of them,
Cannon to | left of them,
Cannon in | front of them,
   Volleyed and | thundered.
Stormed at with | shot and shell,
Boldly they | rode and well,
Into the | jaws of death,
Into the | mouth of hell,
   Rode the six | hundred.*

Tennyson.

Warriors and | chiefs! should the | shaft or the | sword
Pierce me in | leading the | hosts of the | Lord,
Heed not a | corse, though a | king's, in your | path,
Bury your | steel in the | bosoms of Gath.

Byron.

Tell me, thou | bonny bird,
  When shall I | marry me ?
When six braw | gentlemen
Kirkward shall | carry ye.

Scott.

Here we go off on the " London and Birmingham,"
  Bidding adieu to the foggy metropolis !
Staying at home with the dumps in confirming 'em :—
  Motion and mirth are a fillip to life.

G. D.
" Railway Dactyls."

* This famous *Charge of the Light Brigade*, says Mr. Austin Dobson (*Notes and Queries*, 4th series, vol. x., p. 338), was doubtless suggested, both in metre and style, by a short but grand poem by Michael Drayton on the battle of Agincourt, the last stanza of which is as follows :—

Upon St. Crispin's day
Fought was this noble fray,
Which fame did not delay
  To England to carry.
O when shall Englishmen
With such acts fill a pen,
Or England breed again
  Such a King Harry !

Onward she | glides amid | ripple and | spray
Over the | waters a | way and a | way !
Bright are the | visions of | youth ere they | part,
Passing a | way like a | dream of the | heart.

　　　　　　　　　　　　　　　Hervey

Sea-king's | daughter from | over the | sea.
　　　　　　Alexandra !
Saxon and | Norman and | Dane are | we,
But | all of us | Danes in our | welcome of | thee,
　　　　　　Alexandra !
Welcome her, | thunders of | fort and of | fleet !
Welcome her, | thundering | cheer of the | street !
Welcome her, | all things | youthful and | sweet !
Scatter the | blossom | under her | feet !

　　　　　　　　　　　　　　　Tennyson.

Brightest and | best of the | sons of the | morning,
　Dawn on our | darkness and | lend us thine | aid ;
Star of the | East, the hor | izon a | dorning,
　Guide where our | Infant Re | deemer is | laid.

　　　　　　　　　　　　　　　Heber.

The following examples will be found to run
more in the measure of *Amphibrachs,* though by
regarding the first foot as an Iambus it would become
Anapestic, while by beginning with a single syllable
it becomes Dactylic. The general character of the
rhythm as interpreted by a trained ear is the sole
test.

　　　Thĕ Bōurbŏn ! | thĕ Bōurbŏn !
　　　　Săns cōuntrў | ŏr hōme,
　　　We'll follow | the Bourbon
　　　　To plunder | old Rome.

　　　　　　　　　　　　Byron.

　　　Thĕ dēw ŏf | thĕ mōrnĭng
　　　　Sank chill on my brow.
　　　It felt like | the warning
　　　　Of what I | feel now.

Thy vows are | all broken,
And light is | thy fame,
I hear thy | name spoken,
And share in | its shame.

Byron.

This is perhaps better scanned as follows :

Thĕ | dēw ŏf thĕ | mōrnĭng sănk | chīll ŏn mў | brōw,
It | felt like the | warning of | what I feel | now.

Macgregor, | Macgregor, | remember | our foemen !
The morn ri | ses broad from | the brow of | Ben Lomond ;
The clans are | impatient | and chide thy | delay.
Arise, let | us bound to | Glenlyon | away.

Hogg.

In the extracts which follow, all of which are full
of melody, the rhythm is so varied that it is difficult to pronounce with certainty which of the measures predominates.

Now silently poised o'er the war of the main,
Like the spirit of Charity brooding o'er pain ;
Now gliding with pinion all silently furled,
Like an angel descending to comfort the world.

Gerald Griffin.

Mount Blanc is the monarch of mountains,
We crowned him long ago,
On a throne of rocks, in a robe of clouds,
With a diadem of snow.
Around his waist are forests braced,
The av'lanche in his hand ;
But ere it fall, that thundering ball
Must pause for my command.

Byron.

There came to the beach a poor exile of Erin ;
  The dew on his thin robe was heavy and chill ;
For his country he sighed when at twilight repairing,
  To wander alone by the wind-beaten hill.
Campbell.

  I was a child, and she was a child,
    In this kingdom by the sea ;
  But we loved with a love that was more than love,
    I and my Annabel Lee ;
  With a love that the winged seraphs of heaven
    Coveted her and me.
Poe.

I silently laugh at my own cenotaph,
  And out of the caverns of rain,
Like a child from the womb, like a ghost from the tomb,
  I arise and unbuild it again
Shelley.

MIXED METRES.

WRITERS of verse are under no necessity to a slavish adherence to metrical rules. The muse may soar high with steady wing and stately swoop, or flutter about the lower grounds in fantastic mazes; but his movements must always be rhythmical and his utterances musical. Linguistic difficulties and the 'seductive chains of linked sweetness,' urge him to the adoption of every possible variety of measure that lends freedom to the movement, and relieves the monotony of regularity. We have already pointed out the addition or omission of short syllables, the interchange of feet of one kind for those of another. Now we have to illustrate, in addition to these variations, the mingling of long and short measures in elegant complexity, together with the fitful ring of rhymes, the combined effect of which often adds to the melody of the rhythm the richness of harmony.

Amongst the simpler of these combinations are the Iambic with Anapestic, Trochaic with Dactylic, in both of which the swing of the melody is uninterrupted, *e.g :*

My life | is cold | and dark | and drear | y ;
It rains | and the wind | is nev ' er wear | y.

My thoughts | still cling | to the mould | ering past,
And the hopes | of youth | fall thick | in the blast,
    And the days | are dark | and drear | y.
Longfellow.

And Willy, my eldest born, is gone, you say, little Annie ?
Ruddy and white, and strong on his legs, he looks like a man.
And Willy's wife has written—she never was overwise—
Never the wife for Willy—he wouldn't take my advice.
Tennyson.
" The Grandmother."

In the following, Iambic and Trochaic verses alternate regularly.

> When the lamp is shattered,
>   The light in the dust lies dead ;
> When the cloud is scattered,
>   The rainbow's glory is shed ;
> When the lute is broken,
>   Sweet tones are remembered not ;
> When the lips have spoken,
>   Loved accents are soon forgot.

Shelley.

In *L'Allegro* and *Il Penseroso* the measures are mingled irregularly.

> Sometimes with secure delight
> The upland hamlets will invite,
> When the merry bells ring round,
> And the jocund rebecs sound,
> To many a youth and many a maid
> Dancing in the chequer'd shade ;
> And young and old come forth to play
> On a sunshine holiday,
> Till the livelong daylight fail ;
> Then to the spicy nut-brown ale.

Milton.

As also in the following :

> There be none of Beauty's daughters
>   With a magic like thee ;
> And like music on the waters
>   Is thy sweet voice to me.
> When, as if its sound were causing
> The charmèd ocean's pausing,
> The waves lie still and gleaming,
> And the lulled winds seem dreaming !
> *Byron.*

> Happy the man, and happy he alone,
>   He who can call to-day his own,
> He who, secure within, can say,
>   To-morrow do thy worst, for I have lived to-day.
> *Dryden.*

A combination of the same species of verse is made by those which differ in the number of their feet, as in the examples here given, where the figures denote the number of feet in each verse.

Combinations in the Iambic.
- 5. In realms long held beneath a tyrant's sway,
- 4. Lo ! Freedom hath again appear'd !
- 3. In this auspicious day
- 6. Her glorious ensign floats, and high in Spain is rear'd.

In the Trochaic.
- 4. Banded despots hate the sight ;
- 2. And in spite
- 4. Arm their slaves for war and plunder.
- 4. But the British lion's roar,
- 3. Heard on every shore,
- 5. Soon shall break their impious league asunder.

In the Anapes-tic.

- 3.   Then Spaniards shall set at defiance
- 2.   Their foes that advance :
- 4.   They shall laugh at the threats of the Holy Alliance,
- 4. And baffle, indignant, th' invasion of France.

In th'e Dactylic.

- 2.   On to the field !
- 4. Heaven will assist the defenders of Freedom ;
- 4. Prayers and arms in your cause, if you need 'em
- 3.   Every Briton will yield !

Other combinations are those of different kinds of verse, viz. the iambic with the three others ; the trochaic with the anapestic and dactylic, and the two last together. These combinations are made according to the fancy of the writer, in a variety of degrees : sometimes no greater than single verses, or parts of a verse, as in this of Dryden's Ode, the anapestic with the iambic :

And amazed | he stares | around.

Another line in the same ode is of ambiguous measure. The latter half is anapestic ; so the first may be, but it reads and scans better as trochaic :

These are | Grecian | ghosts that in | battle were | slain.

Such combinations are to be observed as matters of curiosity rather than imitated.

Ariel's Song in the *Tempest* combines the trochaic with the dactylic :

On the bat's back I do fly
After summer merrily ;
Merrily, merrily shall I live now
Under the blossom that hangs on the bough.

The ode just quoted has, within the compass of six lines, half as many combinations :

> Behold **a** ghastly band,
> Each a torch in his hand :
> These are Grecian ghosts that in battle were slain,
> And unburied remain
> Inglorious on the plain :
> Give the vengeance due.

In *Love's Labour's Lost* there is a stanza formed by a curious combination of verses, some of them of a measure very uncommon, being trochaics of five feet, the last curtailed.

> Clear wells spring not, sweet birds sing not,
> Green plants bring not forth their dye ;
> Herds stand weeping, flocks all sleeping,
> Nymphs black peeping fearfully.
> All our pleasure known to us poor swains,
> All our merry meetings on the plains,
> All our evening sport from us is fled ;
> All our love is lost, for love is dead.
> Farewell, sweet love, thy like ne'er was,
> For a sweet content, the cause of all my woe ;
> Poor Coridon must live alone,
> Other help for him I see that there is none.

A very extraordinary combination of English verse is a song by Campion, who will be quoted at length hereafter. Campion was eminent as a musician as well as a poet, which may account for so singular a specimen of metre.

> What if a day, or a month, or a year,
> Crown thy delights with a thousand wish'd contentings ;
> Cannot a chance of a night or an hour,
> Cross thy delights with a thousand sad tormentings ?

Fortune, honour, beauty, youth, are but blossoms dying;
Wanton pleasure, doting love, are but shadows flying.
     All our joys are but toys,
      Idle thoughts deceiving;
     None hath power of an hour,
      In their live bereiving.

In every combination there should be a design
of producing some effect; to introduce a combination without any design is a mark of carelessness,
or lack of patience and resource. The effect
designed may be merely to please, by a change
of the measure, for the sake of variety; but the
change is made more properly when it is done
to accommodate the verse to the sentiments; to
express, for example, what is grave by a suitable
kind, as the iambic; what is sprightly by the
trochaic, and the like. Gray, in his ode on the *Progress of Poesy*, has produced a very striking and
happy effect by such a combination of verses;
the tripping measure which represents the *frisky
dance* of the Cupids, is finely contrasted with the
smooth iambic which describes the gentle gait of
Venus.

    Nów pursúing, nów retréating,
     Nów in círcling tróops they méet:
    Tó brisk nótes in cádence béating
     Glánce their mány twínkling féet.
  Slow mélting stráins their quéen's appróach decláre;
  In glíding státe she wíns her éasy wáy.

A disagreeable and jarring effect would be produced if they were made contrariwise to this, *i.e.*

if, in this instance, the trochaic and iambic should change places.

Combinations may be esteemed good or bad, according as they preserve or break the measure and flow of the verse. The following is good:

> The listening Muses all around her
> Think 'tis Phœbus' strains they hear.

Here is an iambic line, with a redundant syllable followed by a trochaic. This satisfies the ear; for the verses flow smoothly on to the end of the period, because the iambic measure is continued unbroken. The combination below is not good.

> A mind that's truly brave
> Stands despising
> Storms arising,
> And can't be made a slave.

The last line, being an iambic, which follows a trochaic, not curtailed, but full, produces an un-pleasing effect; for it seems to have a syllable too much. It offends the ear, because the measure is broken: strike out that syllable, and the offence will be removed; the trochaic measure will be pre-served to the end. In fact, the objectionable line is owing to a mistake of Bysshe. In his Art of Poetry, he quoted the passage from Dryden incor-rectly; in that author, the last line runs thus:

> And can ne'er be made a slave,

which is a trochaic verse, and gives the measure desired.

In serious poetry the combination is bad, generally speaking, which subjoins a short line to a long one, especially if they rhyme together; as,

> Be thou thine own approver; honest praise
> Oft nobly sways
> Ingenuous youth.
>
> *Akenside.*

One reason is, that such a combination wants dignity, which is the more apparent in this instance, because the preceding line is the stately heroic verse. To give another example:

> By Euphrates' flowery side
> We did bide;

and

> When poor Sion's doleful state,
> Desolate.

In these lines the quick return of the rhyme nearly destroys the gravity of the matter. Another reason why these combinations are faulty, is the disproportion between the length of the lines. And upon this account, if lines as disproportionate as these were set in a contrary order, the combination would still be unpleasing, as in this instance:

> As if great Atlas from his height
> Should sink beneath his heavenly weight,
> And with a mighty flow the flaming wall,
> As once it shall,
> Should gape immense, and, rushing down, o'erwhelm this nether ball.
>
> *Dryden.*

But a good combination is made by two lines, or more, increasing, as they proceed, in a moderate degree: *i.e.* by one or two feet; example:

> All real here the bard had seen
> The glories of his pictured queen :
> The tuneful Dryden had not flatter'd here,
> His lyre had blameless been, his tribute all sincere.
> > *Warton.*

It is this gradual increase above the preceding lines which makes the Alexandrine so graceful in the close ; for it has no beauty if set in the beginning of a poem or stanza, as it has been by some of our poets.

After this manner the verse of fourteen syllables may be brought in, and follow the Alexandrine with good effect :

> The sylvans to their shades retire ;
> Those very shades and streams new shades and streams require,
> And want a cooling breeze of wind to fan the raging fire.
> > *Dryden.*

The lighter sorts of poetry are not to be considered as necessarily subject to this rule. In epigrams, for instance, where wit is often most happily expressed by brevity, the point or concluding line may very properly be shorter than the preceding; as in this :

> What a frail thing is beauty ! says Baron le Cras,
> Perceiving his mistress had one eye of glass :

And scarcely had he spoke it,
When she, more enraged as more angry she grew,
By a negligent rage proved the maxim too true:
    She dropt the eye and broke it.

                                    Prior.

The concluding specimens of mixed metres from Dryden's *Alexander's Feast*, Tennyson's *Ode on the Death of the Duke of Wellington*, and *The Sisters* furnish illustrations of still greater complexity.

Soothed with the sound the king grew vain,
Fought all his battles o'er again,
And thrice he routed all his foes, and thrice he slew the slain,
    The master saw the madness rise,
    His glowing cheeks, his ardent eyes;
    And when he heaven and earth defied,
    Changed his hand and checked his pride.
        He chose a mournful muse,
        Soft pity to infuse:
    He sang Darius great and good,
        By too severe a fate,
        Fall'n, fall'n, fall'n, fall'n,
        Fallen from his high estate,
    And weltering in his blood.

                                    Dryden.

        O divine light!
Through the cloud that roofs our noon with night,
    Through the blotting mist, the blinding showers,
Far from out a sky for ever bright,
    Over all the woodland's flooded bowers,
    Over all the meadows drowning flowers,
    Over all this ruined world of ours,
        Break, divine light!

                                    Tennyson.

F

But while the races of mankind endure,
    Let his great example stand,
    Colossal, seen of every land,
And keep the soldier firm, the statesman pure';
    Till in all lands, and through all human story
    The path of duty be the way to glory :
And let the land whose hearths he saved from shame
For many and many an age proclaim,
At civic revel and pomp and game,
And when the long-illumined cities flame
Their ever-loyal iron leader's fame,
With honour, honour, honour, honour to him,
    Eternal honour to his name.

                       Tennyson.

COMBINATIONS OF VERSES.

VERSES are combined to form poems either in continuous unbroken runs, extending in some instances to thousands of lines, or in detached groups of a varying number of lines, which are called stanzas.* The former consist of verses of the same metre, generally of iambic pentameter, without division or metrical complexity, and in this amorphous form, as it may be termed, all the great poems of our own and other tongues are embodied. The latter includes all our lyric poetry, and nearly all other minor poetic forms.

I.—CONTINUOUS VERSE.

In continuous verse are the heroic measures of Chaucer, Dryden, Pope, Goldsmith, Keats, &c., and the noble blank verse of Milton, Shakspere, Addison, Cowper, Wordsworth, and Tennyson. All the great masters of song have clothed their lofty imaginings and philosophy in this form, since it allowed them the widest freedom of rhythmic roll, and harassed them with the fewest verbal diffi-

* A *verse* is a succession of feet forming one line of a poem ; a *stanza* a group of verses constituting a regular division of a poem,

culties. Poets, like their brother artists the pain-
ters, have availed themselves of larger canvas and
freer methods of treatment when depicting continuous heroic action, or in portraying the chequered
drama of life; the minuteness and polish of the
miniature picture is bestowed for the most part
upon lyrical efforts.

Of epic and dramatic verse, which embraces
nearly all the continuous forms of poetry, we have
spoken elsewhere.

2.—STANZAIC VERSE.

We now proceed to illustrate the various forms
of stanza into which poets have moulded their
verses with infinite variety. As these groups of
verses not only vary in number from two to sixteen,
and the verses themselves range in length from
one to eight feet, it is obviously impossible to exhibit specimens of all varieties that may be found.
We have, however, selected with care as many
and as varied illustrations of each kind as the
subject demands.

(a). Stanzas of Two Verses.

These are called *distichs* or *couplets.*

> Hard he laboured, long and well :
> Over his work the boy's curls fell.

> Then back again his curls he threw,
> And cheerful turned to work anew.

> *R. Browning.*
> " The Boy and the Angel."

From their nests beneath the rafters hung the swallows wild
   and high ;
And the world beneath me sleeping, seemed more distant
   than the sky.

Longfellow.
" Belfry of Bruges."

Love took up the glass of Time, and turned it in his glowing
   hands ;
Every moment, lightly shaken, ran itself in golden sands.

Love took up the harp of life, and smote on all the chords with
   might ;
Smote the chord of Self, that, trembling, passed in music out
   of sight.

Tennyson.
" Locksley Hall."

(*b*). STANZAS OF THREE VERSES.

These are known as *tercets*, and when rhyming
together are called *triplets*.

A still small voice spake unto me,
" Thou art so full of misery,
Were it not better not to be " ?

Then to the still small voice I said,
" Let me not cast in endless shade
What is so wonderfully made."

Tennyson
" Two Voices."

Thy silver locks, once auburn bright,
Are still more lovely in my sight
Than golden beams of orient light.

Cowper.
" My Mary."

There's a palace in Florence the world knows well,
  And a statue watches it from the square,
And this story of both do our townsmen tell.
                              R. Browning.
                        " The Statue and the Bust."

        When I tie about thy wrist,
        Julia, this my silken twist,
        For what other reason is't,

        But to show thee how, in part,
        Thou my pretty captive art ?
        —But thy bond-slave is my heart.
                              Herrick.
                           " The Bracelet."

I made a posy while the day ran by ;
Here will I smell my remnant out, and tie
        My life within this band.

But Time did beckon to the flowers, and they
By noon most cunningly did steal away,
        And withered in my hand.
                              Herbert.
                        " Life and the Flowers."

      There's a being bright whose beams
      Light my days and gild my dreams,
      Till my life all sunshine seems—
            'Tis the Ladye of Lee.
                          Francis Mahony
                            (Father Prout).

      Beautiful faces are those that wear—
      It matters little if dark or fair—
      Whole-souled honesty printed there.
                              Anon.

      Maiden ! with the meek, brown eyes !
      In whose orbs a shadow lies,
      Like the dusk in evening skies !

O thou child of many prayers !
Life hath quicksands—life hath snares !
Care and age come unawares !
Longfellow.

Mrs. Browning's *Vision of Poets* consists of upwards of three hundred stanzas of rhymed triplets.

(c). STANZAS OF FOUR VERSES.

These are designated *quatrains*, and are more common than any other arrangement of verses. The first four examples illustrate the various dispositions of the rhymes, what follows of the lengths.

Weep no more, or sigh, or moan,
Grief recalls no hour that's gone ;
Violets plucked, the sweetest rain
Makes not fresh or grow again.
Beaumont and Fletcher.

I hold it true, whate'er befall,
I feel it when I sorrow most,
'Tis better to have loved and lost,
Than never to have lovd at all.
Tennyson.
" In Memoriam."

I hear the trailing garments of the night
Sweep through her marble halls !
I saw her sable skirts all fringed with light
From the celestial walls !
Longfellow.
" Hymns to the Night."

Then shook the hills with thunder riven;
Then rushed the steed, to battle driven;
And louder than the bolts of Heaven
 Far flashed the red artillery.
      Campbell.
      " Hohenlinden "

 Let's contend no more, Love,
  Strive nor weep;
 All be as before, Love,
  —Only sleep!
      R. Browning.
      " A Woman's Last Word.

Now all is hushed save where the weak-eyed bat
With short shrill shriek flits by on leathern wing,
 Or where the beetle winds
 His small but sullen horn.
      Collins.
      " Ode to Evening."

 We three archers be,
Rangers that move through the north countree,
Lovers of ven'son and liberty,
 That value not honour or money.
      Anon.

 The rising morn has hid the stars;
 Her level rays, like golden bars,
  Lie on the landscape green,
  With shadows brown between.
      Longfellow.
      " Endymion."

That fawn-skin dappled hair of hers,
  And the blue eye,
  Dear and dewy,
And that infantine fresh air of hers!
      R. Browning.
      " A Pretty Woman."

Another year is swallowed by the **sea**
　　Of sunless waves !
Another year, thou past eternity !
　　Has rolled o'er new-made graves.
　　　　　　　　Ebenezer Elliott
　　　　　　　" A New Year."

　　　　Give me now my lyre !
I feel the stirrings of a gift divine ;
Within my bosom glows unearthly fire,
　　　Lit by no skill of mine.
　　　　　　　Eliz. Lloyd.
　　　　　　"Milton's Last Verses."

I do not ask, O Lord, that thou should'st shed
　　　Full radiance here ;
Give but a ray of peace, that I may tread
　　　Without a fear.
　　　　　　Adelaide Anne Procter.
　　　　　　" Per pacem ad lucem."

My days are in the yellow leaf ;
　　The flowers and fruits of love are gone.
The worm, the canker, and the grief,
　　　Are mine alone !
　　　　　　Byron
　　　　　(In his 36th year).

Four heroics rhyming alternately, as in Gray's
Elegy, constitute the *Elegiac stanza.*

Full many a gem of purest ray serene
　　The dark unfathomed caves of ocean bear ;
Full many a flower is born to blush unseen,
　　And waste its sweetness on the desert air.
　　　　　　Gray.

Four and three **iambics** alternate are known as
Ballad or Service stanza. A slight variation of the
latter goes by the name of *Gray's stanza.*

> All melancholy lying
>   Thus wailed she for her dear ;
> Replied each blast with sighing,
>   Each billow with a tear.
>
>   *Gay.*

(*d*). STANZAS OF FIVE VERSES.

These are called *quintains*, and have been employed
by our poets in great variety of rhyme and length
of verse.

> That was I you heard last night,
>   When there rose no moon at all,
> Nor, to pierce the strained and tight
>   Tent of heaven, a planet small :
> Life was dead, and so was light.
>
>   *R. Browning.*
>   " A Serenade."

> Who is the honest man ?
> He that doth still and strongly good pursue ;
> To God, his neighbour, and himself most true.
>   Whom neither force nor fawning can
> Unpin, or wrench from giving all their due.
>
>   *Herbert.*
>   " The Steadfast Life."

> You meaner beauties of the night,
>   That poorly satisfy our eyes
> More by your number than your light
>   You common people of the skies.
> What are you when the moon shall rise ?
>
>   *Wotton.*
>   " To Elizabeth, Queen of Bohemia."

Love flew in at the window
  As Wealth walked in at the door.
" You have come as you saw Wealth coming," said I
But he fluttered his wings with a sweet little cry,
  " I'll cleave to you rich or poor."
                Tennyson.
                " The Foresters."

      Go, lovely Rose !
  Tell her, that wastes her time and me,
    That now she knows,
  When I resemble her to thee
  How sweet and fair she seems to be.
                Waller.
             " The Rose's Message."

Oh, a lady might have come there,
Hooded fairly like her hawk,
With a book or lute in summer,
And a hope of sweeter talk.
Listening less to her own music than for footsteps on the walk
                Mrs. Browning.
             "The Lost Bower."

    Yes, the year is growing old.
      And his eye is pale and bleared !
    Death, with frosty hand and cold
    Plucks the old man by the beard,
      Sorely, sorely !
              Longfellow.
      " Midnight Mass for the Dying Year."

We look before and after,
  And pine for what is not ;
Our sincerest laughter
  With some pain is fraught :
Our sweetest songs are those that tell of saddest thought.
              Shelley.
      " Ode to a Skylark."

Ah ! wretched and too solitary he
Who loves not his own company !
　He'll feel the weight of't many a day,
Unless he calls in sin or vanity
　To help to bear't away.

Cowley.

Two lovers by a moss-grown spring :
　They leaned soft cheeks together there ;
　Mingled the dark and sunny hair,
And heard the wooing thrushes sing.
　O budding time ! O love's blest prime.

George Eliot.

Beautiful flowers ! to me ye fresher seem
　From the Almighty hand that fashioned all,
　Than those that flourish by a garden wall ;
And I can image you, as in a dream,
　Fair, modest maidens, nursed in hamlets small—
　　I love ye all !

Nicholl.
" Wild Flowers."

Stranger ! however great,
　With lowly reverence bow ;
There's one in that poor shed,
One by that paltry bed,
　Greater than thou.

Bowles.
" The Pauper's Deathbed."

(e). Stanzas of Six Verses, called the Sestet

The pale, the cold, and the moony smile
　Which the meteor-beam of a starless night
Sheds on a lonely and sea-girt isle,
　Ere the dawning of morn's undoubted light,
Is the flame of light so fickle and wan
That flits round our steps till their strength is gone.

Shelley.
" Death."

Such is the fate of artless maid,
Sweet flow'ret of the rural shade !
By love's simplicity betrayed
　　And guileless trust,
Till she, like thee, all soiled, is laid
　　Low i' the dust.

Burns.
" Mountain Daisy."

Beside the ungathered rice he lay,
　　His sickle in his hand ;
His breast was bare, his matted hair
　　Was buried in the sand.
Again in the mist and shadow of sleep
　　He saw his Native Land.

Longfellow.
"The Slave's Dream."

O Mary, go and call the cattle home,
　　And call the cattle home,
　　And call the cattle home,
Across the sands o' Dee.
The western wind was wild and dark with foam,
　　And all alone went she.

Kingsley.

And thou hast walked about (how strange a story !)
　　In Thebes's streets three thousand years ago.
When the Memnonium was in all its glory,
　　And time had not begun to overthrow
Those temples, palaces, and piles stupendous
Of which the very ruins are tremendous !

Horace Smith.
" Address to a Mummy."

Fair pledges of a fruitful tree,
　　Why do you fall so fast ?
　　Your date is not so past,

But you may stay yet here awhile
　　To blush and gently smile,
　　　　And go at last.
　　　　　　　　　　Herrick.
　　　　　　　　　" To Blossoms."

Is there a man whose judgment clear
Can others teach the course to steer,
Yet runs himself life's mad career
　　Wild as the wave ?
Here pause, and through the starting tear
　　Survey this grave.
　　　　　　　　　Burns.
　　　　　　　" A Bard's Epitaph."

I was not ever thus, nor prayed that Thou
　　Should'st lead me on ;
I loved to choose and see my path—but now
　　Lead Thou me on.
I loved the garish day, and, spite of fears,
Pride ruled my will : remember not past years.
　　　　　　　　　Newman.

I love snow, and all the forms
　　Of the radiant frost ;
I love waves, and winds, and storms,
　　Everything almost
Which is Nature's, and may be
Untainted by man's misery.
　　　　　　　　　Shelley.
　　　　　　　　" Invocation."

(ƒ). Stanzas of Seven Verses.

Seven heroics, the first five rhyming at intervals, the last two in succession, form what is known as *Rhyme Royal.* This stanza was much used by early writers, Chaucer, Spenser, &c., but has found few imitations in modern poets, *e.g.* :

So every spirit as it is most pure,
　And hath in it the more of heavenly light,
So it the fairer body doth procure
　To habit it, and is more fairly dight
　With cheerful grace and amiable sight ;
For of the soul the body form doth take
For soul is form and doth the body make.
　　　　　　　　　　Spenser.

　Awake, awake my lyre !
And tell thy silent master's humble tale
　In sounds that may prevail—
Sounds that gentle thought inspire ;
　　Though so exalted she
　　And I so lowly be,
Tell her such different notes make all thy harmony.
　　　　　　　　　Cowley.
　　　　　　　" The Lover to his Lyre."

　Oh, what a dawn of day !
How the March sun feels like May !
　　All is blue again,
　　After last night's rain,
And the south dries the hawthorn spray—
　　Only, my love's away !
I'd as lief that the blue were grey.
　　　　　　　R. Browning.
　　　　　　" A Lover's Quarrel."

Three corpses lay out on the shining sands
　In the morning gleam as the tide went down ;
And the women were weeping and wringing their hands
　For those who will never come back to the town.
　For men must work, and women must weep,
　And the sooner it's over, the sooner to sleep,
　　And good-bye to the bar and its moaning.
　　　　　　　　Kingsley.
　　　　　　" The Three Fishers."

In the convent clad in grey,
   Sat the monks in lonely cells,
Paced the cloisters, knelt to pray,
   And the poet heard their bells;
         But his rhymes
         Found other chimes
Nearer to the earth than they.

Longfellow
" Olive Basselin.'

Swiftly walk over the western wave,
         Spirit of Night!
Out of the misty eastern cave,
Where, all the long and lone daylight,
Thou wovest dreams of joy and fear,
Which make thee terrible and dear,
         Swift be thy flight !

Shelley.
" To Night."

We are so unlike each other
   Thou and I, that none could guess
We were children of one mother
   But for mutual tenderness.
Thou art rose-lined from the cold,
And meant, verily, to hold
Life's new pleasures manifold.

Mrs. Browning.
" Bertha in the Lane."

Though, like a wanderer,
   The sun gone down,
Darkness be over me,
   My rest a stone ;
Yet in my dreams I'd be
Nearer, my God, to Thee—
   Nearer to Thee.

Sarah Flower Adams

The flower that smiles to-day
   To-morrow dies ;
All that we wish to stay
   Tempts and then flies :
What is this world's delight ?
Lightning that mocks the night,
Brief even as bright.

Shelley.
" Mutability."

(*g*). Stanzas of Eight Verses.

Eight heroics, the first six rhyming alternately, the last two in succession, are known as *Ottava Rima*. Many of the great poems of Italy, Spain, and Portugal are arranged in this stanza : Byron's translation of *Morgante Maggiore* and his *Don Juan* are the best English examples of it.

But the Consul's brow was sad,
   And the Consul's speech was low,
And darkly looked he at the wall,
   And darkly at the foe.
"Their van will be upon us
   Before the bridge goes down ;
And if they once may win the bridge,
   What hope to save the town ? "

Macaulay.
" Horatius."

A wizard is he !
   Do you see, d'ye see ?
Temples arise in the upper air :
   Now they are gone,
   And a troop comes on
Of plumed knights and ladies fair ;

They pass—and a host of spirits grey
Are floating onward—away! away!

Sarah Flower Adams.
" March Song."

I'm wearin' awa', John,
Like snaw wreaths in thaw, John,
I'm wearin' awa'
   To the land o' the leal.
There's nae sorrow there, John,
There's neither cold nor care, John,
The day's aye fair
   I' the land o' the leal.

Lady Nairn.

I climbed the dark brow of the mighty Helvellyn,
   Lakes and mountains beneath me gleamed misty and wide;
All was still, save, by fits, when the eagle was yelling,
   And starting around me the echoes replied.
On the right, Striden-edge round the Red-tarn was bending,
And Catchedicam its left verge was defending,
One huge nameless rock in the front was ascending,
   When I mark'd the sad spot where the wanderer had died.

Sir Walter Scott.
" Helvellyn."

Welcome, maids of honour!
   You do bring
   In the spring,
And wait upon her.
   She has virgins many
   Fresh and fair;
   Yet ye are
More sweet than any.

Herrick.
" To Violets."

He saw my anger was sincere,
   And lovingly began to chide me ;
And wiping from my cheek the tear,
   He sat him on the grass beside me.
He feigned such pretty amorous love,
   Breathed such sweet vows one after other,
I could but smile while whispering low—
   Be quiet, do, I'll call my mother.

C. M.

   Stone walls do not a prison make,
      Nor iron bars a cage ;
   Minds innocent and quiet take
      That for a hermitage :
   If I have freedom in my love,
      And in my soul am free,
   Angels alone that soar above
      Enjoy such liberty.

Lovelace.
" To Althea, from prison."

'Twas twilight, and the sunless day went down
   Over the waste of waters ; like a veil,
Which, if withdrawn, would but disclose the frown
   Of one whose hate is masked but to assail.
Thus to their hopeless eyes the night was shown,
   And grimly darkled o'er the faces pale,
And the dim desolate deep : twelve days had Fear
Been their familiar, and now Death was here !

Byron.
" Don Juan."

   Draw near,
     You lovers that complain,
     Of Fortune or Disdain,
   And to my ashes lend a tear ;
Melt the hard marble with **your groans,**
And soften the relentless stones,

Whose cold embraces the sad subject hide,
Of all Love's cruelties and Beauty's pride !

T. Stavley.

    Sweetest love ! I do not go
      For weariness of thee,
Nor in hope the world can show
    A fairer love to me :
        But since that I
    Must die at last, 'tis best
    Thus to use myself in jest,
      By feigned death to die.

Donne.
" To his Love, on going a Journey."

She spoke and wept : the dark and azure well
   Sparkled beneath the shower of her bright tears,
And every little circlet where they fell,
   Flung to the cavern-roof inconstant spheres
And intertangled lines of light :—a knell
   Of sobbing voices came upon her ears
From those departing Forms, o'er the serene
Of the white streams and of the forest green.

Shelley.
" Witch of Atlas."

    On the door you will not enter,
      I have gazed too long—adieu !
    Hope withdraws her peradventure—
      Death is near me,—and not *you !*
        Come, O lover,
        Close and cover
    These poor eyes, you called, I ween,
    " Sweetest eyes were ever seen."

Mrs. Browning.
" Catarina to Camoens.'

    Speak, speak, thou fearful guest !
    Who, with thy hollow breast
    Still in rude armour drest,

> Comest to daunt me !
> Wrapt not in Eastern balms,
> But with thy fleshless palms
> Stretched, as if asking alms,
> Why dost thou haunt me ?
>
> *Longfellow.*
> " The Spectre in Armour."

(*h*). Stanzas of Nine Verses.

One particular arrangement of nine-line verse is known as the *Spenserian stanza,* being first used by Spenser in his *Fairie Queene.* It consists of eight heroics followed by an Alexandrine, and these are made to rhyme in three sets, 1, 3 ; 2, 4, 5, 7 ; 6, 8, 9. Though it is thus complex in structure, there is sufficient variety in its stately swing to render it suitable, either for lengthy or short compositions, and to make it a favourite form with most of our poets. Besides the *Fairie Queene,* Thomson's *Castle of Indolence,* Beattie's *Minstrel,* Burns's *Cotter's Saturday Night,* Byron's *Childe Harold,* and Shelley's *Revolt of Islam,* are written in it. A stanza from each of these poems follows :

> His life was nigh into death's door yplast,
> And thread-bare cote and cobbled shoes he wore ;
> Ne scarce good morsell all his life did taste ;
> But both from backe and bellie still did spare,
> To fill his bags, and richesse to compare :
> Yet childe ne kinsman living had he none
> To leave them to ; but thorough daily care
> To get, and nightly feare to lose, his owne,
> He led a wretched life, unto himselfe unknowne.
>
> *Spenser.*
> " Avarice."

I care not, Fortune, what you me deny ;
You cannot rob me of free Nature's grace ;
You cannot shut the windows of the sky,
Through which Aurora shows her morning face ;
You cannot bar my constant feet to trace
The woods and lawns, by living stream, at eve :
Let health my nerves and finer fibres brace,
And I their toys to the great children leave ;
Of fancy, reason, virtue, nought can me bereave.

Thomson.

Ah ! who can tell how hard it is to climb
The steep where Fame's proud temple shines afar ;
Ah ! who can tell how many a soul sublime
Has felt the influence of malignant star,
And waged with Fortune an eternal war ;
Checked by the scoff of Pride, by Envy's frown,
And Poverty's unconquerable bar,
In life's low vale remote has pined alone,
Then dropped into the grave, unpitied and unknown.

Beattie.

Dr. Beattie says of this stanza : "I am surprised
to find the structure of Spenser's complicated stanza
so little troublesome. I think it the most harmonious that ever was contrived. It admits of more
variety of pauses than either the couplet or the
alternate rhyme [he means the stanza of four], and
it concludes with a pomp and majesty of sound
which to my ear is wonderfully delightful. It seems
also very well adapted to the genius of our language,
which from its irregularity of inflexion and number
of monosyllables, abounds in diversified terminations
and consequently renders our poetry susceptible of
an endless variety of legitimate rhymes.*

* Forbes's " Life of Beattie."

O happy love ! where love like this is found !
O heart-felt raptures ! bliss beyond compare !
I've pacèd much this weary, mortal round,
And sage experience bids me this declare—
If Heaven a draught of heavenly pleasure spare,
One cordial in this melancholy vale,
'Tis when a youthful, loving, modest pair
In other's arms breathe out the tender tale,
Beneath the milk-white thorn that scents the evening gale
                              Burns.

Roll on, thou deep and dark blue Ocean—roll !
Ten thousand fleets sweep over thee in vain ;
Man marks the earth with ruin—his control
Stops with the shore ; upon the watery plain
The wrecks are all thy deed ; nor doth remain
A shadow of man's ravage, save his own,
When, for a moment, like a drop of rəin
He sinks into thy depths with bubbling groan,
Without a grave, unknelled, uncoffined, and unknown.
                              Byron.

Specimens of other nine-line stanzas, not Spenserian, follow.

If thou beest born to strange sights,
    Things invisible to see,
Ride ten thousand days and nights
    Till age snow white hairs on thee ;
Then, when thou return'st wilt tell me
All strange wonders that befell thee,
        And swear,
        Nowhere,
    Lives a woman true and fair.
                    Donne.
                " Fair and False."

It's wiser being good than bad ;
   It's safer being meek than fierce ;
It's fitter being sane than mad.
   My own hope is, a sin will pierce
The thickest cloud earth ever stretched ;
   That after Last returns the First,
Though a wide compass round be fetched ;
   That what began best can't prove worst,
Nor what God blessed once, prove accurst.

                      R. Browning.
                    " Apparent Failure.

Alas ! I have nor hope, nor health,
   Nor peace within, nor calm around,
Nor that content, surpassing wealth,
   The sage in meditation found,
   And walked with inward glory crowned ;
Nor fame, nor power, nor love, nor leisure,
   Others I see whom these surround,—
Smiling they live, and call life pleasure :
To me life's cup has been dealt in another measure
                      Shelley.

(*i*). Stanzas of Ten Verses.

To each his sufferings ; all are men
   Condemned alike to groan,
The tender for another's pain,
   Th' unfeeling for his own.
Yet ah ! why should they know their fate ?
Since sorrow never comes too late,
   And happiness too swiftly flies ;
Thought would destroy their paradise.—
No more ;—where ignorance is bliss
   'Tis folly to be wise.

                      Gray.
            " On a Distant Prospect of Eton College."

Fair daffodils, we weep to see
 You haste away so soon ;
As yet the early rising sun
 Has not attained his noon.
 Stay, stay,
 Until the hast'ning day
 Has run,
 But to the even-song !
And having prayed together, we
 Will go with you along.

Herrick.
" To Daffodils."

Freeze, freeze, thou bitter sky,
Thou dost not bite so nigh
 As benefits forgot ;
Though thou the waters warp,
Thy sting is not so sharp
 As friends remember'd not.
Heigh ho ! sing heigh ho ! unto the green holly,
Most friendship is feigning, most loving mere folly
 Then heigh ho ! the holly !
 This life is most jolly.

Shakspere.

The time I've lost in wooing,
In watching and pursuing
 The light that lies
 In woman's eyes,
Has been my heart's undoing.
Tho' wisdom oft has sought me,
I scorned the love she brought me.
 My only books
 Were woman's looks,
And folly's all they taught me.

Moore.

She passed like summer flowers away.
 Her aspect and her voice
 Will never more rejoice,
For she lies hushed in cold decay;
 Broken the golden bowl,
 Which held her hallowed soul :
It was an idle boast to say
 " Our souls are as the same,"
 And stings me now to shame ;
Her spirit went, and mine did not obey.

      Thos. Woolner.
      "My Beautiful Lady."

I'm no slave to such as you be ;
 Neither shall a snowy breast,
Wanton eye, or lip of ruby,
 Ever rob me of my rest.
 Go, go, display
 Thy beauty's ray
To some o'er-soon enamoured swain ;
 These common wiles
 Of sighs and smiles
Are all bestowed on me in vain.

      Wither.

For thou wert born of woman !   Thou didst come,
O Holiest ! to this world of sin and gloom,
Not in Thy omnipotent array ;
 And not by thunders strewed
 Was Thy tempestuous road ;
Nor indignation burnt before Thee on Thy way.
 But Thee, a soft and naked child,
 Thy mother undefiled,
 In the rude manger laid to rest
 From off her virgin breast.

      Milman.

How beautiful is night !
A dewy freshness fills the silent air ;
No mist obscures, nor cloud, nor speck, nor stain,
Breaks the serene of heaven.
In full-orbed glory yonder moon divine
Rolls through the dark-blue depths ;
Beneath her steady ray
The desert-circle spreads,
Like the round ocean girdled with the sky.
How beautiful is night !

Southey.

(*j*). STANZAS OF ELEVEN VERSES.

I said—Then, dearest, since 'tis so,
Since now at length my fate I know,
Since nothing all my love avails,
Since all my life seemed meant for, fails,
Since this was written and needs must be—
My whole heart rises up to bless
Your name in pride and thankfulness !
Take back the hope you gave—I claim
Only a memory of the same,—
And this beside, if you will not blame,
Your leave for one more last ride with me.

R. Browning.
" The Last Ride Together."

The hour was late ; the fire burned low,
The landlord's eyes were closed in sleep,
And near the story's end a deep
Sonorous sound at times was heard,
As when the distant bagpipes blow.
At this all laughed ; the landlord stirred,
As one awakening from a swound,
And, gazing anxiously around,

Protested that he had not slept,
But only shut his eyes, and kept
His ears attentive to each word.

Longfellow.
"Good Night."

God be with thee, my beloved.   God be with thee!
        Else alone thou goest forth,
        Thy face unto the north.—
Moor and pleasance, all around thee and beneath thee,
        Looking equal in one snow!
        While I, who try to reach thee,
        Vainly follow, vainly follow,
        With the farewell and the hollo,
        And cannot reach thee so.
        Alas! I can but teach thee,
God be with thee, my beloved.   God be with thee!

Mrs. Browning.
" A Valediction."

(*k*). STANZAS OF TWELVE VERSES.

You'll come to our ball; since we parted,
    I've thought of you more than I'll say;
Indeed, I was half broken-hearted
    For a week, when they took you away.
Fond fancy brought back to my slumbers
    Our walks on the Ness and the Den,
And echoed the musical numbers
    Which you used to sing to me then.
I know the romance, since it's over,
    'Twere idle, or worse to recall;
I know you're a terrible rover,
    But, Clarence, you'll come to our ball?

Praed.

        O what a plague is love!
            I cannot bear it;
        She will inconstant prove,
            I greatly fear it.

It so torments my mind
   That my heart faileth ;
She wavers with the wind
   As a ship saileth.
Please her as best I may,
   She loves still to gainsay ;
Alack ! and well-a-day !
   Philinda flouts me !

Anon.

Here was I with my arm and heart
   And brain, all yours for a word, a want,
Put into a look—just a look, your part—
   While mine to repay it . . . valiant vaunt.
Were the woman that's dead alive to hear,
Had her lover, that's lost, love's proof to show !
But I cannot show it ; you cannot speak
   From the churchyard neither, miles removed,
Though I feel by a pulse within my cheek,
   Which stabs and stops, that the woman I loved
Needs help in her grave, and finds none near,
   Wants warmth from the heart which sends it—so !

R. Browning.
"Too Late."

With blackest moss the flower-plots
   Were thickly crusted, one and all :
The rusted nails fell from the knots
   That held the pear to the gable-wall.
The broken sheds look'd sad and strange :
   Uplifted was the clinking latch ;
   Weeded and worn the ancient thatch
Upon the lonely moated grange.
     She only said, " My life is dreary ;
     He cometh not," she said ;
     She said, " I am aweary, aweary,
     I would that I were dead !"

Tennyson.
" Mariana."

See, O see,
How every tree,
Every bower,
Every flower,
A new life gives to others' joys :
Whilst that I,
Grief-stricken, lie,
Nor can meet
With any sweet,
But what faster mine destroys.
What are all the senses' pleasures,
When the mind has lost all measures ?

(*l*). STANZAS OF MORE THAN TWELVE* VERSES.

Long years of toil and care,
And pain and poverty, have passed
Since last I listened to her prayer,
And looked upon her last.
Yet how she looked, and how she smiled
Upon me, while a playful child,
The lustre of her eye,
The kind caress, the fond embrace,
The reverence of her placid face,
Within my memory lie
As fresh as they had only been
Bestowed, and felt, and heard, and seen
Since yesterday went by.
                                    John Bethune.
                                    " My Grandmother."

A glorious people vibrated again
   The lightning of the nations : Liberty
From heart to heart, from tower to tower, o'er Spain,
   Scattering contagious fire into the sky,

---

* For a full account of the *Sonnet*, see page 203.

Gleamed.   My soul spurned the chains of its dismay
     And, in the rapid plumes of song,
     Clothed itself, sublime and strong ;
As a young eagle soars the morning clouds among,
     Hovering in verse o'er its accustomed prey ;
          Till from its station in the heaven of fame
     The Spirit's whirlwind rapt it, and the ray
          Of the remotest sphere of living flame
Which paves the void was from behind it flung.
     As foam from a ship's swiftness, when there came
     A voice out of the deep : I will record the same.
                              Shelley.
                         " Ode to Liberty.'

          With deep affection,
          And recollection,
          I often think of
               Those Shandon bells,
          Whose sounds so wide would
          In my days of childhood,
          Fling round my cradle
               Their magic spells.
          On this I ponder,
          Where'er I wander,
          And thus grow fonder,
               Sweet Cork, of thee ;
          With thy bells of Shandon,
          That sound so grand on
          The pleasant waters
               Of the river Lee.

                         Francis Mahony
                         Father Prout).

   Shelley's beautiful ode, *The Cloud*, is built up of
stanzas of twelve, fourteen, and eighteen verses, the
first of which is here given.

I bring fresh showers for the thirsting flowers
    From the seas and the streams;
I wear light shade for the leaves when laid
    In their noon-day dreams;
From my wings are shaken the dews that waken
    The sweet birds every one,
When rocked to rest on their mother's breast,
    As she dances about the sun.
I wield the flail of the lashing hail,
    And whiten the green plains under;
And then again I dissolve in rain,
    And laugh as I pass in thunder.

                        Shelley.

Terza Rima, in which Dante's *Divine Comedy* is written, furnishes another variety of verse arrangement intermediate between the continuous and stanzaic forms. It consists of heroics with three rhymes at intervals. In the first tercet the first line rhymes with the third, and the second with the first and third of the following tercet, and so on continuously throughout. Even when the groups are separated, as in Shelley's *Triumph of Life,* the sense is continuous, and it is therefore usual to present them in unbroken succession. The following extract from Byron's *Prophecy of Dante* furnishes an excellent example :

Many are the poets who have never penned
    Their inspiration, and perchance the best:
They felt, and loved, and died, but would not lend
    Their thoughts to meaner beings; they compressed
The good within them, and rejoined the stars
    Unlaureled upon earth, but far more blest

Than those who are degraded by the jars
  Of passion, and their frailties linked to fame,
Conquerors of high renown, but full of scars.
  Many are the poets, but without the name ;
For what is poesy but to create
  From overfeeling good or ill, and aim
At an eternal life beyond our fate,
  And be the new Prometheus of new men,
Bestowing fire from heaven, and then too late
  Feeling the pleasure given repaid with pain,
And vultures to the heart of the bestower,
  Who, having lavished his high gift in vain,
Lies chained to his bare rock by the seashore.

Byron.

There was a youth, who, as with toil and travel,
  Had grown quite weak and grey before his time ;
Nor any could the restless griefs unravel

Which burned within him, withering up his prime
  And goading him, like fiends, from land to land.
Not his the load of any secret crime,

For nought of ill his heart could understand,
  But pity and wild sorrow for the same ;—
Not his the thirst for glory or command

Baffled with blast of hope-consuming shame ;
  Nor evil joys which fire the vulgar breast
And quench in speedy smoke its feeble flame,

Had left within his soul their dark unrest :
  Nor what religion fables of the grave
Feared he,—Philosophy's accepted guest.

Shelley.

H

(*m*). IRREGULAR STANZAS.

Most of the finest odes in our language are exceedingly complex in structure, both in variety of
metre and length of verse, and they are usually
broken up into stanzas of varying length, from four
to upwards of twenty lines.   Amongst the most
noted compositions of this kind may be enumerated
Milton's *Ode on the Nativity of Christ*, Dryden's
Alexander's Feast, Pope's *Ode on St. Cecilia's Day*,
Gray's *Bard* and *On a Distant Prospect of Eton Col-
lege*, Shelley's *West Wind* and *The Cloud*.   Collins's
Ode on the Passions is here quoted at length as a
typical specimen.

THE PASSIONS.

> When Music, heavenly maid, was young,
> While yet in early Greece she sung,
> The Passions oft, to hear her skill,
> Thronged around her magic cell.
>
> Exulting, trembling, raging, fainting,
> Possess'd beyond the Muse's painting;
> By turns they felt the glowing mind
> Disturbed, delighted, raised, refined;
> Till once, 'tis said, when all were fired,
> Fill'd with fury, rapt, inspired,
> From the supporting myrtles round
> They snatch'd her instruments of sound;
> And as they oft had heard apart
> Sweet lessons of her forceful art,
> Each, for madness ruled the hour,
> Would prove his own expressive power.

First Fear his hand, its skill to try,
  Amid the chords, bewilder'd laid ;
And back recoil'd, he knew not why,
  E'en at the sound himself had made.
Next Anger rush'd, his eyes on fire,
  In lightnings own'd his secret stings ;
In one rude clash he struck the lyre,
  And swept with hurried hand the strings.

With woeful measure wan Despair—
  Low sullen sounds his grief beguiled ;
A solemn, strange, and mingled air ;
  'Twas sad by fits, by starts 'twas wild.

But thou, O Hope ! with eyes so fair
  What was thy delighted measure ?
  Still it whispered promised pleasure,
And bade the lovely scenes at distance hail.
  Still would her touch the strain prolong ;
And from the rocks, the woods, the vale,
  She call'd on Echo still through all the song ;
And where her sweetest theme she chose,
A soft responsive voice was heard at every close ;
And Hope enchanted, smiled and waved her golden hair :
  And longer had she sung—but with a frown
    Revenge impatient rose ;
He threw his blood-stained sword in thunder down
    And with a withering look,
    The war-denouncing trumpet took,
    And blew a blast so loud and dread,
Were ne'er prophetic sounds so full of woe ;
    And ever and anon he beat
    The double drum with furious heat ;
And though sometimes, each dreary pause between,
    Dejected Pity at his side
    Her soul-subduing voice applied,
Yet still he kept his wild unalter'd mien,
While each strain'd ball of sight seem'd bursting from his
    head.

Thy numbers, Jealousy, to nought were fix'd;
　Sad proof of thy distressful state;
Of diff'ring themes the veering song was mix'd,
　And now it courted Love, now raving call'd on Hate.

With eyes upraised, as one inspired,
Pale Melancholy sat retired,
And from her wild sequester'd seat,
In notes by distance made more sweet,
Pour'd through the mellow horn her pensive soul;
　And dashing soft from rocks around,
　Bubbling runnels join'd the sound;
Through glades and glooms the mingled measure stole:
　Or o'er some haunted streams with fond delay,
　　Round a holy calm diffusing,
　　Love of peace and lonely musing,
　In hollow murmurs died away.

But oh! how alter'd was its sprightly tone
　When Cheerfulness, a nymph of healthiest hue,
Her bow across her shoulder flung,
　Her buskin gemmed with morning dew,
Blew an inspiring air that dale and thicket rung,
The hunter's call, to fawn and dryad known
　The oak-crowned sisters, and their chaste-eyed queen,
　Satyrs and sylvan boys, were seen
　Peeping from forth their alleys green;
Brown Exercise rejoiced to hear,
And Sport leap'd up, and seized his beechen spear.

Last came Joy's ecstatic trial:
　He with viny crown advancing,
　First to the lively pipe his hand address'd;
But soon he saw the brisk awakening viol,
　Whose sweet entrancing voice he loved the best.
They would have thought who heard the strain,
　They saw in Tempe's vale her native maids,
　Amid the festal sounding shades,
　　To some unwearied minstrel dancing:

While, as his flying fingers kiss'd the strings,
Love framed with Mirth a gay fantastic round,
Loose were her tresses seen, her zone unbound :
   And he, amidst his frolic play,
   As if he would the charming air repay,
Shook thousand odours from his dewy wings.

   O Music ! sphere-descended maid,
   Friend of pleasure, wisdom's aid !
   Why, goddess ! why, to us denied,
   Lay'st thou thy ancient lyre aside ?
   As in that loved Athenian bower,
   You learn an all-commanding power ;
   Thy mimic soul, O nymph endeared
   Can well recall what then it heard,
   Where is thy native simple heart,
   Devote to virtue, fancy, art ?
   Arise, as in that elder time,
   Warm, energic, chaste, sublime !
   Thy wonders in that godlike age
   Fill thy recording sister's page—
   'Tis said, and I believe the tale,
   Thy humblest reed could more prevail,
   Had more of strength, diviner rage,
   Than all that charms this laggard age
   Even all at once together found,
   Cecilia's mingled world of sound.
   Oh, bid our vain endeavours cease.
   Revive the just designs of Greece ;
   Return in all thy simple state ;
   Confirm the tales her sons relate.

POETIC LICENCES.

IN this chapter we are called upon to deal with all the departures from normal exactitude of which writers of verse avail themselves. We shall find that it is not so much an enquiry into the nature and extent of the liberty the poet is allowed, as of the kind and amount he thinks fit to take. Verse-making preceded prosodial laws, as speech and writing existed before the rules of grammar were drawn up. The poet presents us with the verses he has framed to his own sweet will, and all that is left to prosaic mortals is to approve or condemn them. The restrictions and difficulties that the artist, whose material is words, has to contend with are at once so embarrassing and unavoidable, that what are called licences would be more truly designated necessities. The versifier is expected to conform to strict grammatical rule; he has to manipulate sounds and their symbols which bristle with irregularities and difficulties of many kinds, and yet he must produce melody which is pleasing and varied. To accomplish all this he is compelled to become, in a sense, a law unto himself, and therefore he makes no scruple in surmounting obstacles to trespass the boundaries laid down for ordinary observance.

These so-called poetic licences may be conveniently grouped together and considered under three heads—*Grammatical, Orthographical,* and *Metrical.*

1.—GRAMMATICAL LICENCES.

These embrace deviations from ordinary forms of expression, or the strict grammatical structure of sentences. In prose most of them would be considered *solecisms,* but in verse they are allowable in order to meet the exigencies of rhythm, or to add variety and elegance to the composition.

(*a*). ELLIPSIS.

This is the omission of words which are necessary to complete the construction though not to convey the sense.

> Cold, cold, my girl ?
>> " *Othello.*"

> What ! all my pretty chickens and their dam
> At one fell swoop ?
>> " *Macbeth.*"

> Is there for honest poverty,
> That hangs his head, and a' that ?
>> *Burns.*

A form of ellipsis in which the consequence is suppressed to be supplied by the hearer's mind is called *Aposiopesis, e.g.* :

> If she sustain him and his hundred knights
> When I have shown the unfitness——: How now, Oswald ?
>> " *King Lear.*"

They fell together all as by consent ;
They dropped as by a thunder stroke.   What might,
Worthy Sebastian ? O what might ?—No more :
And yet, methinks, I see it in thy face
What thou should'st be : the occasion speaks thee ; and
My strong imagination sees a crown
Dropping upon thy head.

" Tempest."

Omission of conjunctions is called *Asyndeton.*

(*b*). PLEONASM

is the introduction of superfluous words, in order
to strengthen the expression or to keep the mind
dwelling upon the thought, *e.g. :* What a length of
tail *behind !* The *sea-girt* isle. In prose these would
be condemned as tautological.

Nor to these idle orbs does day appear,
Or sun, or moon, or stars, throughout the year,
Or man, or woman.

Milton.

Now all these things are over—yes, all thy pretty ways—
Thy needlework, thy prattle, thy snatches of old lays.

Macaulay.

Such repetitions as these, says Coleridge, constitute beauty of the highest kind.

(*c*). ENALLAGE

is the use of one part of speech for another, adjectives for adverbs, the past tense for the participle,
as :

Those move easiest who have learned to dance.

Pope.

The idols are broke in the temple of Baal.
Byron.
They fall successive, and successive rise.
Pope.

(d). HYPERBATON

is the transposition of words beyond what would be allowable even in rhetorical prose, *e.g. :*

> Idle after dinner, in his chair,
> Sat a farmer, ruddy, fat, and fair.
> *Tennyson*

> From morn
> To noon he fell, from noon to dewy eve,
> A summer's day.
> *Milton.*

> High on a throne of royal state, which far
> Outshone the wealth of Ormuz or of Ind,
> Or where the gorgeous East, with richest hand
> Showers on her kings barbaric pearl and gold,
> Satan exalted sat.
> *Milton.*

> Far along,
> From peak to peak, the rattling crags among,
> Leaps the live thunder.
> *Byron.*

(e). ANACOLUTHON.

This is the want of proper sequence in the construction of a compound sentence, as :

> My name is Edgar, and thy father's son.
> *" King Lear."*

Why I do trifle thus with his despair
Is done to cure it.

" King Lear."

God from the Mount of Sinai, whose gray top
Shall tremble, he descending, shall himself,
In thunder, lightning, and loud trumpets' sound,
Ordain them laws.

Milton.

2.—ORTHOGRAPHICAL LICENCES.

These are deviations from the ordinary spelling, and therefore in the pronunciation of words, their object being to shorten or lengthen a verse by a syllable.

(*a*). ELISION

is the omission of a letter or syllable at the beginning, middle, or end of a word, *e.g.* : 'gainst, 'scape, o'er, ta'en, ope', th'. At the beginning this is known as *aphæresis*, in the middle *syncope*, at the end *apocope*.

(*b*). PROSTHESIS

is prefixing an expletive syllable to a word; as, yclad, beweep.

(*c*). PARAGOGE

adds an expletive syllable to a word; as withouten, lovèd.

(*d*). SYNÆRESIS

is the merging of two syllables into one, as may be done with such words as alien, flower, familiar, amorous, murmuring, mouldering.

(*e*). DIÆRESIS

is the separation of a diphthong into two sounds, as is occasionally found in our older poets; such as regarding the endings tion, sion, and words like hire, dire as dissyllables.

> And so by many winding nooks he strays,
> With willing spirit to the wide o-*cean*.

(*f*). TMESIS

is the insertion of a word between the parts of a compound; as, to us ward, on which side soever.

To these may be added the use of archaisms, *i.e.* old forms of words that have become otherwise obsolete; as wis for know, e'en or eyne for eyes.

Some of these orthographical licences present difficulties which have given rise to so much diverse opinion that it may be useful to illustrate them more in detail. Elisions, generally speaking, should not be such as to create words of unpleasing sound or difficult pronunciation. The following verse is somewhat harsh, for instance :

> Then 'gan th' obstrep'rous mob to rage.

Whereas in the opening line of *The Paradise Lost* the last two syllables of *disobedience* are merged without any unpleasant effect.

> Of man's first disobedience, and the fruit—

One complaint made against our language is that its consonants are too numerous in proportion to the vowels, and the effect of elision is to increase that proportion.

The second person singular of our verb terminates with letters that do not well accommodate themselves to elisions, when the verb itself ends with a consonant;

> Ill thou consider'st that the kind are brave.

> That usher'st in the sun, and still prepar'st its way.

> Thou mourn'st them living, as already dead.

These elisions are harsh: but where the verb is regular, as love, loved, fear, feared, &c., the same person in the past time presents an obstacle almost insurmountable to any elision. Yet some few have attempted it, making indeed two elisions, as,

> Thou shar'd'st their nature, insolence, and fate,

But to others this rough assemblage of consonants has appeared so formidable that, rather than meet it, they have ventured to trespass upon their grammar rules. For instance, in Pope's *Messiah* this passage occurs—

> O Thou, my voice inspire,
> Who *touch'd* Isaiah's hallowed lips with fire !

—where touch'd is used for touch'd'st.

The occasions for making such elisions as this ought to be avoided; but unfortunately they occur oftenest in those kinds of poetry where they are least admissible. For with respect to elisions. it is to be observed that, as in familiar discourse we use without scruple those which we should not allow in the solemn recital of a grave composition, so in familiar verse we may admit those which are to be excluded from the higher species—from epic and lyric poems and the like.

The elisions which we meet with as frequently as any are of the verbs, substantive and auxiliary. Many of these are improper in grave poetry.

> From Paran's height the One that's holy came.

> But have evoked them oft, I'm sure in vain.

> Kill him, and thou'rt secure ; 'tis only he.

These elisions of the verb substantive are none of them suitable to the rank of the poems in which they stand ; neither are those made of the auxiliary verbs, as I'll, for I will, he'd, for he would, &c., but they might all enter into light pieces without offence ; as into satires, as here:

> 'Tis sad
> To say you're curious when we say you're mad.

> I'm very sensible he's mad in law.

We find in some of our poets other elisions which are faulty, because the letters which are left do not meet and coalesce, as they ought, into one syllable The following is such :

> We' allow'd you beauty, and we did submit,
> Shame and woe to us. if we' our wealth obey.

But a fault still greater is here :

> Sha'n't I return the vengeance in my power ?

This term, *sha'n't,* is so deformed and vulgarized by elision as to be altogether unfit to appear in poetry. In justice to the poets of the present time, it is to be acknowledged that they are more correct and guarded against these blemishes ; and to collect them we are forced to go back to a former age.

Other elisions, not much practised by our moderns, are made in words of more than one syllable, by cutting off the last, like these in Milton : *

> Th' specious deeds on earth which glory' excites,
> To be invulnerable' in those bright arms,
> So he with difficulty' and labour hard.

But among our earliest poets this sort of elision was common ; Gower used it :

> For ever I wrastle', and ever I am behind,
> As pray unto my Lady' of any help.

So did Chaucer :

> Then help me, Lord, to-morrow' in my battaille.

> Winnen thy cost, take her ensample' of me.

> My body' is ay so redy' and so penible.

* See *Hiatus,* p. 115.

For trouble' in earth take no meláncholy.
Be rich in patience, gif thou' in goods be poor ;
Who livis merry' he livis mightily :
Without gladnéss availis no treasúre.

The reader will not fail to observe that, after all
these elisions, the next word begins with a vowel,
and that in general the syllables cut off are short.

Contractions are made, as has been said, of syllables which are not separated by any consonant; these
our language contains in great number and variety ;
particularly a large class from the Latin, as *motion,
region, occasion.* The two last syllables of these
and other such words are now always contracted
into one, when used in a verse. It was not so formerly :

His name was heavenly contemplation ;
Of God and goodness was his meditation.
Spenser.
" Fairy Queen."

Some willing men that might instruct his sons,
And that would stand to good conditions.
"Hall's Satires."

Examples in other words :

To fly his step-dame's love outrageous.
Spenser.
" Fairy Queen."

This siege that hath engirt his marriage.
Shakspere.
" Rape of Lucrece."

Should bleed in his own law's obedience.

Syllables like these were divided whenever it suited the poet's convenience. Shakspere in all his rhymed poetry makes them rhyme double, as :

> To kill myself, quoth she, alack ! what were it
> But with my body my poor soul's pollution ?
> They that lose half with greater patience bear it,
> Than they whose whole is swallow'd in confusion.
> > *" Rape of Lucrece."*

> I will drink
> Potions of eysel 'gainst my strong infection ;
> No bitterness that I will bitter think,
> Nor double penance to correct correction.
> > Sonnet iii.

This division of syllables is found in our poetry as late as Cowley's time ; but he was a licentious versifier :

> At thy strong charms it must be gone,
> Though a disease, as well as devil, were call'd legion,
> > *Cowley.*

A different manner of lengthening the word is seen in this example :

> O, how this spring of love resembleth
> The' uncertain glory of an April day !
> > *Shakspere.*
> > " Two Gentlemen of Verona," act i. sc. 3.

—where the word resembleth is pronounced resemble-eth, as having four syllables. But such licence would not be now permitted. In our early poets it could not be accounted a licence, for it was according to the ordinary pronunciation of many such words:

> He came at his commandément on hie.
> > *Chaucer.*
> > " Knight's Tale "

> Right in the middest of the threshold lay.
> > *Spenser.*
> > "Fairy Queen."

It may here be pointed out that in our older poetry final syllables were sounded which have since entirely disappeared or become mute, such as *é, és, éd, e.g.* :

> The smalé fowlés maken melodie—*

and also that many words were differently accented three hundred years ago; for instance, fárewell, revénue, twilíght, canónized, aspéct, cómplete.

---

* This is further illustrated by presenting the opening lines of the Prologue to the " Canterbury Tales," scanned :—

' Whăn thăt | Ăprīl | lĕ wĭth | hĭs schŏw | rĕs swoŏte
Thĕ drŏught | ŏf Mărche | hăth pēr | cĕd tŏ | thĕ roŏte,
Ănd bă | thĕd ēve | rȳ vēyne | ĭn swĭch | lĭcoŭr,
Ŏf whĭch | vĕrtue | ĕngēn | drĕd ĭs | thĕ floŭr;
Whăn Zē | phĭrūs | ĕek wĭth | hĭs swē | tĕ breēthe
Ĕnspĭ | rĕd hăth | ĭn ēve | rȳ hŏlte | ănd heēthe
Thĕ tēn | drĕ crŏp | pĕs, ănd | thĕ yŏn | gĕ sŏnne
Hăth ĭn | thĕ Răm | hĭs hal | fĕ coŭrs | ĭ-rŏnne,
Ănd smă | lĕ fŏw | lĕs mă | kĕn mē | lŏdie,
Thăt slē | pĕn ăl | thĕ nĭght | wĭth ŏ pĕn eȳe,
Sŏ prĭ | kĕth hēm | nătūre | ĭn hĕre | cŏrăges:—
Thănne lŏn | gĕn fŏlk | tŏ gŏn | ŏn pĭl | grĭmăges
Ănd păl | mĕrs fŏr | tŏ seē | kĕn străun | gĕ strŏndes,
To fĕr | nĕ hăl | wĕs, koŭthe | ĭn sŏn | drȳ lŏndes;
And spē | cĭallȳ, | frŏm ēve | rȳ schĭ | rés ēnde
Ŏf Eń | gĕlŏnd, | tŏ Căunt | tĕrbūry | thĕy wēnde,
Thĕ hŏ | lȳ blĭs | fŭl măr | tĭr fŏr | tŏ seēke,
Thăt hĕm | hăth hŏlp | ĕn whăn | thăt thĕy | wĕre seēke.'

I

To what has been said of the contraction and lengthening of words may be added, that there are some English words which are not allowed to pass in verse for two syllables, though in sound they are such, and cannot be pronounced in one. Of these the following is an account.

" Our short *u*, sounded as in *but,* is pronounced easiest of all the vowels, and therefore is a great favourite with my countrymen; it is commonly inserted between *e, i, o, u* (when long), and *r*; as n there, fire, more, pure, which we pronounce the*u*r, *fiu*r, mo*u*r, &c. I think *hire* and *dire* have as fair a claim to be counted dissyllables as higher and dyer, though we will not allow them the same rank in verse.* If you repeat

> For high renown the heaven-born poets strive,
> Actors for higher (*hire*) in toils incessant live,

a person may think you mean to reflect upon the players when you intend them a compliment. Or in describing a drunken quarrel, if you end with these lines :

> The blood that streamed from the gash profound,
> With scarlet *dire* distain'd their garments round,
> Sad scarlet *dyer* he who gave the wound.

Should you, in reading them, transpose the *dire, dyer,* into each other's places, you would not per-

---

* Crying that's good that's gone: our rash faults.
> *Shakspere,* " All's Well that Ends Well."

In this line *our* stands for two syllables, which indeed it may fairly claim ; for the organs of speech, after sounding any long vowel or diphthong, cannot proceed to sound the letter *r* without being in a position to sound the short *u* (sometimes, however, represented in writing by *e*), as higher.

ceive the change ; such is the force of custom and imagination to debauch the ear, that it does not know when one and one syllable make two."*

Here we must introduce the consideration of the *hiatus* in verse, which has occupied the attention of writers on versification beyond its due importance. By it is meant the occurrence of a final vowel followed immediately by the initial vowel of another word without the suppression or elision of either by an apostrophe. It is admitted on all hands to be a fault, and though by some writers it is declared to be absolutely inadmissible into our verse, as it is in Italian, yet it is to be found in the works of all our poets. Perhaps the truth lies in regarding it as unavoidable, and the remedy in minimising its occurrence as much as possible. Pope exemplifies it in the line :

> Tho' oft the ear the open vowels tire.
> > *" Essay on Criticism."*

The vowels which he calls open are those that stand one at the end of a word, and the other at the beginning of the next, without any consonant between them. When vowels so meet they cause in the pronunciation a gaping, called after the Latin, an hiatus, which offends the ear in prose as well as in verse.

Two of our own poets, most celebrated for their skill in versification, viz. Pope and Dryden, have repeatedly spoken of the hiatus as a fault; but, as

* Tucker's " Treatise on Vocal Sounds."

they represent it to be of greater magnitude than I think it is in reality, I will here state their opinions respecting it, and their practice. Pope says, "the hiatus should be avoided with more care in poetry than in oratory; and I would try to prevent it, unless where the cutting it off is more prejudicial to the sound than the hiatus itself." Dryden is still more averse to the hiatus. "There is not (says he in his dedication to the *Æneid*), to the best of my remembrance, one vowel gaping on another for want of a *cæsura* (*i.e.* a cutting off) in this whole poem; but where a vowel ends a word, the next begins with a consonant, or what is its equivalent; for our *w* and *h* aspirate, and our diphthongs are plainly such; the greatest latitude I take is in the letter *y*, when it concludes a word, and the first syllable of the next begins with a vowel. Neither need I have called this a latitude which is only an explanation of the general rule; that no vowel can be cut off before another, when we cannot sink the pronunciation of it, as he, she, me, I, &c." In another place he mentions the hiatus with extreme severity. "Since I have named the *synalepha*, which is cutting off one vowel immediately before another, I will give an example of it from Chapman's *Homer*. It is in the first line of the argument to the first *Iliad*.

Apollo's priest to th' Argive fleet doth bring.

Here we see ne makes it not the Argive, but th' Argive; to shun the shock of the two vowels immediately following each other; but in the same page he gives a bad example of the quite contrary kind:

> Alpha the prayer of Chryses sings ;
> The army's plague, the strife of kings.

In these words, the army's, the ending with a vowel, and army's beginning with another vowel, without cutting off the first (by which it had been, th' army's), there remains a most horrible ill-sounding gap betwixt those words. I cannot say that I have every way observed the rule of the synalepha in my translation : but wheresoever I have not, it is a fault in the sound."*

As Dryden acknowledges that, in the verses to which this dedication is prefixed, he has sometimes admitted an hiatus, let us pass to his *Æneid*, where he professes to have avoided it throughout ; only allowing himself a certain latitude. But, indeed, what he allows himself is nothing less than an admission of the hiatus, as will appear by various instances.

> On every altar sacrifice renew.
> *Book* iv. *line* 76.

He claims a latitude in the letter *y* ; but that letter is, here and everywhere else, at the end of a word as much a vowel as any in the alphabet. He says, " W aspirates." It does so at the beginning of a word, but at the end it is either silent or makes a diphthong :

* Dedication to " Translations from Ovid's Metamorphoses."

Or hid within the hollow earth to lie.

Book xii. *line* 1293.

Now low on earth the lofty chief is laid.

Ibid. line 1346.

She drew a length of sighs, nor more she said.

Ibid. line 1280.

He says further, "That no vowel can be cut off before another, when we cannot sink the pronunciation of it, as he, she, me, I, &c." This is very true; but it does not follow that there is no hiatus where such a vowel is left. In each of these lines is an hiatus :

Whoe'er you are, not unbeloved by Heaven.

Book i. *line* 537.

These walls he enter'd, and those words express'd.

Book iv. *line* 515.

False as thou art, and more than false, forsworn.

Ibid. line 523.

Weak as I am, can I, alas! contend?

Book xii. *line* 1262.

So is there when the last consonants of a word are not sounded, as :

One bough it bears; but wond'rous to behold.

Book vi. *line* 210.

In all these, and many similar cases, which occur in every book of his *Æneid*, Dryden has left an hiatus, although he endeavours to explain it away.

Pope, in the poem where he stigmatizes the hiatus as a fault, has repeatedly committed the same fault, and done so in every one of those instances which he exhibits as faulty; they are these:

Though (i) oft the (ii) ear the (iii) open vowels tire.

And these are his own faults:

(i) Though each may feel increases and decays.
"*Ess. on Crit.*" 404.

(ii) And praise the easy vigour of a line.
Ib. 361.

(iii) As on the land while here the ocean gains.
Ib. 54.

As for their frequency, they recur sometimes as often as twice in one line:

Unlucky as Fungosa in the play.
Ib. 328.

Who, if once wrong, will needs be always so.
Ib. 569.

But taking the whole poem, there will be found, upon an average, an hiatus in every eleven lines; and, except the *Æneid* above-mentioned, the hiatus occurs nearly as often throughout all the poetry of Dryden and Pope. This observation is made, not to condemn their practice, but to show partly that the fault is not so great as they seem to represent

it, and partly that it is very difficult, if not imprac-
ticable, to avoid it. In Milton's poetry, to compute
from the fifty first and fifty last lines of *Paradise
Lost* and *Samson Agonistes*, there is an hiatus at
every fifth. In his other poems, it may not be so
frequent perhaps.

It is hardly necessary to say more of the hiatus;
yet this may be added, that, whatever offence it
may give will be less noted if it stands at a pause,
as:

Works without show, and without pomp presides.
Pope.
" Essay on Crit." 75.

Nature, like liberty, is but restrained.
Ib. 90.

Immortal Vida ! on whose honour'd brow.
Ib. 705.

In these instances the hiatus is better managed
than in the three quoted above from the same poem.
On the other hand, the hiatus will be perceived
most when the two vowels which mark it are such
that the organs of speech, in pronouncing them,
keep the same position.

There is a different sort of hiatus, as it may be
termed, which is made when a word or part of it
stands for two syllables that might be contracted
into one ; as, *heaven, tower, violet, evening,* &c. for
then there is a gap, because the verse seems to
want its full measure. The same want appears
still plainer when such words as *glorious, earlier,*

have the two last syllables divided. But this observation is not extended to verse of the anapestic kind; for our language, being somewhat overstocked with consonants, does not readily supply short syllables in the proportion which that verse requires. And therefore to divide syllables like those just mentioned is, in that species of verse, no licence at all.

Many other instances of diverse opinions might be quoted upon the niceties of elision and synæresis, but instead of doing so further, we prefer to impress upon the student the importance of cultivating a refined taste and critical ear as the ultimate test of rhythmic appreciation. For instance, in the following verse of thirteen syllables, the ear instinctively sanctions their reduction to the normal ten, thus :

And man | y a fro | zen, man | y a fi | ery Alp
Milton.

While in the two examples that follow it at once declines to allow any elision in the feet that are marked off.

Canst thou imagine where those spirits live,
Which make such del | *icate mu* | sic in the woods.
Shelley.

And multitu | *dinous as* | the desert sands,
Borne on the storm its millions shall advance.
Ibid.

3.—METRICAL LICENCES.

These embrace all deviations of whatever kind from the normal metre of the verse of which the poem is constructed.   Thus the normal line of heroic verse, the iambic pentameter, is this:

$$| \smile - | \smile - | \smile - | \smile - | \smile - |$$

Any variation, therefore, from this standard is to be regarded as a metrical licence; and the same is the case with all other measures.

We have already been obliged to anticipate to some extent the subject of metrical licences when dealing with the various kinds of metre in detail, and to trespass still further in the same direction in the chapter on mixed metres; but we have only formally stated and inadequately illustrated the three fundamental principles which form the basis of all such licences, viz:

(i) That an additional unaccented syllable, or even two, may be added to the end of a verse.

(ii) That a syllable may be omitted or added at the beginning.

(iii) That feet, other than those of the normal line, may be substituted in nearly any part of the verse.

The application of these general principles, and the restrictions which the best poets have observed in their use, now claim a more detailed examination.

And first, as regards the *Iambic measure*, which embraces the bulk of our poetry. The regular heroic line is common enough, if to have accented syllables in the even places be all that is required to form it:

> Achilles' wrâth, to Gréece the díreful spring
> Of wóes unnúmber'd, heâvenly Góddess, síng;

but if quantity be regarded together with accent; if the syllables in a regular verse ought to be not only accented and unaccented, but also long and short, very few such will be found in our poetry. This line is of the sort:

> On hungry waves that howl around the fold.

So are the following from a celebrated poem whose numbers are most highly polished:

> When o'er the blasted heath the day declined.
> But why prolong the tale; his only child ——
> > *Rogers.*

The next approaches very near the same regularity:

> 'Twas all he gave, 'twas all he had to give.
> > *Ibid.*

It bears a strong resemblance to a line in Gray's *Elegy* which is perfect:

> He gained from heaven, 'twas all he wished, a friend.

It may surprise those who have been taught to depreciate the versification of our earlier poets, to be informed that such perfect verses as are here quoted are not so rare among them as among the moderns. Campion, in his " Art of English Poetry," has these three lines together :

> The more secure, the more the stroke we feel
> Of unprevented harms ; so gloomy storms
> Appear the sterner if the day be clear.

These he calls *pure* iambics; which, considering them according to quantity, they are: the accents too are placed on the even syllables throughout, except on *if*, the sixth in the last verse. Such lines as want this perfection, he distinguishes by the name of *licentiate* iambics; *i.e.* lines in which some other foot is substituted for an iambic; to what extent this is allowable we now proceed to state.

But first, be it remembered that in these feet the syllables are considered as accented or unaccented, not as long or short : and that where quantity is to be noticed, it will be expressly pointed out.

The *pyrrhic* foot (two unaccented syllables ⌣ ⌣) may supply the place of an iambic, and is substituted for it oftener than any other foot. It may stand in any part of the verse, *e.g.* :

> *In the 1st foot.*
> Is he a chúrchman ? thén he's fónd of pówer.

> *In the 2nd foot.*
> A rébel to the véry kíng he lóves.

In the 3rd foot.

Has máde the fáther of a námeless ráce.

In the 4th foot.

But qúite mistákes the scáffold for the píle.

In the 5th foot.

The dúll flát fálsehood sérves for pólicy.
Pope.

This foot may have place twice, or even three times in the same line:

You lóse it in the móment you detéct.
It is a crócket of a pínnacle.
Ibid.

But as unaccented feet weaken a line, this last has the utmost degree of weakness that is consistent with a verse, there being in it only two syllables accented, and for quantity, not one long.

The *spondee* (two accented syllables – –) may be substituted for the iambic, and in as many places as the pyrrhic, *e.g. :*

In the 1st foot.

Tóm strúts a sóldier, ópen, bóld and bráve.

In the 2nd foot.

The pláin róugh héro túrn a crafty knáve.

In the 3rd foot.

When fláttery gláres áll háte it in a quéen.

In the 4th foot.

That gáy freethínker, a fíne tálker ónce

In the 5th foot.
Yet támes not thís, it stícks to our lást sánd.
Pope.

This foot may be repeated, and the following line will show to what extent:

Móre wíse, móre léarn'd, móre júst,—móre éverythíng.

In Milton we have such a line as this:

Rocks, caves, lakes, fens, bogs, dens, and shades of death.

in which the first six syllables are all long, though the even ones alone bear the metrical accent. Such instances merely demonstrate that the measure of a poem cannot be gathered from isolated verses, but is fixed by the *prevalent foot* throughout, and that in poems extending to thousands of lines, such exceedingly licentiate verses form a pleasing break to the monotony rather than a blemish.

The iambic verse admits likewise the trochee, but not in such abundance. Pope, who furnishes all the examples here given from a poem of 260 lines, has not, in that compass, any trochaic foot except in the beginning of a verse. For such examples we must turn to a poem of a different structure, and to a greater master of poetical numbers. Any foot of the heroic verse may be a trochee, except the last, *e.g.* :

In the 1st foot.
Hére in the heart of hell to work in fire.

In the 2nd foot.

Anon, oút of the earth a fabric huge.

In the 3rd foot.

For one restraint, Lórds of the world besides

In the 4th foot.

Abject and lost lay these, cóvering the flood.
Milton.

The same verse will admit two trochaic feet, as:

Hóv'ring on wing únder the cope of hell.

Smóte on him sore besides, vaúlted with fire; *
Ibid.

but not a greater number; for the last foot cannot
be a trochee; neither can two trochees stand close
together in one line; but different feet, as the spondee and pyrrhic, may so stand; and all the three may
be introduced into the same line, instead of iambics.
The beginning of the third book of the *Paradise
Lost* will afford examples :

Háil, hóly Líght! óffspring of Heáven fírst-bórn !
Máy I expréss thee únblámed? sínce Gód is líght,

---

* It is to be noted that in every one of these instances there is a
pause immediately preceding the trochaic foot; the introduction of it
without such a pause is always harsh; as
    Of Eve, whose eye | darted | contagious fire.
            Paradise Lost,
In some places so much so as to destroy the metre; and is therefore not
to be approved, as
    Burnt after them to the | bottom | less pit.
            Ibid.
    Shoots in | visi | ble virtue ev'n to the deep.
            Ibid.

> And néver but in únapproáched líght
> Dwélt from etérnity, dwélt thén in thée,
> Bríght éffluence of bríght éssence íncreáte.
>> *Ibid.*

The licences here taken are so many that they exceed the number of iambic feet in these lines.

Another kind of licence permitted to the heroic verse, is to have an additional syllable at the end, as :

> His wish and best endeavour, us asund | ĕr.
>> *Paradise Lost.*

or even two, as :

> For solitude sometimes is best soci | ĕtў.
>> *Ibid.**

But all such syllables must be unaccented; for an accent upon the last syllable, when two are added, would make an *Alexandrine,* which is another species

---

* This line is quoted because it has been called an *Alexandrine ;* Mitford's " Essay on the Harmony of Language," p. 133, 1st edition, where an Alexandrine is defined to be " a verse of the heroic cadence, and consisting of six feet." By *heroic cadence* is meant such measures (or feet) as an heroic verse is made of. It is true that an Alexandrine must contain six iambic feet; but it is not true that every verse of six such feet, the last being unaccented, must be an Alexandrine. If it must, then it follows that a line of five such feet must be an heroic verse ; and these in Hudibras :

> She laid about in fight more busily,
> Than th' Amazonian dame Penthesilé,
>> *P. i. c.* 2

are not doggerel, as is commonly supposed, but of a higher order, and may claim to be ranked with the heroics of Pope and Dryden. The line in Milton is exactly like the following in Othello :

> For sure he fills it up with great abil | Itў,
> With any strong or vehement importun | Itў ;
>> *Act* iii. *sc.* 3.

and like numberless others that occur in our tragedies, which were never yet reckoned as Alexandrine, but as heroic verses with two redundant syllables.

of verse ; and the addition of an accented syllable to the normal line would destroy any known measure. Hypermetrical syllables should not occur often in serious poems, because the unaccented terminations have the lightness of the trochee and dactyl, which are unsuitable to pieces of a grave character. The drama, which claims greater liberty than any other form of composition, uses them more freely.

The introduction of *trisyllabic feet* in iambic measure is one of the favourite bones of contention with writers on versification, and much ingenuity and learning have been wasted on the matter. It is an undoubted fact that extra unaccented syllables are freely introduced by our standard poets into the body of iambic verse, and whether we attempt to deal with them as troublesome interlopers, or accept them in a friendly spirit as forming metrical feet of another kind, seems to us a mere verbal question of very little importance. Dr. Abbott takes the former view, which he elaborates in his "Shaksperean Grammar," 452—515, and in the "English Lessons for English People," 97—150 ; Mr. J. B. Mason, in his "Chapters on English Verse," takes the latter, and to us the more reasonable one. His summing up of the question leaves little more to be said. "Dactyls and Anapests being recognised feet, it is better to use them where they will serve to explain the metre of a verse, than to have recourse to extra metrical syllables, a licence which, except at the end of a line, is now unknown and not recognised by all, even in Shakspere."

K

The same licences which are given to the heroic line are allowed to the other species of iambic measure; and, by observing upon what ground they stand, it will be seen how many of them may be taken in each species.

From the account of the numerous licences which are permitted by substituting some other foot for that which is fundamental to this measure, the iambic, it will appear what a variety the English heroic verse is capable of exhibiting: much greater than the Latin or Greek hexameter can produce, whatever has been advanced to the contrary. This is a point that does not rest upon opinion, it is a matter of computation; neither is the variety such as is allowable only, and not in usage; it is to be seen in all our poems of that measure; and it will not be foreign to our subject to establish these facts by evidence and proof.

The measures which enter into the composition of an hexameter are the dactyl and spondee, and no other; and the last foot of the verse being invariably a spondee, there remains a line of five feet to receive all the varieties that can be made by two different measures. Now the first foot admits of two, and the second of the same number; which, combined with the first, is four; the third of twice four, viz. eight; the fourth of twice eight, viz. sixteen; the fifth of twice sixteen, viz. thirty-two. And this was precisely the number of varieties which the ancient grammarians recognised in the hexameter. But the English heroic verse admits of four different feet; and according to the same rate of combination, its varieties in the second foot would be four times four, viz. sixteen, and so on; but because, as has been said, two trochees cannot stand together, nor two pyrrhics, the varieties will not be so many; yet they will amount to a much greater number than those of an hexameter.

And that this variety is not imaginary, but continually employed by our poets, may be shown from any of their works. The same epistle of Pope, to which we have already had recourse, will afford the proof. The *first two feet* of each verse will be sufficient for the purpose, *e.g.*:

Two Iambics.

And yét | the fáte | of all extremes is such. Line 9.

Trochee and Iambic.

Gránt but | as ma | ny sorts of mind as moss. Line 18.

Spondee and Iambic.

Quick whirls | and shifting eddies of our minds. Line 24.

Pyrrhic and Iambic.

And in | the cún | ning truth itself's a lie. Line 68.

Pyrrhic and Spondee.

Nor will | life's stréam | for observation stay. Line 7.

Iambic and Spondee.

We grów | móre pár | tial for the observer's sake. Line 12.

Trochee and Spondee.

Sée the | sáme mán | in vigour and the gout. Line 71.

Iambic and Pyrrhic.

His prin | ciple | of action once explore. Line 27.

In this example, taken from a poet who is more distinguished for the smoothness than the variety of his measures, the varieties in two feet amount to eight, which is double the number that the hexameter is capable of making within the same compass ; the varieties of our entire heroic line must therefore exceed those of the hexameter in a still greater proportion.

Next with regard to *Trochaic measure.* There being some affinity between the trochaic and iambic measures, the licences permitted in each will be similar, as far as consists in the substitution of some other foot for that which is characteristic of the kind. But beside these, there is another licence very generally extended to the trochaic; viz. that of cutting off part of the concluding syllable. This is allowed in every species of the trochaic verse, whether of two, three, or four feet ; so that we have lines of three, five, and seven syllables, and many specimens of them have been given already.

The pure trochaic line is composed of trochees without the intermixture of any other foot: thus the normal trochaic tetrameter line is this—

$$| - \smile | - \smile | - \smile | - \smile ;$$

and if quantity concurs with accent to form the measure, it is then perfect ; as in the following example, where the accented syllables are all long and the unaccented all short :

Richly paint the vernal arbour.

Gray.

A perfect line is not oftener found in this kind than in the heroic verse.

Now as to the licences which we will exemplify from lines of eight and seven syllables indiscriminately.

The *first foot* admits a pyrrhic,

On a | rock, whose haughty brow;

Gray.

or a spondee:

No, blést | chiefs! a hero's crown;

Sir W. Jones.

or an iambus:

To brisk | notes in cadence beating.

Gray.

The *second foot* admits a pyrrhic:

Mute, but | to the | voice of anguish;

Gray.

or spondee:

Wakes thee | nów, thoúgh | he inherit.

Gray.

The *third foot* admits the same.

Pyrrhic:

With Harmodius | shall re | pose;

spondee:

Rome shall perish— | write thát | word.

Cowper.

In the line of eight syllables, the last foot is necessarily a trochee, and therefore the seventh syllable accented; but in the line of seven, the last syllable may be short; as:

> And with godlike Diomed.

We do not find an iambic in the second or third foot of any authentic composition. In the first, it has obtained a place by the authority of Gray and others; it is nevertheless so harsh a violation of the regular foot as hardly to be approved of.

Anapestic verse allows but few licences. One is a redundant syllable at the end of a line; another, an iambic, or spondee, in the first foot. And where the former of these is introduced, the other ought to be taken in the line next following, as in this example:

> To invite the gods hither they would have had rea | son,
> And Jove | had descended each night in the season.
> *Byrom.*

This rule, though but little attended to, is good and proper; because the observance of it will keep the measure entire, which otherwise is sometimes over-loaded, and produces a bad effect on the ear.

> Prithee, pluck up a good resolution,
> To be cheerful and thankful in all.
> *Byrom*

The second line begins with an anapest; and by the word *to*, the measure is broken; omit it, and the whole will run smoothly and agreeably.

Another licence claimed by some writers is that of dropping a syllable in the middle of the verse; Swift takes it very often, as here:

> And now my dream's out; for I was a dream'd
> That I saw a huge rat—O dear how I scream'd!

But this licence is questionable at least; it may be called unwarrantable, because it occasions such halting metre.

Diæresis is a licence more suitable to this kind of verse than to the dissyllabic metres, *i.e.* to make a dissyllable into a trisyllable, a monosyllable into a dissyllable wherever possible, *e.g.* :

> Whose humour, as gay as the *fire*-fly's light.
> > *Moore.*

> Would feel herself *happier* here,
> By the nightingale *warbling* nigh.
> > *Cowper.*

Drayton makes *April* three syllables.

Such a division of syllables helps the line to move lightly, and is a reasonable indulgence to a measure which, more than others, is apt to suffer by the clogging of accented words and consonants.

Any long or accented syllable, standing first or second in the foot, is a deviation from this measure; but it is less offensive to the ear in the second place than in the first:

Whíle a par | cel of verses the hawkers were hollowing.

Wíne the sov | ereign cordial of God and of man

Far above | áll the flowers | of the field,
When its leaves | are áll dead | and its col | ours áll lost.

And while | a fálse nymph | was his theme,
A willow supported his head.

The licences taken in *Dactylic verse* are sometimes such that they disguise the measure and render it equivocal, as in this uncommon specimen :

> Oh ! what a pain is love !
>   How shall I bear it ?
> She will unconstant prove,
>   I greatly fear it.
> Please her the best I may,
> She looks another way ;
> Alack and well-a-day,
>   Phillida flouts me !
>
> *Ellis's " Specimens."*
> v. iii. p. 338.

Every line of this stanza but the last is divisible into iambic feet, and they all make verses in that measure; they are nevertheless designed for the dactylic, as appears by these next, which cannot be so divided without violence:

> Thou shalt eat curds and cream
>   All the year | lasting ;
> And drink the crystal stream,
>   Pleasant in | tasting.

But this great confusion of measure is not often made. The allowed licences are to curtail the last foot, sometimes by one syllable, as in the lines quoted above, but more usually by two, which, as compositions of this kind are chiefly for music, makes a better close: such is:

Under the blossom that hangs on the | bough.

It is allowed in the beginning of a line to substitute for the proper foot a trochee, as :

Songs of | shepherds and rustical roundelays.
Old Ballad.

Or a single accented syllable may stand for it, even for two feet together, as:

Come, | see | rural felicity.

The question of metrical licences as it affects the Heroic measure will be further considered when we come to deal with *Blank verse* (see p. 185).

POETIC PAUSES.

I⊤ is perhaps necessary to insist again here that
verse is rhythmic *articulate speech*, just as music in
its broadest definition is rhythmic *sound*. A
printed sheet of notes on a stave is no more
music than is a page of poetry verse. We have
to deal throughout with poems as read or recited;
with the body, not with the soul of poetic creation.

The rhythm or musical flow of verse depends not
only upon the metrical arrangement of accented
and unaccented syllables, but in no little degree
upon breaks or pauses, which divide it into phrases
of different lengths. These *pauses* are identical
in many instances with the grammatical *stops*, but
they are also independent of them, and occur
where there are no stops at all. Metrical pauses
must, therefore, be clearly distinguished from sen-
tential stops at the outset of this enquiry. The
one is as essential to the melody as the other is to
the sense. With the latter we have no further
concern.

Metrical pauses are of two kinds, the one *final*
at the end of a verse, the other *cæsural*, which cuts
it into equal or unequal parts.

1.—THE FINAL PAUSE.

When the verse is rhymed the final pause is unmistakable, and is absolutely necessary to bring out the jingle of the rhymes; but in blank verse, and especially in the dramatic form, it is not so clearly marked, and is often omitted entirely. A good reader, however, will hardly ever fail to mark the end of the lines, however slightly, in reciting two consecutive verses, and if one line is run into another here and there, the occurrence is never continuous. Sheridan, in his "Art of Reading," says that if the first thirteen lines of the *Paradise Lost* were printed as prose and read by some one who had never seen the poem, they would be read as prose. We are certain that the judgment of most educated men would condemn this assertion. As well might we take the opinion of a Chinaman upon one of Beethoven's sonatas as of an illiterate person upon a question of verse and prose. We may safely conclude that verse which will not stand such a test as this is well deserving of being considered prose.

2.—THE CÆSURAL PAUSE.

Cæsural pause is the rest or halt of the voice in reading verses aloud at other points than the end of the line. It is independent of the same, and may occur at almost any part of the line, and even in the middle of a foot. No precise rules can be laid down as to its position, although it is generally found in one kind of verse, the heroic, for example, at one part of the line rather than at another. Sometimes there are two or even three metrical pauses in a line, one more marked than the other, and, occasionally, there are verses with no break in the middle at all. Here are a few examples of the diversity of their occurrence:

> Over them triumphant Death | his dart
> Shook, | but delayed to strike.

> The quality of mercy | is not strained.

> This | in a moment | brings me to an end.

> I'd rather be a kitten | and cry mew.

> Sweet | are the uses of adversity.

> Damn with faint praise, | assent with civil leer.

> Pleased with the danger | when the waves went high.

> A man to all succeeding ages curst.   (None.)

The pause is often preceded by the strongest accent of the line, and when both these are combined, and on the most important word, the emphasis thus produced gives as it were the keynote to the rhythm. When the occurrence of these is skilfully arranged to take place in different positions in succeeding verses, the monotonous melody of the measure is broken into something approaching harmony.

Pope, whose verse is remarkable for smoothness

and polish, has been greatly censured for arranging his pauses in the same, or very nearly the same, position for many lines in succession. Thus, in the following example from his *Rape of the Lock*, it occurs at the end of the second foot in each line :

> The busy sylphs | surround their darling care,
> Those set the head | and these divide the hair ;
> Some fold the sleeve, | while others plait the gown,
> And Beauty's praised | for labours not her own.

The swing of hundreds of lines such as these becomes sleepily wearisome. He seldom varies it beyond the fourth, fifth, or sixth syllable. Here is an instance, very rare with him, where it occurs at the end of the third :

> Offend her | and she knows not to forgive,
> Oblige her | and she'll hate you while you live.

Dryden, whose heroic measures are somewhat less polished but more vigorous than Pope's, varies the position of his pauses more, and correspondingly diversifies his rhythm, *e.g.* :

> A man so various that he seemed to be   (None.)
> Not one | but all mankind's epitome :
> Still in opinions | always in the wrong.
> Was everything by starts | and nothing long :
> But in the course of one revolving moon,   (None.)
> Was chemist, | fiddler, | statesman, | and buffoon.

It is blank verse, however, as has been already said, whose rhythm is most diversified by the varying position of the pauses. Milton uses them

with great skill, seldom placing them in the same
position in any three or four consecutive lines.
They occur with him very frequently after the
second and third syllable.   Here are two examples
from *Paradise Lost,* and one from the Sonnets :

> From branch to branch the smaller birds | with song
> Solaced the woods | and spread their painted wings
> Till even : | nor then the solemn nightingale
> Ceased warb | ling, but all night tuned her soft lays : |
> Others | on silver lakes and rivers | bathed
> Their snowy breasts.

> Now morn | her rosy steps in Eastern clime
> Advancing | sowed the Earth with orient pearl, |
> When Adam waked | so customed | for his sleep
> Was airy light | from pure digestion bred |
> And temperate vapours bland.

> In thy book record their groans |
> Who were thy sheep, | and in their ancient fold |
> Slain by the bloody Piedmontese | that rolled
> Mother with infant down the rocks. | Their moans
> The poles redoubled to the hills | and they
> To heaven.

With Shakspere the pauses are still more irregularly distributed throughout the lines, the result
being a still greater mobility to the rhythm.   They
are to be met with in his work after every syllable
of the verse, even immediately before the fifth
accent, which is very rare, *e.g. :*

> And so his peers upon this evidence
> Have found him guilty of high treason. | Much
> He spoke and learnedly for life.
>
> "*Henry VIII.*"

Alas! alas!
Why, | all the souls that were | were forfeit once ; |
And He | that might the vantage best have took |
Found out the remedy. | How would you be
If He | who is the top of judgment | should
But judge you as you are ? | O think of that, |
And mercy, then, | will breathe within your lips, |
Like man new made.

" Measure for Measure."

From his cradle
He was a scholar, | and a ripe and good one ; |
Exceeding wise, | fair spoken, | and persuading ; |
Lofty and sour | to them that loved him not, |
But to those men that sought him, | sweet as summer. |
And though he was unsatisfied in getting, |
Which was a sin, | yet in bestowing, | madam, |
He was most princely.

" Henry VIII."

In an *Alexandrine verse* the pause should always occur at the end of the sixth syllable, or after the seventh if that syllable is strongly accented. In any other position the long majestic march of the measure is broken.

Rarely the pause may take the place of a syllable, *e.g.* :

Spreads his | light wings | and | in a mo | ment flies.

A few examples from our modern poets are added :

He heard it | but he heeded not ; | his eyes
Were with his heart, | and that was far away ; |
He recked not of the life he lost, | nor prize, |
But where his rude hut by the Danube lay ; |

There | were his young barbarians all at play, |
There | was their Dacian mother | —he, their sire,
Butchered | to make a Roman holiday. |
All this rushed with his blood. | Shall he expire,
And unavenged ?—Arise, | ye Goths, and glut your ire !

Byron.
"Childe Harold."

They never fail | who die
In a great cause : | the block may soak their gore ; |
Their heads | may sodden in the sun ; | their limbs
Be strung | to city gates and castle walls | —
But still their spirit walks abroad. | Though years
Elapse, | and others share as dark a doom, |
They but augment | the deep and sweeping thoughts |
Which overpower all others, | and conduct
The world | at last | to freedom.

Byron.

Small service | is true service, | while it lasts : |
    Of friends, however humble, | scorn not one ; |
The daisy | by the shadow that it casts, |
    Protects | the lingering dew-drop | from the sun.

Wordsworth.

Yet think not | that I come to urge thy crimes : |
I do not come to curse thee, | Guinevere, |
I, | whose vast pity al | most makes me die |
To see thee laying there | thy golden head, |
My pride in happier summers, | at my feet. |
The wrath | which forced my thoughts on that fierce law, |
The doom of treason | and of flaming death, |
(When first I learnt thee hidden here) | is past, |
The pang, | which while I weighed thy heart with one |
Too wholly true | to dream untruth in thee, |

Made my tears burn | —is also past, | in part : |
And all is past, | the sin is sinned, | and I, |
Lo ! | I forgive thee, | as Eternal God
Forgives : | do thou for thine own soul | the rest.

Tennyson.
" Guinevere."

The third line is best scanned, perhaps, in this way—

ſ ! whŏse văst | pĭtў ăl | mŏst măkes | mĕ dĭe. |

RHYME.

HAVING considered the essentials of verse, and the chief variations and combinations thereof, we have now to enquire into the accidents which largely enter into its composition as ornaments to its melody. The chief of these is *rhyme*, or rime, as the word was formerly, and more correctly, spelled. Rhyme may be defined as a similarity of sound in the final syllable or syllables of two or more verses, or, as Milton speaks of it, as the "jingling sound of like endings." In words that rhyme there must be difference as well as similarity of sounds. Words that are identical in sound, however different their appearance may be, do not form rhyme in English poetry, though we occasionally find them there on account of the fewness of rhyming words in our tongue. For instance, such words as I, eye; hie, high; oar, ore, o'er, are *assonances*, not rhymes. On the other hand, however unlike each other words may look, if their sounds be similar without being identical, they form perfectly good rhymes, of which the following are examples—girl, pearl, curl; box, locks; cow, bough, frau. In order to arrive at a clear conception of the elements which make up a good rhyme we will take the three words *nose*, *toes*, *rose*. In each of these we have the same vowel sound, the open *o*, followed by the same sibillant consonant, but preceded by the different consonant sounds of *n*, *t*, *r*. Now, as these words rhyme correctly we can gather from this brief examination of their constituent parts what is essential to a perfect rhyme. This is—

(i) Identity in the vowel sound.

(ii) Identity in the consonant sound that follows it, if any.

(iii) Difference in the consonant sounds that precede; and to these must be added similarity in accent; *e.g. sing* rhymes with *ring*, but not well with *thinking*.

When confined to one syllable, rhymes are called *single*, as: *swing*, *bring*; when embracing two, *double*, as: *duty*, *beauty*; when extended to three, *triple*, as: *slenderly*, *tenderly*. In double rhymes the last syllable is unaccented, and in triple the last two.

Rhymes may be classed as perfect, imperfect, and false or bad, each of which kinds requires detailed consideration.

1.—PERFECT RHYMES.

Faultless rhymes are—

(i) Such as have an exact agreement in sound in the vowel and the consonants, if any, that follow, *e.g. :*

Did God set His fountain of light in the sky,
That man should look up with the tear in his eye?
Did God make this earth so beauteous and fair,
That man should look down with a groan of despair?

J. C. Prince.

(ii) Such as have a marked and sensible differ-ence between the consonants preceding the vowel; that is, consonants not of the same class, like these, *b, p*; *d, t*; *c, g*; *f, v*; *s, z*; which would rhyme in *bit, pit*; *den, ten*; *come, gum*; *fan, van*; *seal, zeal.* Such rhymes differ, indeed, in the sound pre-ceding the vowel, and therefore, strictly taken, are regular; but the difference is so slight that they are not to be commended.

The want of sufficient difference is likewise per-ceptible in such rhymes as *bled, bed*; *pray, pay*, where the second consonant is dropped, and both words begin with the same letter; but the rhymes *bled, led*; *pray, ray*, are perfectly good, because the consonants with which they begin are different.*

(iii) Such as are made by syllables that are long and full-sounding, in preference to their opposites; among which last are the terminations of polysyllabic words.

Compounds do not rhyme well with their simples, as, *resound* with *sound.* The greater variety also

---

* Dr. Johnson, in one of his poems, has used a very uncommon rhyme:

Such bribes the rapid Greek o'er Asia whirl'd,
For such the steady Roman shook the world.

" *Vanity of Human Wishes.*"

One of these words is aspirated and the other not; so that here is a dif-ference; but they make the nearest approach to identity that can be allowed, or, indeed, that can be uttered.

in the length of the rhyming words the better,
as *hound* with *rebound*.

The observations of Mitford on this topic of good
rhymes are worthy of attention. He says : "According to our preceding definitions, euphony and
cacophony, in language, mean sound, pleasing and
unpleasing. English speech has rarely any material cacophony in the middle of words, but in
terminations it too certainly abounds. A well-
eared poet will avoid cacophony in rhymes, and in
the conspicuous parts, especially the last syllable,
of any verse. Pope has had generally credit for
what are called rich poems; though his higher
respect, justly directed to that powerful closeness
of phrase, in which he singularly excels, has
led him to admit some rhymes rather cacophonous.
The word *king* is certainly not euphonous, nor of
dignified sound; the vowel is short and close, and
the following consonant, one consonant expressed
by two characters, the most cacophonous in our
pronunciation. Whether it was for the dignity
of the idea conveyed, or for the opposite quality of
the sound, that Pope chose it for the first rhyme
of his *Essay on Man*, with cacophony doubled by
an added *s*, appears doubtful. He has, indeed,
not scrupled to use the same *ing* for the first
rhyme of his translation of the *Iliad ;* but the example is not to be recommended. Terminations
in a long vowel, or a liquid consonant, preceded
by a long vowel, will be most euphonous. The
termination in a liquid consonant preceded by a
short vowel, though less rich, will make a plea-

sant variety. That of a mute preceded by a long vowel will be wholly unobjectionable, rich without any cacophony, if a vowel begin the following word, as in the first verse of *Paradise Lost*. These, however, would, in our language, be limits too narrow for the poet; and the ear practised in our versification will take no offence at the conclusion of the second line of *Paradise Lost*, where a long vowel is followed by two consonants within the same syllable, and two consonants begin the next verse. The judicious poet, however, will be sparing of such accumulation of consonants."

We are not to expect that such good and approved rhymes as are here advocated should constitute the major part in any composition. The difficulty of rhyming well, and the propriety of sacrificing what is merely ornamental to what is more important, must always plead for as much indulgence as can be granted.

2.—IMPERFECT RHYMES.

We now proceed to pass in review imperfect rhymes, viz., such as are admissible into verse, but are not of the best quality. These form a most extensive class; they are found in the works of all our poets, and into some of them they enter very largely. They are admissible, but they generally labour under some defect; either they want the proper correspondence of sound, or they are made of little insignificant words, or they are stale and hackneyed. Examples will be given of all these.

According to what has been already said of rhyme, it is evident that a word may fail of making an exact one, in three parts :

(i) In the letters which go before the vowel.

(ii) In the vowel itself.

(iii) In the letters (if any) that follow it.

By failing in the first part, viz. by making no difference before the vowel, the rhyme will be inadmissible, because it will form an assonance. A failure in either of the other parts may yet give a rhyme which is passable, though defective. And as it is this particular defect, more than any other imperfection, that mars our poetry, as far as rhyme goes, it will not be unfit to enlarge thereon. By a broad computation of the possible rhyming combination of our vowels, diphthongs, and consonants, it has been ascertained that there are upwards of six hundred of them at the rhymester's disposal. Yet, notwithstanding this ample field for choice and variety, there will not be found one, among all our poets, who within the compass of thirty rhymes, does not usually make some repetition upon an average taken of the whole of his works in rhyme.

In support of this assertion, which perhaps may surprise some readers, we will exhibit a specific account of such repetitions, and also of imperfect rhymes, taken from a considerable number of poets, from Dryden to Goldsmith. These have been pitched upon for two reasons ; one, to obviate what otherwise might be objected, that such faults do not occur in our best versifiers; the other, to prevent young writers from being misled by examples of such high and deserved authority.

The table subjoined shows the number of repeated rhymes, and of those which are imperfect, in the works of the authors whose names are in the margin, taken from the first sixty rhymes of the pieces there specified.

Authors.	Translations.	Rhymes repeated.	Rhymes imperfect.
Dryden .	Translation of Homer's Iliad, B. 1	18 .	9
Pope .	,, ,, .	24 .	6
Dryden .	,, Virgil's Æneid, B. 1	19 .	10
	Originals.		
Pope .	Moral Essays, Epist. . . .	19 .	9
Swift .	Baucis and Philemon . . .	10 .	2
Prior .	Solomon	18 .	11
Goldsmith	Traveller	26 .	2
Cowper .	Retirement	15 .	2

This selection has been made from pieces written in couplets, because, in such pieces, the rhymes being unconnected with other rhymes or lines, the versifier is less restricted in his choice than he would be if composing in any kind of stanza. The repetitions are, nevertheless, very frequent. In stating the imperfections, the smallest have been taken into account. They are, generally, a difference in the vowel-sound; which, in most cases, is less offensive to the ear than a difference in the consonants. The imperfect rhymes in the extract from Pope's original piece are these:—gross, moss; view, do; desert, heart; charron, buffoon;

revere, star; impell'd, field; breast, east; retreat, great; and one identical, known, none.

Some of these imperfections are very slight, and none of them less tolerable than this in the consonants:

> For Britain's Empire, boundless as the main,
>> Will guard at once domestic ea*se*,
>> And awe th' aspiring nations into pe*ace*.

When there is a double imperfection, and the vowel-sound and consonant are both different, as in this couplet, the rhyme is bad:

> Nor did your crutch give battle to your d*uns*,
> And hold it out where you had built a sc*once*.
>> *Butler.*

From a review of the extract given above, it will appear that in the points under consideration, our later versifiers, to speak of them generally, have improved upon their predecessors, with an exception to Swift alone, who as a correct rhymer has never been excelled by any.

The introduction of little insignificant words to make rhyme is a blemish which is not often chargeable on our modern poets. It was very common before the beginning of the last century; nor do such rhymes appear to have been considered then as any imperfection. The instances are numerous:

> Who with his word commanded all to be,
> And all obeyed him, for that word was he;
> Only he spoke, and everything that is
> From out the womb of fertile Nothing ris'.
>> *Cowley.*

A frequent rhyme in Waller is the word *so,* which has been noted and censured by Johnson :

> Thy skilful hand contributes to our woe,
> And whets those arrows which confound us so :
> A thousand Cupids in those curls do sit,
> Those curious nets thy slender fingers knit.
> > *" Verses to Saccharissa's Maid "*

> Who, naming me, doth warm his courage so,
> Shows for my sake what his bold hand would do.
> > *" Verses for Drinking Healths."*

We find in Dryden rhymes of the same class.

> The Panther smiled at this, " and when," said she,
> " Were those first councils disallow'd by me ?
> 'Tis dangerous climbing ; to your sons and you
> I leave the ladder, and its omen too.—
> Why all these wars to win the book, if we
> Must not interpret for ourselves, but she ?
> > *" Hind and Panther."*

They occur more frequently in his prologues and epilogues ; but examples enough have been given ; for they are not introduced for the purpose of censure, but only to show what, in the present day, ought to be avoided.

Another defect in this part of versification is the employment of such rhymes as are become hackneyed by overmuch use. What these rhymes are, is described and exemplified by Pope ; he calls them " the sure returns of still-expected rhymes ; " as in this couplet :

Where'er you find the cooling western *breeze*,
In the next line it whispers through the *trees*.
"Essay on Criticism."

His own verses, however, sometimes fall under this censure, as is shown in the following :

Her fate is whisper'd by the gentle breeze,
And told in sighs to all the trembling trees.

In some still evening, when the whispering breeze
Pants on the leaves, and dies upon the trees.
"Fourth Pastoral."

The dying gales that pant upon the trees,
The lakes that quiver to the curling breeze.
"Eloisa to Abelard."

There are some rhymes, and also some ends of verses, so hackneyed that we might, at the first recital of them, do in the same manner as Demetrius Phalerus informs us the Athenians did sometimes towards those orators who composed their speeches in studied and artificial periods. "The hearers were disgusted," says he, "and being well aware how the sentence would end, they would often forestall the speaker, and utter it aloud."

Many subjects for verse have these common rhymes accompanying, and, as it were, belonging to them. For example, in prologues and epilogues it is perhaps necessary to mention the *stage ;* this, being a very easy word to rhyme with, is readily taken ; and then its partner shall be *age* or *rage*, and stand with it after this manner :

The plays that take on our corrupted stage,
Methinks, resemble the distracted age.

While you turn players on the world's great stage,
And act yourselves the force of your own age.
Dryden.

In his prologues and epilogues, which are about forty, these two words rhyme above a dozen times. In the same pieces the term *play* occurs as naturally as *stage*, and is made as serviceable; for its termination in *ay* affords as many rhymes as any in the language.

Pope's *Prologue to Cato* is another instance in point. It consists of twenty-three couplets, in which we find these rhymes: stage, age; stage, rage; fate, state; great, state; draws, was; cause, laws; laws, cause.

Here are a few specimens of commonly recurring imperfect rhymes:

war	wound	arms	ease	river
shore	ground	warms	increase	ever
returned	prove	thought	come	pass
mourned	love	wrote	tomb	face
hear	face	flood	increase	peace
pair	rays	brood	breathe	piece

3.—BAD RHYMES.

Of rhymes that are classed as *bad* very little need be said beyond quoting a few typical examples, and pleading the difficulty of rhyming in Eng-

lish, as compared with some other tongues, as
ground for indulgence.

Of such are those that are widely different in the
vowel sound, as :

> Beauty and youth, and wealth and luxu*ry*,
> And sprightly hope, and short-enduring *joy*.
> > *Dryden.*

Or which are different, both in the vowel-sound and
in the consonants which follow it, as :

> All trades of death that deal in steel for gains
> Were there; the butcher, armourer, and sm*ith*,
> Who forges sharpen'd falchions or the scy*the*.
> > *Dryden.*

Or those in which the consonants preceding the
vowel are of the same sound, as :

> But this bold lord, with manly strength endued,
> She with one finger and a thumb subdued.
> > *Pope.*

The last is an instance of pure assonance, which
is not admissible into modern poetry, though it
was common enough with our earlier writers, and
is still allowable in French verse.

Another gross violation of the requirements of
rhyme is where the preceding consonants have the
same sound, and the vowel and what follows it
different ones, as in atttempting to make a rhyme
of *scenes* and *sense*.

4.—DOUBLE AND TRIPLE RHYMES.

Under the name of *Double and Triple rhymes* are comprehended all those which are made by more than one syllable, of how many syllables soever they may consist. And they may consist of as many syllables as follow the last accented syllable of a word, together with that syllable, as *glory, story; beautiful, dutiful; censurable, commensurable.* As in single rhymes it is required that all which follows the vowel shall be identical in sound; so in double rhymes all which follow the *last accented vowel,* both consonants and syllables, should in sound be identical, as in the examples above.

Double rhymes are but sparingly used in our serious poetry; the reason may be that they are considered as having too sprightly a character to accord with it, the rhyme of two syllables forming a trochee, and that of three, a dactyl; but in earlier times this unfitness was either not perceived or not regarded. The double rhymes in Shakspere's *Rape of Lucrece* sometimes occupy an entire stanza, as this:

> Besides, the life and feeling of her passion
> She hoards, to spend when he is by to hear her:
> When sighs, and groans, and tears may grace the fashion
> Of her disgrace, the better so to clear her
> From that suspicion which the world might bear her.
> To shun this blot, she would not blot the letter
> With words, till action might become them better.

The rules or custom of a more correct age

abridged, in serious poems, this large use of double rhymes; and what was still allowed, was under certain limitations : as, first, that the rhyme should not consist of more than two syllables; and second that it should not, like some in the stanza above, be made of two words. Under these restraints the double rhyme often appears, and not without grace, in our lyric poetry, as here :

> O lyre divine ! what daring spirit
> Wakes thee now ? though he inherit
> Nor the pride, nor ample pinion,
> That the Theban eagle bear,
> Sailing with supreme dominion
> Through the azure deep of air.
>
> *Gray.*

A fine example of double rhyming is to be seen in Shelley's *Cloud.* But the most suitable place for the exhibition of double rhymes is where ludicrous subjects are treated of in a burlesque style, as in Butler's *Hudibras*, Hood's *Whims and Oddities*, or Gilbert's *Bab Ballads*, in which numerous examples of double and triple rhymes may be found, as in the following stanzas taken at random from the latter :

> For Burglars, Thieves, and Co.,
>   Indeed I'm no a*pologist,*
> But I, some years ago,
>   Assisted a phre*nologist.*

> Wild croquêt Hooper banned,
>   And all the sports of Mammon !
> He warred with cribbage, and
>   He exorcised back*gammon.*

In verses of this class, the rhyming syllables may be as many as follow the last accented syllable of a verse, including that syllable. We mean here that verse which ends with polysyllables. Our language has not many polysyllables where the accent is thrown farther back than the antepenultimate ; and therefore we have but few rhymes of four syllables, and these are only met with in whimsical and far-fetched expressions.

When more words than one are taken to make up the rhyme, it gives opportunity, by the combination, to frame new rhymes, the novelty of which is pleasing, as in the following by Butler :

> The oyster-women lock'd their fish up,
> And trudg'd away, to cry No Bishop.
>
> *Hudibras.*

And again—

> You have said my eyes are blue ;
> There may be a fairer hue,
>   Perhaps—and yet
> It is surely not a sin
> If I keep my secrets in—
>   Violet.
>
> *Mortimer Collins.*

To produce this novelty is a species of wit, though of an inferior order, yet such as cannot be exercised without great facility in composition and command of language. There are poems of a very modern date which will prove this assertion, whence we conclude that our contemporaries, some of them

at least, are superior in these points to the gener-
ality of former writers. The following verses of
Swift, upon the ancient dramatic authors, exhibit
this faculty in a remarkable degree. He had superior abilities in rhyming, and he appears to have
set himself down to this piece merely for the purpose of exerting them :

> I went in vain to look for Eupolis,
> Down in the Strand, just where the new pole is ;
> For I can tell you one thing, that I can,
> You will not find it in the Vatican.
> He and Cratinus used, as Horace says,
> To take his greatest grandees for asses.
> Poets, in those days, used to venture high ;
> But these are lost full many a century.
> Thus you may see, dear friend, *ex pede* hence,
> My judgment of the old comedians.
>   Proceed to tragics : first, Euripides
> (An author where I sometimes dip a' days)
> Is rightly censured by the Stagirite,
> Who says his numbers do not fadge aright.
> A friend of mine that author despises
> So much, he swears the very best piece is,
> For aught he knows, as bad as Thespis's ;
> And that a woman, in these tragedies,
> Commonly speaking, but a sad jade is.
> At least, I'm well assured, that no folk lays
> The weight on him they do on Sophocles.
> But, above all, I prefer Eschylus,
> Whose moving touches, when they please, kill us
>   And now I find my muse but ill able
> To hold out longer in trisyllable.
>   *" To Dr. Sheridan."*

Here follow a few instances of whimsical combi-

M

nations in the way of rhyming, mostly by modern
writers :

> Just so romances are, for *what else*
> Is in them all but love and *battles.*
> > *Butler.*

> And pulpit, drum ecclesiastic,
> Beat with fist instead of á stick.
> > *Butler.*

> Sun, moon, and thou, vain world, adieu,
> That kings and priests are plotting in ;
> Here, doomed to starve on water gru—
> el, never shall I see the U—
>   niversity of Gottingen—
>   niversity of Gottingen.
> > *Gifford.*

> But, oh ! ye lords of ladies intellectual !
> Inform us truly, have they not henpecked you all ?
> > *Byron.*

> May no rude hand deface it,
> And its forlorn *hic jacet.*
> > *Wordsworth.*

> I hate all critics ; may they burn all,
> From Bentley to the Grub-street Journal.
> > *Fielding.*

> Some say, compared to Bonnocini,
> That Mynheer Handel's but a ninny ;
> Others aver, that he to Handel
> Is scarcely fit to hold a candle.
> Strange all this difference should be
> 'Twixt Tweedledum and Tweedledee.
> > *Byrom.*

An hour they sat in *Council;*
　At length the Mayor broke *silence:*
For a guilder I'd my ermine *gown sell,—*
　I wish I were a *mile hence.*
　　　　　　　Browning.

Having reached the summit, and managed to *cross it, he*
Rolled down the hill with uncommon *velocity.*
　　　　　　　Barham.

　　Grown blind, *alas ! he'd*
　　Some prussic *acid,*
And that put him out of his pain.
　　　　　　　Barham.

　　Careless rhymer, it is true
　　That my favourite colour's blue;
　　　　But am I
　　To be made a victim, sir,
　　If to puddings I prefer
　　　　Cambridge π.
　　　　　　　Mortimer Collins.

Here are some stanzas from an amusing satire
which rhymes throughout on the long e :

Says 'My Lord' to our Captain, " Now, Captain," says he,
" On my life, I was never before at sea,
But, hang it ! that's not at all necessaree
For the very First Lord of the Admiraltee."

We sailed to the eastward but miles two or three,
When somehow 'My Lord' took as ill as could be :
" If you take me much further, now steward," cries he,
" I shall throw up my post at the Admiraltee."

> " Bout ship ! " shouts the Captain, immediatelee,
> " And bear the ' First Lord ' to his own countree ;
> If our vessel went down, no matter to we,
> But what would become of the Admiraltee ! "
>
> *A. J.*

We shall conclude this subject of double rhymes with laying before the reader what Dryden has said upon it. "The double rhyme (a necessary companion of burlesque writing) is not so proper for manly satire ; for it turns earnest too much to jest, and gives us a boyish kind of pleasure. It tickles awkwardly, with a kind of pain to the best sort of readers ; we are pleased ungratefully, and, if I may say so, against our liking. He (Butler, of whom he is writing) might have left that task to others, who, not being able to put it in thought, can only make us grin with the excrescence of a word of two or three syllables in the close. It is, indeed, below so great a master to make use of such a little instrument. But his good sense is perpetually shining through all he writes ; it affords us not the time for finding faults. We pass through the levity of his rhyme, and are immediately carried to some admirable, useful thought."

5.—FAULTS IN RHYMING.

The faults in rhyming, which have hitherto been noticed, arise from some imperfection in the rhymes themselves ; but there are other usages deserving censure, which are independent of any such imperfections.   Of these, some may be attributed to the inadvertence or negligence of the writer.   Of this sort is the recurrence of the same rhymes at short distances.   By the *same* rhymes is meant, all those which rhyme together, though consisting of different words, as bay, day ; lay, may ; pay, say.

> Our age was cultivated thus at *length*,
> But what we gain'd in skill we lost in *strength* :
> Our builders were with want of genius curst ;
> The second temple was not like the first ;
> Till you, the best Vitruvius, come at *length*,
> Our beauties equal, but excel our *strength*.
>   *Dryden.*

Here the same rhymes occur, and are even made by the same words, separated by one couplet only.

A fault similar to this is the frequent repetition of the same rhymes, as in this example :

> Shall funeral eloquence her colours spread,
> And scatter roses on the wealthy *dead ?*
> Shall authors smile on such illustrious days,
> And satirise with nothing—but their *praise ?*
>   Why slumbers Pope, who leads the tuneful train,
> Nor hears that virtue, which he loves, complain ?
> Donne, Dorset, Dryden, Rochester, are *dead,*
> And guilt's chief foe, in Addison, is fled ;
> Congreve, who, crown'd with laurels, fairly won,
> Sits smiling at the goal, while others run :
> He will not write ; and (more provoking still !)
> Ye gods ! he will not write, and Mævius *will.*
>   Doubly distrest, what author shall we find,
> Discreetly daring, and severely kind,
> The courtly Roman's shining path to tread,
> And sharply smile prevailing folly *dead ?*

Will no superior genius snatch the quill,
And save me, on the brink, from writing *ill ?*
Though vain the strife, I'll strive my voice to raise ;
What will not men attempt for sacred *praise ?*

Young.

Here, within the distance of ten couplets, are two rhymes twice repeated, and one three times. Again :

For when the tender rinds of trees dis*close*
Their shooting gems, a swelling knot there *grows :*
Just in that space a narrow slit we make,
Then other buds from bearing trees we take :
Inserted thus, the wounded rind we *close,*
In whose moist womb th' admitted infant *grows.*
But when the smoother bole from knots is free,
We make a deep incision in the tree ;
And in the solid wood the slip en*close ;*
The battening bastard shoots again and *grows.*

Dryden.

The fault is still greater when two couplets together have the same rhyme, as :

With soothing words to Venus she be*gun :*
High praises, endless honours you have *won,*
And mighty trophies with your worthy *son :*
Two gods a silly woman have un*done.*

Dryden.

Nor is the fault much less when the rhymes, though not the same, are so near as to differ only by a single letter, as in this instance :

The lofty skies at once come pouring down,
The promised crop and golden labours drown.

The dikes are fill'd, and with a roaring sound
The rising rivers float the nether ground.

Dryden.

The following couplets in Pope's *Rape of the Lock* are very remarkable:

The doubtful beam long nods from side to side;
At length the wits mount up, the hairs subside.
See, fierce Belinda on the Baron flies,
With more than usual lightning in her eyes:
Nor fear'd the chief th' unequal fight to try,
Who sought no more than on his foe to die.
But the bold lord, with manly strength endued,
She with one finger and a thumb subdued.
Just where the breath of life his nostrils drew,
A pinch of snuff the wily virgin threw:

Canto 5.

The first three couplets have nearly the same rhymes, so have the two others; and to mark the poet's negligence in this passage, the rhymes of the first and fourth couplets have the additional fault of being identical.

These are faults which, though not inexcusable in a long work, are by no means to be allowed in short pieces; for in such, to be correct and polished makes a considerable part of their merit. This frequent repetition of rhymes may be perhaps allowed or at least will not be severely condemned in lyric compositions, where the return of the regular stanza lays the author under a greater restraint. An instance of such repetition occurs in Gray:

> Ambition this shall tempt to rise,
> Then whirl the wretch from high,
> To bitter Scorn a sacrifice,
>   And grinning Infamy.
> The stings of Falsehood these shall try,
> And hard Unkindness' alter'd eye.
> > " *Ode on the Prospect of Eton Coll.*"

Another fault to be mentioned here is the introduction of words merely for the sake of rhyme. This is done in various ways—first, by making use of unnecessary and superfluous words, as :

> Rome, the terror of the world,
> At length shall sink, in ruin *hurled*.

Again :

> So, when a smooth expanse receives *impressed*
> Calm Nature's image on its watery breast.

That is, when a smooth piece of water reflects natural objects. Now in both these instances the rhymes are made by words that had better been omitted ; and the last not only clogs the sentence, but gives a false idea ; for the objects which are reflected by a mirror are not *impressed* upon it.

This arises sometimes when a rhyme is wanted for a word that has but few rhymes to it in the language. The term *world* is one of these ; there are not above five that will pair with it ; two of which are *furled* and *hurled*, and these being more pliable than the others, are therefore often worked up into some distorted phrase to furnish a rhyme ; for example :

Let Envy in a whirlwind's bosom hurled,
Outrageous, search the corners of the world.

In him He all things with strange order hurled ;
In him, that full abridgment of the world.

Another form of this blemish is, by pitching upon some rhyme, to which all the rest of the sentence is to be held subservient; and then, for want of a proper word to match with the rhyme already determined, the poet is often obliged to substitute such as he can get. Butler ridicules this in the couplet :

But those that write in rhyme still make
The one verse for another's sake.

A couplet from the *Epistle of Eloisa to Abelard* will explain and exemplify what we mean. Pope had to express in rhyme and measure this sentence: "I would rather be the mistress of the man I love, than the empress of Cæsar." Of this he took the strong energetic part for his close, "Make me mistress to the man I love," and having thus fixed his rhyme, he sacrifices the other line to it; for, as the sentence afforded him no second word to match with the rhyme he had taken, he was driven to make out the sense as well as he could by some substitute. He therefore substituted the term *prove* as an equivalent to *be ;* and the ardent sentiment of Eloisa was enfeebled by these expressions :

Not Cæsar's empress would I *deign to prove ;* *
No, make me mistress to the man I love.

Pope.

* All who have dabbled in amatory verse must have felt the want of more words to rhyme with *love.*

The notice taken of this imperfection leads to the mention of another very similar to it. Our versifiers, for the most part, are well acquainted with poetical language, and possess a store of terms and phrases which are very fit and proper to be employed in the composition of verse; but they often commit mistakes in the application of them. Among their errors one arises from this : that they consider certain words to be synonymous which are only partially so. For instance, a head of hair and tresses frequently mean the same thing ; but we cannot properly give the name of tresses to every head of hair. Again, waves and water are the same : every wave is water; but water in every situation and quantity is not to be called a wave. The misapplication of such terms as these, and the indifferent use of one for the other, as if they had the same signification in all cases, is a blemish in our poetry, and it deserves animadversion. It is admitted, sometimes for the purpose of supposed poetical ornament, and sometimes for the more urgent purpose of supplying a rhyme. Tyros in the art of versifying are the worst offenders in this respect, yet traces of it are to be seen in writers of a much higher order. In Pope's *Windsor Forest* the river Thames is described thus :

> In that blest moment from his oozy bed
> Old Father Thames advanced his reverend head.
> His *tresses* dropp'd with dews, and o'er the stream
> His shining horns diffused a golden gleam.

Tresses are braided hair, and the term is gen

erally, if not always, used to signify the hair of a
female head.   They would make an incongruous
appearance in the head-dress of a *reverend old
man*, but they are here put for hair of the head
in general, which is a misuse of the word.   Milton
had occasion to use this word when describing
Adam and Eve in Paradise; and he marks, by
many distinguishing circumstances, the wide difference between the male and female head of hair
in those whom he represents as perfect models of
human beauty.

> His hyacinthine locks
> Round from his parted forelock manly hung
> Clustering, but not beneath his shoulders broad :
> She, as a veil, down to the slender waist,
> Her unadorned golden *tresses* wore
> Dishevell'd, but in wanton ringlets waved,
> As the vine curls her tendrils.

Besides these faults it has been reckoned another
to make the great majority of rhymes with monosyllables.   Goldsmith has been censured for this,
and Gray, in his remarks on the poems of Lydgate,
says : "We (the English) are almost reduced to
find our rhymes among the monosyllables, in
which our tongue too much abounds.   In Pope's
Ethic epistles (that to Lord Burlington), I find, in
the compass of forty lines, only seven words at
the end of a verse which are not monosyllables.
That it is undesirable to rhyme with such monosyllables as are trifling and insignificant words, is
acknowledged, as has been already observed; but
to object to monosyllables for rhymes, merely

because they are so, is fastidious, nor can the objection, as applied to our language, be justified."

6.—ARRANGEMENT OF RHYMES.

Before closing the chapter on rhymes, some remarks appear necessary as to their *arrangement* in verse, and as to the *kinds of poetry* to which their introduction seems suitable and necessary. Rhymes are arranged either:

(i) *Consecutively* in couplets and rarely in triplets, or

(ii) *Alternately*, as in the elegiac stanza and ballad metre, or

(iii) At irregular intervals, or *crossed*, of which numerous examples will be found in "Combinations of Verse," and the "Sonnet." Puttenham, in his "Art of Poetry," adopted an elaborate system of angular and wavy lines to illustrate such arrangements, a plan which we decline to adopt as unnecessary and disfiguring to verse presentation. The student, who is accustomed to read with pencil in hand, will know how and when to mark the points on which his attention should rest.

By arrangement is to be understood the order in which rhymes ought to stand to produce the best effect, *i.e.* to satisfy the ear; for the ear will be better pleased with the rhymes that are perfect, if they stand in one order rather than another, and a skilful managment in ordering those that are imperfect will render them less displeasing. The quick return of the same sound, however

pleasing to the ear and suitable to the nature of
the lighter kinds of verse, is inconsistent with the
gravity and sublimity that characterise the higher
forms of poetic expression. At the same time if
the interval that separates the rhyming words be
too great, their correspondence on the ear, which
is the main purpose of rhyme, would be lost.
When three heroic lines intervene, they seem to
be set as far asunder as can be allowed with propriety. No definite rules bearing upon the subject can be deduced from the writings of our best
poets, and little more can be said with certainty
beyond the two broad principles stated above.
The remarks that are made as to the disposition
of rhymes in the pure Italian form of the sonnet,
and in the Spenserian stanza, may be appropriately
referred to here. In the case of imperfect rhymes,
if the broader and longer vowel sound be arranged
to come before the corresponding shorter one, and
a hard consonant sound precede the corresponding
soft sound, the discordance between them is not
so disagreeable as when this order is reversed. And
the same applies to a word of many syllables, the
last, of course, being unaccented, rhyming with
a monosyllable, the light ending should always
come last.

Rhyme is a non-essential element in verse.
Minstrels poured forth their lays of war and love
long before the chiming of similar sounds had been
thought of. In our own language traces of it are
to be found as far back as the tenth century, and
although Chaucer may be said to have popularised

it in his *Canterbury Tales* towards the end of the fourteenth century, and all succeeding poets have made use of it more or less, it was long looked down upon as a barbarous innovation, and is still regarded by some as a meretricious aid to "poesie divine." All the very greatest poems in all languages are rhymeless. The additional restrictions that it imposes upon the freedom of the poet have caused it to be discarded in all the masterpieces of poetic art. Some few noble and lengthy poems, like Spenser's *Fairie Queen* and Byron's *Childe Harold*, no doubt owe much of their charm to its embellishments, but its use seems more suitably restricted to lyrical pieces of all kinds, as well as to verse of a descriptive and humorous kind.

ALLITERATION.

ALLITERATION is the frequent recurrence of the same letter or sound at the beginning of words in a verse, forming a kind of initial rhyme, *e.g.* :

> Carking care,
> Green-eyed grief, and dull despair.
> > > *Kirke White.*

It was an essential element in Anglo-Saxon and Old English poetry, which, for the most part, consists of short couplets containing three or four accented syllables, linked together by alliterative consonance.* Here is a specimen from the opening lines of *Piers the Plowman's Vision*, written by Willam Langlande about 1362 :

> In a somer seson,
> When softe was the sonne,
> I shope me in shroudes
> As I a shepe were ;
> In habit as an hermit,
> Unholy of workes.

Again, from the same poem :

> There preached a pardoner,
> As he a prieste were ;
> Brought forth a bull
> With many bishops' seals.

* See **Development of Versification**, p. 256.

When Chaucer began to reform our versification, and introduced the regular rhythmic flow of accented syllables and the new element of rhyme, alliteration ceased to be an essential to English verse, but it has always retained its hold as an aid and embellishment to its melody. The Elizabethan poets evinced a marked fondness for its " artful aid," and used it with great taste and skill, as for example :

> Sitting by a river's side,
> Where a silent stream did glide,
> Muse I did of many things
> That the mind in quiet brings.
>
> *Greene.*

> Repining courage yields
> No foot to foe : the flashing fire flies
> As from a forge.
>
> *Spenser.*

In the fashionable craze called *Euphuism** of Queen Elizabeth's reign, alliteration was carried to a ridiculous excess, which furnished occasion for

---

* Ephuism takes its name from *Euphies, or the Anatomy of Wit* by John Lily, a minor dramatist of Elizabeth's reign (1554-1600). It was written in a ridiculously ornate style, abounding in conceits, classical allusions, forced antitheses, and alliterations. It took the popular fancy of the time, and became much in vogue with the wits and dandies of Elizabeth's Court. Sir Walter Scott parodies its use in the *Monastery* in the person of Sir Percie Shafton ; here is an example :

" And now having wished to my fairest Discretion those pleasant dreams which wave their pinions around the couch of sleeping beauty, and to this comely damsel the beauties of Morpheus, and to all others the common good night, I will crave your leave to depart to my place of rest."

Euphuism should not be confounded with *Euphemism*, which is an expression in which the offensiveness of a thought is somewhat hidden : *e.g.,* " He has gone to that other world which is not heaven."

Shakspere's mock imitation of it in *Love's Labour's Lost.* Holofernes, the pedantic pedagogue, writes some verses which he calls "An Extemporal Epitaph on the Death of the Deer:" they run:

> The praiseful princess pierced and pricked a pretty
> Pleasing pricket ;
> Some say, a sore ; but not a sore till now made
> Sore with shooting.

He ridicules the excessive use of it again in the bombastic words of Bottom :

> Whereat, with blade, with bloody, blameful blade,
> He bravely broached his boiling, bloody breast.
> *"Midsummer Night's Dream."*

Nevertheless he avails himself of this simple ornament with rare felicity throughout his entire works.

> This precious stone set in a silver sea.
> *"Richard II."*

> Our dreadful marches to delightful measures.
> *"Richard III."*

> He capers nimbly in his lady's chamber
> To the lascivious pleasing of a lute.
> *"Richard III."*

> Myself could else out-frown false fortune's frown.
> *"King Lear."*

> Whose influence, like a wreath of radiant fire,
> On flickering Phœbus front.
> *"King Lear."*

N

Poor naked wretches, wheresoe'er you are,
That bide the pelting of this pitiless storm.
                              " King Lear."

I'll look to like, if looking liking move.
                              " Romeo and Juliet."

                    Jocund day
Stands tiptoe on the misty mountain tops.
                              " Romeo and Juliet."

                    His virtues
Will plead, like angels, trumpet-tongued, against
The deep damnation of his taking off.
                              " Macbeth."

But now I'm cabin'd, cribb'd, confined.
                              " Macbeth."

After life's fitful fever he sleeps well.
                              " Macbeth."

Life is as tedious as a twice-told tale,
Vexing the dull ear of a dying man.
                              " King John."

                    My story being done,
She gave me for my pains a world of sighs :
She swore—in faith, 'twas strange, 'twas passing strange,
'Twas pitiful, 'twas wondrous pitiful.
                              " Othello."

Then the whining schoolboy, with his satchel,
And shining morning face, creeping like snail,
Unwillingly to school.
                              " As You Like It."

They are not a pipe for Fortune's finger
To sound what stop she please.
                              " Hamlet."

Make thy two eyes like stars start from their spheres.
> "*Hamlet.*"

Milton's use of alliteration is not so marked in his epics as in the minor poems. He also employs various devices to tone down the alliterative effect by (1) employing it with unaccented syllables; (2) with syllables other than the initial one; and (3) by the use of consonants similar but not identical in sound, as *b*, *p*, *t*, &c. His exquisite skill in the choice of words for all the purposes of picturesque and melodic effect is unsurpassed by any of our poets. The very sound of many of his verses, even apart from the sense, has a distinct pleasurable effect.

> Deep on his front engraven
> Deliberation sat, and public care.
> > "*Paradise Lost.*"

> The rising wind of waters, dark and deep.
> > "*Paradise Lost.*"

> That soil may best
> Deserve the precious bane . . . .
> > "*Paradise Lost.*"

> Moping melancholy,
> And moon-struck madness.
> > "*Paradise Lost.*"

> Perhaps some cold bank is her bolster now.
> > "*Comus.*"

> Or 'gainst the rugged bark of some broad elm.
> > "*Comus.*"

> Yet they in pleasing slumber lulled the sense.
> *" Comus."*

> Sweetest Shakspere, Fancy's child,
> Warble his native wood-notes wild.
> *" L' Allegro."*

> Lap me in soft Lydian airs,
> Married to immortal verse.
> *" L' Allegro."*

> Sweet bird, that shunn'st the noise of folly,
> Most musical, most melancholy.
> *" Il Penseroso."*

Sometimes we have instances of *vowel allitera-tion,* e.g. :

> Where awful arches make a noonday night.
> *Pope.*

> Tho' oft the ear the open vowels tire.
> *Pope.*

> With sudden adoration and blank awe.
> *Milton.*

> Sleep on, thou mighty dead,
>   A glorious tomb they've found thee,—
> The broad blue sky above thee spread,
>   The boundless ocean round thee.
> *Lyte.*

Dryden and Pope both avail themselves freely of this poetic ornament; the latter seems specially to have taken care to make the consonance less obvious by separating the words more than usual :

Deep in a dungeon was the captive cast,
Deprived of day, and held in fetters fast.
Dryden.

So, speechless, for a little space he lay.
Dryden.

One laced the helm, another held the lance.
Dryden.

The bookful blockhead, ignorantly read,
With loads of learned lumber in his head.
Pope.

Speed the soft intercourse from soul to soul,
And waft a sigh from Indus to the Pole.
Pope.

Soft as the slumbers of a saint forgiven.
Pope.

Who shall decide when doctors disagree?
Pope.

We conquered France, but felt our captive's charms.
Pope.

In the following verse Pope employs it skilfully in an elaborate onomatopeia:

Up the high hill he heaves a huge round stone.

Alliteration enters largely as a melodic element into all our modern poetry, but for the most part its effect is more artfully concealed. No doubt it is often employed unconsciously, for in the choice of words association as well as sound affects the taste in selection. Here follows a selection from our nineteenth-century poets:

> Back to the struggle, baffled in the strife.
>
> *Byron.*

> Beneath its base are heroes' ashes hid.
>
> *Byron.*

> There is a pleasure in the pathless woods.
>
> *Byron.*

> Foiled, bleeding, breathless, furious to the last,
> Full in the centre stands the bull at bay.
>
> *Byron.*

> Drank the last life drop of his bleeding breast.
>
> *Byron.*

> Sounds sweet as if a sister's voice reproved.
>
> *Byron.*

> Like a glow-worm golden
> In a dell of dew.
>
> *Shelley.*

> Our sincerest laughter
> With some pain is fraught:
> Our sweetest songs are those that tell of saddest thought.
>
> *Shelley.*

> The lustre of the long convolvuleses.
>
> *Tennyson.*

> Havelock baffled, or beaten, or butchered, for all that we knew

> This truth came borne with bier and pall,
> I felt it when I sorrowed most,
> 'Tis better to have loved and lost
> Than never to have loved at all.
>
> *Tennyson.*

Abou Ben Adhem (may his tribe increase !)
Awoke one night from a deep dream of peace.

Leigh Hunt.

Alone, alone, all, all alone,
Alone on a wide, wide sea.

Coleridge.

The fair breeze blew ; the white foam flew,
The furrow followed free.

Coleridge.

The sentinel stars set their watch in the sky.

Campbell.

BLANK VERSE.

THIS term, although it includes all unrhymed measures, is generally restricted to Heroic verse, or Iambic pentameter. In it are embalmed the masterpieces of English poetry, Milton's epics and Shakspere's dramas. It was first employed in English verse by the Earl of Surrey, who also introduced the sonnet, during the reign of Henry VIII., in a translation which he made of the second and fourth books of the *Æneid*, the opening lines of which are as follows:

> They whisted all, with fixed face attent,
> When Prince Æneas from the royal seat
> Thus 'gan to speak : O Queen, it is thy will
> I should renew a woe cannot be told.

These lines are not an unfavourable specimen of the kind of verse ; they run smoothly, and the pause is varied—in fact they would bear comparison with the blank verse of all but the greatest masters.

Blank verse is less trammelled by artificial restrictions, and its rhythm is improved by the introduction of a greater number of deviations from normal regularity than any other measure in English, or indeed of any other language, ancient or modern. It admits into its composition a free use of at least five different kinds of feet, whereas in the most commonly used classical measure, the hexameter, only two kinds, dactyls and spondees, find place. The simplicity of its structure, and the almost infinite variety of rhythmic effect of which it is capable, render it the noblest vehicle of poetic expression which the melodic instincts of mankind have conceived. Each great poet that has employed it to any extent has given to it a distinctive character, which even an untrained ear would readily detect. Read aloud, for instance, a passage from Wordsworth's *Excursion*, or Cowper's *Task*, and follow it by a full-mouthed piece from Milton, and then by some verses of Shakspere's, free and mellifluent as a summer breeze ; the marked contrast in the rhythmic flow is unmistakable.

1.—LICENCES.

The chief *licences* allowable in standard blank verse have already been enumerated and illustrated, p. 122, but it will be as well here, for the sake of completeness, to recapitulate and supplement what has there been said.

(i) *A pyrrhic foot* ($\smile \smile$) may take the place of an iambus in any part of the line, though rarely in the fifth foot ; two, and (very rarely) three, such substitutions may occur in the same verse, but then the approach to prose is dangerously close.

(ii) *Spondees* ($- -$) may also find place in any part of the line, though the metrical accent is only given to the second syllable of each. Two spondees often occur together, and occasionally as many as three or four.

(iii) *Trochees* (− ⌣) are occasionally admissible, but much more sparingly than either of the former, as their run from strong to weak breaks the regular iambic flow weak to strong. Two trochees should never occur together, and not more than two in the same line. They are to be found frequently in the first foot, occasionally in the third and fourth, but rarely in the second and fifth.

(iv) Trisyllabic feet are also frequently used for iambic, especially *anapests* (⌣ ⌣ −), which have the same rhythmic run from weak to strong ; the utmost limit of such substitution is three to five.

(v) An additional unaccented syllable is frequently found at the end of a verse, and occasionally a twelfth syllable is added, but there must be no sixth accent. This liberty is mostly confined to dramatic verse.

The canons here concisely laid down have been carefully deduced from the usage of our best poets, and are in agreement with the views of the most recent authorities on our versification. Mr. Ellis says,* "The number of syllables may therefore be greater than ten, and the accents may be, and generally are, less than five. If there be accent at the end of the third and fifth group, or at the end of the second and fourth, other accents may be distributed almost at pleasure." Dr. Abbott† states that about one

---

* Ellis, " Essentials of Phonetics," p. 77.
† Abbott, " Shaksperian Grammar," p. 453.

line in three has the full number of emphatic accents, about two in four have four, and one out of fifteen three.

Mr. Conway* has drawn out with elaborate precision a table in which he gives thirty-five different arrangements of the accents found in heroic lines of approved authors, seven with the full number of five, fifteen with four, eleven with three, and ten with two. Now, if to all these allowable variations in the arrangement of the accented syllables we add the practically limitless change that may be made in the position of the pauses in successive lines, we shall at once realise the boundless capabilities of rhythmical variety that this measure presents. Well may it be selected as the most suitable form of verse for lofty and continuous poetical utterance.

2.—EPIC OR HEROIC BLANK VERSE.

MILTON.

The singular excellence of *Milton's blank verse* being generally admitted, we will here point out some of its causes, or at least some of those qualities which are most apparent and eminent in his versification. He has availed himself of the use of mixed metre to the utmost possible extent, such as these :

Draw after him the third | pãrt ŏf | Heaven's host.

Deliberate valour breath'd | fĩrm ănd | unmoved.

* Gilbert Conway, " Treatise on Versification," p. 24. (Longmans, London, 1878.)

Of Eve, whose eye | dărtĕd | contagious fire.

How art thou lost! | hŏw ŏn | a sudden lost !

Uni | vērsăl | reproach, far worse to bear.

Anon, | oūt ŏf | the earth, a fabric huge.

Bĕttĕr | to reign in hell than serve in heaven.

These licences are all of one kind; viz. the substitution of the trochaic for the iambic foot, and it
is this which offends the ear in some of Milton's
lines, as in this:

Yet fell ; remember, and | fēar to | transgress.

But it offends only because there is no pause before
it ; the following, which has exactly the same feet,
is a musical line :

In wood or wilderness, | fōrĕst | or den.

This trochaic substitution being the direct opposite to the fundamental measure of the heroic line
should be used most sparingly, and never occur
in the last foot, though a pyrrhic or spondee may
so stand, as in the two following lines :

Till even, nor then the solemn night | ĭngăle
Ceased warbling, but all night tuned her | sŏft lāys.

Here are examples of other substituted feet in
Milton's verse :

Ănd thĕ | shrīll soūnds | ran echoing through the wood,

Mŭrmŭrĭng, | and with him fled the shades of night,

Innu | mĕrăblĕ | before th' Almighty's throne.

Gămbollĕd | before | thĕm ; thĕ | unwieldy el | ĕphănt.

All beasts | ŏf thĕ eārth | since wild, | ănd ŏf | āll chāse.

> Through man | y a dārk | and dreary vale
> They passed, and man | y a rē | gion do | lŏroŭs,
> O'er man | y a frō | zen, man | y a fî | ĕry Ālp,
> Rŏcks, cōves, | lākes, fēns, | bōgs, dēns, | and shades of
>   death.

Next to the variety of feet may be noticed the variety of pauses with respect to their position in the line. Here again Milton's excellence appears :

> However, some tradition they dispersed
> Among the heathen, of their purchase got,
> And fabled how the serpent, whom they call'd
> Ophion, with Eurynome, the wide-
> Encroaching Eve, perhaps, had first the rule
> Of high Olympus, thence by Saturn driven
> And Ops, e'er yet Dictæan Jove was born.

In this passage the pause is so varied that no two lines together have it in the same place ; and within the compass of seven lines it stands in six different places. This is by no means a singular instance ; a variety, similar if not so great, is one characteristic of this poem.

> Millions of spirits for his fault amerced
> Of heaven, and from eternal splendours flung
> For his revolt ; yet faithful how they stood,
> Their glory wither'd : as when heaven's fire

> Hath scathed the forest oaks or mountain pines,
> With singed top their stately growth, though bare,
> Stands on the blasted heath.

Here, from the second line to the sixth, there are as many different pauses as lines.

When a pause falls on the third, or fifth, or seventh syllable of a verse, the foot in which it stands will generally be a pyrrhic, because the connecting words of our language, as conjunctions, &c., are all unaccented; it would therefore be a weak foot, which is sometimes to be guarded against, in order to preserve what Pope calls " the full resounding line, the majestic march," of the heroic measure. To this Milton has attended in many passages; for example :

> Tórments | him, roŭnd | he throws | his bale | ful eyes.

> For these | rebell | ious, hēre | their prison | ordain'd.

> Breaking | the horrid silence, thūs began.

> When Je | sus, sōn of Ma | ry, sēcond Eve.

> Convulsions, ēpilepsies, fiērce catarrhs,
> Intestine stone and ulcer, cōlic-pangs,
> Demoniac phrensy, mōping melancholy,
> And moon-struck madness, pīning atrophy,
> Marasmus, and wide-wasting pestilence.

In every line here, except the last, the syllable following the pause is accented; this makes the foot an iambic, and gives a fulness to the measure. No modern poet would venture to construct a passage such as the last one.

Another circumstance remarkable in Milton's versification is his use of elisions. The practice of cutting off a vowel at the end of a word was not introduced by him into our poetry, but he revived it when it had become obsolete ; so that his manner appeared as a novelty, and was indeed clearly different from that of other poets, and even from his own earlier productions. In his *Comus* there occur no elisions like these :

His temple right against the temple' of God—

Anguish, and doubt, and fear, and sorrow', and pain—

Abominable', unutterable', and worse.

The length of periods, occasionally and judiciously introduced, is another distinguishing feature. Such is the following :

Sing, heavenly Muse, that on the secret top
Of Oreb, or of Sinai, didst inspire
That shepherd who first taught the chosen seed,
In the beginning, how the heavens and earth
Rose out of chaos.

To these may be added the frequent inversions, as this, which is most remarkable :

God, from the Mount of Sinai, whose gray top
Shall tremble, he descending, shall himself,
In thunder, lightning, and loud trumpet's sound,
Ordain them laws.

But in Milton's versification nothing is more remarkable than the skilful manner by which his lines are connected and run one into another. This is done by ending the line in that part of a sentence where there is no sensible pause. But to explain this it will be necessary to consider how, for this purpose, a sentence may be divided, and also what makes a pause. And first to mention what, in a simple sentence, will produce a pause. Take a sentence in its natural order of words : viz. 1st, the article ; 2nd, the nominative case, and what may be joined with it, as adjective or genitive case; 3rd, the verb ; 4th, the noun, or other word governed by it, *e.g. :*

> The affable archangel had forewarn'd
> Adam.

Whatever disturbs this natural order creates a pause, as :

(i) Transposition ; *i.e.* any change of that order, *e.g. :*

> The sojourners of Goshen, who beheld
> *From the safe shore* their floating carcases.

> Ahaz his sottish conqueror, whom he drew
> *God's altar* to disparage.

(ii) The insertion of any phrase, or word, not necessary to make out the sentence :

> ———— the selfsame place where he
> *First* lighted from his wing.

> ——— my sudden hand
> *Prevented*, spares to tell thee yet by deeds.

On a sudden open fly
With impetuous recoil and jarring sound
The infernal doors.

———— on each hand the flames
Driven backward, slope their pointing spires.

(iii) Apposition, or the introduction of a second
word having the same signification as the former;
this differs but little from the preceding, *e.g. :*

———— or that sea-beast
Leviathan, which God of all his works—

———— yea, often placed
Within his sanctuary itself their shrines,
Abominations, and with cursed things.

Hid Amalthea, and her florid son,
Young Bacchus, from his step-dame Rhea's eye.

By any of these means a pause is made, even in a
simple sentence.

Dramatic writers sometimes end a line with
such words as would hardly be allowed in other
kinds of serious poetry; such are the articles, the adjective pronouns, and conjunctions. Now there is no
pause between the article and its noun, nor between
the pronoun adjective and its substantive; on the
contrary, these have too close a connexion to be
separated. But verses may be made to run into
one another by dividing a sentence in other parts,
where yet there is no pause.

(1) Between two substantives.

(2) Between the nominative case and the verb.

o

(3) Between the verb and the accusative case.

(4) Between two verbs. These breaks are of the most frequent occurrence, but there are others, as

(5) Between the adjective and its substantive.

(6) Between certain pronouns and the verb.

(7) Between some prepositions and the word governed by them.

The following instances are subjoined to show Milton's use of these divisions :

(1.) Of man's first disobedience, and the fruit
Of that forbidden tree.

(2.) ———— whose mortal taste
Brought death into the world.

(3.) Sing, heavenly muse that
———— didst inspire
That shepherd.

(4.) ———— He now prepared
To speak ; whereat their doubled ranks they bend

(5.) God their creator and th' invisible
Glory of him that made them to transform.

———— the gray
Dawn, and the Pleiades before him danced.

(6.) And feel thy sovran vital lamp ; but thou
Revisit'st not these eyes.

———— that thou art naked, who
Hath told thee ? hast thou eaten of the tree ?

(7.) That were an ignominy and shame beneath
This downfall.

Sole Eve, associate sole, to me beyond
Compare above all living creatures dear.

These prepositions are dissyllables; the smaller seldom, if ever, occur at the end of a line. We find, but very rarely, the auxiliary separated from its verb:

That with reiterated crimes he might
Heap on himself damnation.

And once a compound epithet is divided at the end of a verse:

Ophion, with Eurynome, the wide-
Encroaching Eve perhaps.

All these qualities enumerated above appear throughout Milton's versification, which indeed he himself has described in his note prefixed to the *Paradise Lost,* in these words, " True musical delight consists only in apt numbers, fit quantity of sylla-bles, and the sense variously drawn out from one verse into another." Such, according to his judg-ment, are the essential elements to good verse, and by due attention to what he here laid down he attained to his distinguished eminence in this, which is the highest species of English versifica-tion.

3.—DRAMATIC BLANK VERSE.

SHAKSPERE.

With respect to dramatic verse very little consideration of what is requisite for effective stage representation is necessary to show that the utmost freedom and variety of treatment must be allowed in this species of composition. The verse is not the language of the poet, but of the characters whom he introduces upon the stage. Words of the deepest passion and pathos have to be altered at times, but without causing incongruity with the everyday surroundings of life. The poet sinks his own individuality altogether, while his puppets speak and act as real men and women do on the great world's stage. The dialogue, elevated and heroic as it must sometimes be, should also be natural and easily comprehended; hence involved constructions, and unusual inversions, and stilted diction are out of place. The natural order of words in a sentence ought not to be violated for the sake of metre beyond what would be deemed suitable in rhetorical oratory. The audience must readily grasp the sense of the words as they are uttered — there is no time for reflection. To accomplish all this the dramatist avails himself freely of every kind of poetic licence, already enumerated and illustrated, and, in true Bohemian spirit, trespasses the conventionalities of versification still further, whenever it suits his purpose. Such as :

(i) The free use of one or two hypermetrical syllables:

> Thou marshal'st me the way that I was go | ĭng.
> > " *Macbeth.*"

> To-day | hĕ pŭts fŏrth
> The tender leaves of hope, to-morrow blos | sŏms,
> And bears his blushing honours thick upon | hĭm.
> > " *Henry VIII.*"

> He were much goodlier ; is't not a handsome gen | tlĕmăn ?
> > " *All's Well that Ends Well.*"

> Your honour and your goodness is so ev | ĭdĕnt.
> > " *Winter's Tale.*"

The use of these additional syllables increases in Shakspere's later plays.

(ii) The use of extra mid-syllables before the cæsural pause, which also becomes more marked in the latter plays of Shakspere :

> This is his Majesty ; say your mind to him.
> > " *All's Well.*"

> Then when I feel and see her, no further trust her.
> > " *Winter's Tale.*"

> And first-fruits of my body, from his presence
> I am barred.
> > " *Winter's Tale.*"

> The marigold, that goes to bed wi' the sun,
> And with him rises weeping ; these are flowers
> Of middle summer.
> > " *Winter's Tale.*"

> There is no more such masters : I may wonder.
>   " *Cymbeline.*"

(iii) Imperfect lines are admissible, *i.e.* verses of only one, two, or three feet—rarely four.   When these *hemistichs,* as they are called, come together, they require to be scanned as a continuous line :

> *Ophelia.* I pray you now receive them.
> *Hamlet.*   No, not **I** ;
>   I never gave her aught.
>   " *Hamlet.*"

> Of but a sickly part of one true sense
> Could not so mope.
> O shame, where is thy blush ?
>   " *Hamlet.*"

Occasionally, *Alexandrines* are blended with the five-foot verse :

> *Hamlet.*   Honeying and making love
>   Over the nasty sty,—
> *Queen.*   O, speak to me no more !
>   " *Hamlet.*"

(iv) What are known as " light " and " weak " endings are freely used, especially in the choicest specimens of Shakspere's verse.   By the former is meant the termination of a line with personal or relative pronouns, or auxiliary verbs, that admit but a very slight pause ; by the latter the verse is ended by prepositions or conjunctions which allow of no break whatever ; the line is forced to run both in sound and sense into the closest connection with the opening words of the succeeding verse, *e.g.* :

> The power I serve
> Laughs at your happy Araby, or the
> Elysian shades.
>
> *Massinger.*

> If by your art, my dearest father, you have
> Put the wild waves in this roar, allay them.
> Had I been any god of power, I would
> Have sunk the sea within the earth, or e'er
> It should the good ship so have swallowed, and
> The freighting souls within her.
>
> *" Tempest."*

At this point the *versification of Shakspere* claims our special attention, beyond what has already been said upon blank verse generally and dramatic verse in particular, he being the acknowledged master of poetic art both as regards matter and form. His unrivalled series of dramas—thirty-seven in all—the pride of our mother tongue, are not only an inexhaustible source of pleasure to the successive generations of English-speaking people all the world over, but they furnish a field of ever-increasing interest and enquiry into the methods of his art and the development of his genius. The attempt to fix the chronological order of his plays has, of late years, led Shaksperean students to pay special attention to his versification, and their united labours have resulted in such an arrangement of

his works in the order of their production, as
further enquiry will, in all probability, never
alter. If we take a number of passages from the
known works of his 'prentice hand, the early
comedies, such, for instance, as *Love's Labour's
Lost*, *The Comedy of Errors*, *The Two Gentlemen of Verona*, and compare them with selections
from the great tragedies of his matured powers,
like *Hamlet*, *Lear*, and *Macbeth*, and again with
others from *The Tempest* and *The Winter's Tale*,
creations of the calm sunset of his life, a clearly
marked change will be observable in the nature
and rhythmic movement of the verses.   In the
first set the numbers flow with a smoothness
approaching the monotony of rhymed heroics; extra
syllables rarely occur, the tenth usually has an
emphatic accent, and the pause comes regularly at
the end of the line : the verses are *end-stopt*, as they
have been appropriately called.   In the other
selections we shall find this regularity gradually
disappearing.   Light and weak endings and
extra syllables occur in increasing numbers;
the pauses are, for the most part, removed from
the end, and find place in any part of the line,
even varying; the sense as well as the sound is
continuous from one line to the next; the verse
is *run-on*, as it is called, to distinguish it from the
former kind.   These marked characteristics are
clearly discernible in the following selections :

> The more thou damm'st it up, the more it burns ;
> The current, that with gentle murmur glides

Thou know'st, being stopped, impatiently doth rage ;
But when his fair course is not hinderèd,
He makes sweet music with the enamell'd stones,
Giving a gentle kiss to every sedge
He overtaketh in his pilgrimage ;
And so, by many winding nooks he strays,
With willing sport to the wild oce-an.
> *" Two Gentlemen of Verona."*

The air is full of noises,
Sounds, and sweet airs, that give delight and hurt not.
Sometimes a thousand twanging instruments
Will hum about mine ears ; and sometimes voices,
That, if I then had waked after long sleep,
Will make me sleep again ; and then, in dreaming,
The clouds, methought, would open and show riches
Ready to drop upon me : that, when I waked,
I cried to dream again.
> *" Tempest."*

O Proserpina,
For the flowers now that, frighted, thou lett'st fall
From Dis's waggon ! daffodils
That come before the swallow dares, and take
The winds of March with beauty ; violets dim,
But sweeter than the lids of Juno's eyes,
Or Cytherea's breath ; pale primroses,
That die unmarried ere they can behold
Bright Phœbus in his strength,—a malady
Most incident to maids ; bold oxlips, and
The crown imperial ; lilies of all kinds,
The flower-de-luce being one !
> *" Winter's Tale."*

The proportion of run-on to end-stopt lines has
been ascertained by Mr. Furnival to be one in
eighteen in *Love's Labour's Lost*, and to gradually

increase to one in two in *Cymbeline* and *The Winter's Tale.* According to Professor Ingram there is no single light or weak ending in the *Two Gentlemen of Verona* and *The Comedy of Errors*, and only one in *Midsummer-Night's Dream.* They begin to appear plentifully in *Macbeth*, and in the later plays they amount to from five to seven per cent. of the whole number of endings. Again, in his early plays the youthful poet made free use of *rhyme*, but gradually discarded it as his skill in rhythmic melody grew. In *Love's Labour's Lost* there are two rhymed lines to each one without ; but in the *Tempest* there is only one couplet throughout, and in *Winter's Tale* not one.

The blank verse of Shakspere's latest plays, we thus see, is the result of careful labour and ripened judgment, directed by an instinctive sense and faculty divine for beauty and melody. His choicest efforts are inimitable, and remain unique in our literature, for they defy analysis ; their beauty must be felt rather than reasoned out. The clear sweet ring of his lyrics is perhaps equalled by some of his contemporaries, and nearly approached by Burns and Shelley, but the grace and ever-varying music of his rhythmic numbers must be regarded as a lost art.

THE SONNET.

THE sonnet, being a distinct kind of poem, demands separate treatment, and is therefore not dealt with here as a mere fourteen-line stanza. Besides, its nature and construction are so complex, and it occupies at the present time such an important and popular part in our poetic literature, that a more detailed account of its position in verse seems desirable.

The form of the sonnet is of Italian origin, and came into use in the fifteenth century, towards the end of which its construction was perfected, and its utmost melodious sweetness attained in the verse of Petrarch and Dante. In the perfect Italian type it consists of fourteen decasyllabic lines, which are divided into two unequal groups of eight and six lines, the former the *octave*, the latter the *sestet*. The octave is made up of two *quatrains*, and the sestet of two *tercets*. The rhymes throughout are unequally blended, and in the normal type are rigidly adhered to, their arrangement being based upon well-tested laws of melody. In the octave only two rhymes are admissible, one for the first, fourth, fifth and eighth lines, the other for the second, third, sixth, and seventh. The tercet admits of three pairs of rhyme, the first and fourth lines, the second and fifth, and the third and sixth. This arrangement may be illustrated as follows, the letters a, b, c, d, e representing the rhymes in succession :

> *Octave* a, b, b, a—a, b, b, a.
> *Sestet* c, d, e —c, d, e.

The subject matter of the poem should consist of one idea, or one emotion elaborately and continuously wrought out throughout, and complete in itself. The principal idea should be stated in the first quatrain, and illustrated and elaborated in the second ; then follows a pause. In each of the two tercets it should be again treated differently, and brought to a close with a dignity fully equal to the opening note, combined with epigramatic force.

The following example is constructed on the pure Petrarchan model, and is an ingenious and amusing illustration of the build of the sonnet itself. It is an English version of Lope de Vega's *Sonnet on the Sonnet*, by Mr. James Y. Gibson :

> To write a sonnet doth my Julia press me ;
> I've never found me in such stress or pain ;
> A sonnet numbers fourteen lines, 'tis plain,
> And three are gone ere I can say, God bless me !
>
> I thought that spinning lines would sore oppress me,
> Yet here I'm midway in the last quatrain :
> And if the foremost tercet I begin,
> The quatrains need not any more distress me.

To the first tercet I have got at last,
  And travel through it with such right goodwill,
  That with this line I've finished it, I ween :

I'm in the second now, and see how fast
  The thirteenth line comes tripping from my quill :
  Hurrah ! 'tis done ! Count if there be fourteen.

It was during the early part of the sixteenth
century that the Earl of Surrey and Sir Thomas
Wyatt, who had imbibed a taste for the glowing
poetry of Italy during residence there, first attempted the sonnet structure in English verse.
They found the difficulty of transplanting this
choice exotic from the musical Italian tongue into
the comparatively rough and rhymeless English
so great, that many liberties had to be taken with
it before it could be well adapted to the sterner
English soil. Spenser, Sir Philip Sidney,
Drayton, and others experimented with the new
toy, and introduced a variety of changes in the
arrangement of the rhymes, carrying the same
jingle from the octave into the sestet, thus abolish-
ing the central pause, and they closed the poem
with a couplet. Out of these attempts to acclima-
tise the stranger to the altered conditions of our
speech—attempts which demonstrated the necessity
of freedom from the flowery chains of Italian
tyranny—grew the *English sonnet*, for which some
writers have claimed an indigenous production.

In the following example from Spenser, note
that three rhymes are admitted into the quatrain,
the last of which is carried into the first tercet,
and that the poem ends with a couplet :

Like as the culver on the barèd bough
   Sits musing for the absence of her mate,
And in her songs sends many a wishful vow
   For his return that seems to linger late :
So I alone, now left disconsolate,
   Moan to myself the absence of my Love,
And, wandering here and there all desolate,
   Seek with my plaints to match that mournful dove ;
Ne joy of ought that under heaven doth hove,
   Can comfort me, but her own joyous sight ;
Whose sweet aspect both God and man can move,
   In her unspotted pleasance to delight.
Day by day, whiles her fair light I miss,
And dead my life that wants such lively bliss.

Spenser.

In the next example, entitled *Sleep*, by Daniel, it will be noticed that six rhymes are admitted, the last two forming a couplet, though the break between the two halves is observed :

Care-charmer Sleep, son of the sable Night,
   Brother to Death, in silent darkness born,
Relieve my languish, and restore the light ;
   With dark forgetting of my care return,
And let the day be time enough to mourn
   The shipwreck of my ill-adventured youth.
Let waking eyes suffice to wail their scorn
   Without the torments of night's untruth.
Cease, dreams, the images of day's desires,
   To model forth the passions of the morrow ;
Never let the rising sun approve you liars,
   To add more grief to aggravate my sorrow.
Still let me sleep embracing clouds in vain,
And never wake to feel the day's disdain.

Daniel.

The following, from Drayton, in the exact model

of the Shaksperian sonnet, is worthy of quotation, not only for its intrinsic beauty, but as illustrating the early development of the English form :

> Since there's no help, come let us kiss and part ;
>   Nay, I have done, you get no more of me ;
> And I am glad, yes, glad with all my heart,
>   That thus, so clearly, I myself can free.
> Shake hands for ever—cancel all our vows—
>   And when we meet at any time again,
> Be it not seen in either of our brows,
>   That we one jot of former love retain.
> Now at the last gasp of Love's latest breath,
>   When, his pulse failing, Passion speechless lies,
> When Faith is kneeling by his bed of death,
>   And Innocence is closing up his eyes,
> Now, if thou wouldst, when all have given him over,
> From death to life thou might'st him yet recover.

In the hands of Shakspere the sonnet became the vehicle of poetic expression, differing in almost every respect from the Italian type. While consisting of fourteen lines only, and maintaining the principle of unity of thought, the distinction of quatrain and sestet is altogether ignored, and the arrangement of the rhymes is entirely different. The Shaksperian sonnet is made up of three deca-syllabic quatrains, rhyming alternately, followed and concluded by a couplet ; thus :

a	c	e	
b	d	f	g
a	c	e	g
b	d	f	

However critics may differ as to the superior melodic sweetness of the pure Italian form, there can be no question that this poetic gem, in the hands of our great master, was wrought into a degree of perfection that has never been surpassed in our own or any other tongue. There is an abiding interest in the one hundred and fifty-four short poems of this kind that Shakspere wrote, which is ever attracting the fancy and ingenuity of new students of his genius, inasmuch as it is generally admitted that they embody the real feelings and experiences of the man himself; that in them he lays bare the joys and sorrows and inner workings of his own marvellous personality.*

* Shakspere's Sonnets were published in 1609 by T. T. (Thomas Thorpe) and, like the plays that were published in 4to during his lifetime, without the poet's knowledge. The *Dedication* of them runs " To the only begetter of these ensuing Sonnets, Mr. W. H." Who this W. H. was has given rise to many conjectures, and to much ingenious special pleading, but the truth will probably never be known with certainty. The most plausible conjectures are that the initials stand for (1) Henry Wriothesley, Earl of Southampton, the poet's junior by nine years, who is known to have been his early patron, and to whom he dedicated *Venus and Adonis* and *The Rape of Lucrece*; and (2) William Herbert, Earl of Pembroke, to whom Heminge and Condell dedicated the first folio in 1623.

It is obviously impossible to discriminate to what extent the deeper utterances of a poet are purely subjective, or are the outcome of his objective experience. The sustained, passionate depth of emotion, however, that is clearly perceptible throughout the sonnets, lead almost conclusively to the belief that they embody the poet's own feelings, and portray, though dimly, a series of real occurrences. Mr. Archibald Brown's hypothesis as to the story they tell, modified by Professor Dowden, seems the most natural and reasonable one that has been suggested, and is in accordance with the later developments of the poet's genius. It is to the effect that Sonnets 1 to 127 were addressed to a young man, and that the rest were written to, or about, a " dark lady," imperious, gifted, and fascinating, but unfaithful, who was for a time Shakspere's mistress. The young friend had wealth, rank, great beauty of person and mind, and the poet entertained for him an inordinate affection. They gradually became estranged, however; the younger succumbs to the seductions of the dark lady, and this double faithlessness plunges the poet into profound darkness and sorrow. The bitterness, however, in time passes out of his heart, the friends become reconciled and bound together by a love that is now purged from all earthly dross.

An attempt has been made of late to identify this mysterious lady as Mary Fitton, of Gawsworth, Cheshire, at one time maid of honour to Queen Elizabeth.

This innate attraction, however, is altogether apart from the illustration of metrical laws with which we are concerned, though it furnishes an instance —if instances were required—of the fascination of the materials with which we are dealing. Here follow two choice specimens of his work, the latter of which is regarded by many as the finest sonnet ever written :

> When to the sessions of sweet silent thought
>   I summon up remembrance of things past,
> I sigh the lack of many a thing I sought,
>   And with old woes new wail my dear time's waste.
> Then can I drown an eye, unused to flow,
>   For precious friends hid in death's dateless night,
> And weep afresh love's long-since-cancelled woe,
>   And moan the expense of many a vanished sight.
> Then can I grieve at grievances foregone,
>   And heavily from woe to woe tell o'er
> The sad account of fore-bemoanèd moan,
>   Which I new pay as if not paid before.
> But if the while I think on thee, dear friend,
> All losses are restored and sorrows end.
>
>   *Shakspere* (39).

> The expense of spirit in a waste of shame
>   Is lust in action ; and till action, lust
> Is perjured, murderous, bloody, full of blame,
>   Savage, extreme, rude, cruel, not to trust ;
> Enjoyed no sooner but despisèd straight ;
>   Past reason hunted ; and no sooner had,
> Past reason hated, as a swallowed bait
>   On purpose laid to make the taker mad :
> Mad in pursuit, and in possession so ;
>   Had, having, and in quest to have, extreme ;
> A bliss, in proof, and proved, a very woe ;
>   Before, a joy proposed ; behind, a dream.

P

All this the world knows well ; yet none knows well
To shun the heaven that leads men to this hell.

Shakspere (129).

In his use of the sonnet form Milton departed altogether from the Shaksperian model, and reverted
to the Italian type. He was well read in the literature of Italy, and, recognising the melodious
beauty of the sonnets of Petrarch and Dante, he
adopted their arrangement of the rhymes in the
quatrain, while varying it slightly in the sestet.
He also departed from the archetype by allowing
no break in the melody between the two halves of
the poem, which gives to his productions a majestic
sonority pre-eminently grand. In the two fine
examples quoted below the rhymes of the sestet
in the first vary from the original *c, d, e ; c, d, e,*
being arranged *c, d ; c, d ; c, d.*

ON THE LATE MASSACRE IN PIEDMONT.

Avenge, O Lord, thy slaughtered saints, whose bones
  Lie scattered on the Alpine mountains cold ;
  Even those who kept thy truth so pure of old,
When all our fathers worshipped stocks and stones,
Forget not : in thy book record their groans,
  Who were thy sheep, and in their ancient fold
  Slain by the bloody Piedmontese, who rolled
Mother with infant down the rocks. Their moans
The vales redoubled to the hills, and they
  To heaven. Their martyred blood and ashes sow
O'er all the Italian fields, where still doth sway
  The triple Tyrant ; that from there may grow
A hundredfold, who having learnt thy way,
  Early may fly the Babylonian woe.

Milton.

ON HIS BLINDNESS.

When I consider how my light is spent
  Ere half my days in this dark world and wide,
  And that one talent, which is death to hide,
Lodged with me useless, though my soul more bent
To serve therewith my Maker, and present
  My true account lest He, returning, chide :
  " Doth God exact day labour, light denied ? "
I fondly ask.   But patience, to prevent
That murmur, soon replies : God doth not need
  Either man's work or His own gifts.   Who best
Bear his mild yoke, they serve Him best.   His state
  Is kingly.   Thousands at His bidding speed
And post o'er land and ocean without rest :—
  They also serve who only stand and wait.
                    Milton.

After Milton's time the sonnet was scarcely
cultivated at all by our poets for upwards of a
hundred years, till, early in the present century,
Wordsworth revived its flickering flame, and caused
it to break forth again with a new beauty and sweetness peculiarly his own.   The taste and love that he
enkindled throughout the English-speaking world
for this artistic poetic gem has never since waned,
and it is hardly too much to say that the sonnet is
more sedulously cultivated at the present day than
any other poetic form.   The productions of our
modern poets conform in the main to the Italian type
as regards the structure of the octave, but a variable
arrangement of the rhymes is adopted in the sestet.
Since Wordsworth, Dante G. Rossetti, and Mrs.
Browning may with confidence be mentioned as

the most successful contributors to our wondrously rich store of sonnet literature.

A few modern specimens of great beauty are added to complete the sketch of the subject.

ON THE SONNET.

Nuns fret not at their convent's narrow room ;
  And hermits are contented with their cells ;
  And students with their pensive citadels ;
Maids at the wheel, the weaver at his loom,
Sit blithe and happy ; bees that soar for bloom
  High as the highest peak of Furness fells,
  Will murmur by the hour in fox-glove bells :
In truth the prison unto which we doom
Ourselves, no prison is ; and hence for me
  In sundry moods, 'tis pastime to be bound
  Within the sonnet's scanty plot of ground ;
Pleased if some souls (for such there needs must be)
Who have felt the weight of too much liberty,
  Should find brief solace there as I have found.

                        Wordsworth.

The world is too much with us, late and soon,
  Getting and spending, we lay waste our powers :
  Little we see in Nature that is ours ;
We have given our hearts away, a sordid boon !
The sea that bares her bosom to the moon,
  The winds that will be howling at all hours,
  And are up-gathered now like sleeping flowers ;
For this, for everything we are out of tune ;
It moves us not.—Great God ! I'd rather be
  A pagan suckled in a creed outworn ;
So might I, standing on this pleasant lea
  Have glimpses that would make me less forlorn ;
Have sight of Proteus rising from the sea ;
  Or hear old Triton blow his wreathèd horn.

                        Wordsworth.

NIGHT AND DEATH.

Mysterious Night ! when our first parent knew
   Thee from report divine, and heard thy name,
   Did he not tremble for this lovely frame,
This glorious canopy of white and blue ?
Yet 'neath a curtain of translucent dew,
   Bathed in the rays of the great setting flame,
   Hesperus with the host of heaven came,
And lo ! Creation widened, widened in man's view,
Who could have thought such darkness lay concealed
   Within thy beams, O Sun ! or who could find
Whilst fly and leaf and insect stood revealed,
   That to such countless orbs thou mad'st us blind !
Why do we then shun Death with anxious strife ?
If Light can thus deceive, wherefore not Life ?

                        J. Blanco White.

Note, in the following example, which forms the
introduction to the *Prisoner of Chillon*, a third
rhyme is introduced into the octave.

CHILLON.

Eternal spirit of the chainless mind !
   Brightest in dungeons, Liberty ! thou art,
   For there thy habitation is the heart—
The heart which love of thee alone can bind ;
And when thy sons to fetters are consigned—
   To fetters and the damp vaults' dayless gloom,
   Their country conquers with their martyrdom,
And Freedom's fame finds wings on every wind.
Chillon ! thy prison is a holy place,
   And thy sad floor an altar, for 'twas trod,
Until his very steps have left a trace
   Worn, as if thy cold pavement were a sod,
By Bonnivard ! May none those marks efface !
   For they appeal from tyranny to God.

                        Byron.

SUBSTITUTION.

Where some belovèd voice that was to you
    Both sound and sweetness, fadeth suddenly,
    And silence against which you dare not cry,
Aches round you like a strong disease and new—
What hope ? What help ? What music will undo
    That silence to your sense ? Not friendship's sigh,
    Not reason's subtle count, not melody
Of violo, nor of pipes that Faunus blew ;
Not songs of poets, nor of nightingales
    Whose hearts leap upward through the Cypress-trees
To the clear moon ; nor yet the spheric laws
    Self-chanted, nor the angels' sweet All hails
Met in the smile of God : Nay, none of these.
    Speak *Thou*, availing Christ ! and fill this pause.

                          Mrs. Browning.

LOST DAYS.

The lost days of my life until to-day,
    What are they, could I see them on the street
    Lie as they fell ? would they be ears of wheat
Sown once for good but trodden into clay ?
Or golden coins squandered and still to pay ?
    Or drops of blood dabbling the guilty feet ?
    Or such spilt water as in dreams must cheat
The undying throats of Hell, athirst alway ?
I do not see them here ; but after death
    God knows I know the faces I shall see,
Each one a murdered self, with low last breath.
    " I am thyself—what hast thou done to me ?"
" And I—and I—thyself," (lo ! each one saith,)
    " And thou thyself to all eternity."

                          D. G. Rossetti.

The last two examples are extremely irregular ;
by many they would not be considered sonnets at

all: As a piece of versification the one by Shelley is simply a stanza of fourteen heroics, rhyming alternately, with one couplet introduced. The last one is appended more as a literary curiosity, an experiment in monosyllables.

TO WORDSWORTH.

Poet of Nature, thou hast wept to know
  That things depart which never may return :
Childhood and youth, friendship, and love's first glow,
  Have fled like sweet dreams, leaving thee to mourn.
These common woes I feel. One loss is mine,
  Which thou too feel'st, yet I alone deplore,
Thou wert as a lone star whose light did shine
  On some frail bark in winter's midnight roar :
Thou hast like to a rock-built refuge stood
Above the blind and battling multitude :
In honoured poverty thy voice did weave
  Songs consecrate to truth and liberty.
Deserting these, thou leavest me to grieve,
  Thus. having been, that thou shouldst cease to be.

MONOSYLLABIC SONNET.

Think not that strength lies in the big round word,
  Or that the brief and plain must needs be weak.
For whom can this be true who once has heard
  The cry for help, the tongue that all men speak
When want, or woe, or fear is in the throat,
  So that each word gasped out is like a shriek
Pressed from the sore heart : or a strange, wild note
  Sung by some fay or fiend ! There is a strength
Which dies if stretched too far, or spun too fine ;
  Which has more height than breadth, more depth than
    length.

Let but this force of thought and speech be mine,
   And he that will may take the sleek, fat phrase,
That glows but burns not, though it beam and shine,
   Light, but no heat, a flash, but not a flame.*

* The student who may desire to enter more fully into this interesting corner of poetic literature will find delight and instruction in the following works :

" A Treasury of English Sonnets," by David M. Main (Alexander Ireland & Co., Manchester, 1880). This is the most complete collection of English Sonnets yet published, and is accompanied by critical notes and extracts of an exhaustive and scholarly character.

" Sonnets of this Century," with a critical introduction by William Sharp, being one of the volumes of the Canterbury Poets. (Walter Scott. London. 1888.)

THE SONG.

PERHAPS the most popular of all forms of verse is
the song, and it is easy to understand why this is
so. The sentiment embodied in a song is simple,
direct, and lies on the surface of our common
nature. Love, patriotism, the blended associations
of natural beauty with human feelings, the
buoyant life and dangers of the deep,—these, and
such-like materials of song, are topics that attract
the fancy, and appeal to the hearts of all. Again,
the song, if it is a good one, is short, its rhythm
smooth and exact, its rhymes ring out clear, its
words are simple and natural, and, moreover, it is
generally wedded to a melody which lingers in the
ear long after the sounds have died away. It
makes no appeal to the intellect, but it stimulates
the sensuousness of our nature, and thrills into life
the dormant phantoms of memory.

It does not flavour of the " superior person " to
say that the bulk of human kind do not possess
cultivated artistic tastes : a sonnet of Shakspere's
or a fugue by Bach would doubtless fall flat on the
general ear, while a simple ballad or a pathetic
song rarely fails to touch a sympathetic chord, or
moisten the eye of the most apathetic listener.

Who has not witnessed the almost electrical effect of *The Marseillaise, Rule Britannia,* and the *Wearing of the Green* upon gatherings of the different nationalities !

Song-writing, that to the uninitiated may seem an easy literary effort, is, indeed, one of the most difficult forms of metrical composition to accomplish satisfactorily. Some of our most eminent poets have failed in it entirely, and others have wisely refrained from attempting it. Milton, Pope, and Wordsworth may be cited as proofs of this assertion.

A song should embody some common human sentiment, which should meander through its verses and bind them together like a silken cord. The metre should be carefully selected, and smoothed into regularity, with a view to its musical setting ; and if it be written to an air already composed, much ingenuity and taste are required in arranging the accents to the beats, the open vowel sounds to the long notes. As it is intended for singing rather than recitation, it should be built up of words having as many open vowels and as few guttural and hissing consonants as possible. The utterance of musical sounds requires an open mouth, so that however beautiful the thought and dress of a line of poetry may be, if the sounds of its words keep the mouth closed, it is unsuitable to vocalisation. An instance of this may be taken from Shelley, whose exquisite taste in sensuous poetry is unrivalled :

I love that thou lovest,
Spirit of delight!
The fresh earth in new leaves drest,
And the starry night.

Here the third line of the stanza is a beautiful
poetical image; but it is next to impossible to
vocalise it, as nearly every word shuts the mouth
in utterance. On the other hand, Burns may be
singled out as supreme as a song-writer; the firm-
ness of his rhythm and the musical flow of his
numbers have never been surpassed. And, besides,
his happy selection of open-vowelled words recom-
mends his compositions for vocal purposes. Such
lines as:

Ye banks and braes o' bonny Doon,
How can ye bloom sae fresh and fair?

open the mouth as Italian words would.

The following remarks of Samuel Lover, himself
no mean writer of tender and humorous songs,
may be reproduced here:—"To awaken sympathy
by the simplest words will go farther in a song
than pomp of language and elaborate polish. But
simplicity should never descend into baldness, or
the stringing of nonsensical rhymes together. A
song should have a thought in it, and that thought
gracefully expressed at least; and if the *tone* of
expression touch the head or the heart of the
listener—appeal either to his fancy or his feeling—
it has in it, I believe, the germ of success. If you
preach too much, or philosophise too much, or if

passion, like the queen in the play in *Hamlet*,
'doth protest too much,' the chances are the song
is overdone.   The feelings you want to excite in a
song should be rather *suggested* than ostentatiously
paraded, and in proportion as this is skilfully done,
the song, I believe, proves successful."

It has been said that the songs of a nation are as
potent as its laws, and doubtless there is no little
truth in the saying.

> How small of all that human hearts endure,
> That part which kings or laws can cause or cure !

Laws become obsolete and are abrogated, but the
passionate words of a song that embody national
sentiments, or have touched the nation's heart,
pass into its "household words," and live on for
ever.

> The seasons change, the winds they shift and veer ;
> The grass of yester-year
> Is dead ; the birds depart, the groves decay ;
> Empires dissolve, and peoples disappear ;
> Songs pass not away.

Thackeray has said that Gray, the writer of the
well-known *Elegy*, passed on to immortality with
the thinnest volume under his arm of any English
author.   This truth might well be extended still
further, to the effect that some few of our humblest
bards have been admitted amongst the " Im-
mortals " upon the strength of one or two songs
only, inscribed upon a single sheet of paper.   And
upon an eminence scarcely lower than the national

songwright is he whose simple words and pregnant thoughts have embodied the universal joys, sorrows, and aspirations of the human heart in strains that, once heard, can never be forgotten. Nor, indeed, is it a small thing to charm with song the social circle; to excite, soothe, and thrill the jaded heart and soul; to enliven and keep sweet the home-life when the day's work is done, and to make

> The night to be filled with music,
>   And the cares that infest the day
> To fold their tents like the Arabs,
>   And as silently steal away.

To attempt to enumerate our song-writers, and present choice and representative specimens of their lyric art, greatly as it might enhance the charm of this volume to the general reader, would extend it beyond the limits of our main object, which is didactic. Besides, this has been already accomplished by several competent hands, and *Anthologies* of our lyric muse are both numerous and exhaustive. It will be sufficient, therefore, for our purpose to point out the chief varieties of songs, and the characteristics of each kind, with brief allusions to some of the best specimens.

i.—THE SACRED SONG OR HYMN.

"A good hymn should have simplicity, freshness, and reality of feeling, a consistent elevation of tone, and a rhythm easy and harmonious, but not jingling or trivial. Its language may be homely, but should not be slovenly or mean. Affectation or visible artifice is worse than excess of homeliness ; a hymn is easily spoiled by a single falsetto note. Nor will most exemplary soundness of doctrine atone for doggerel, or redeem from failure a prosaic didactic style." These words of Lord Selborne's express nearly all that can be said as to the requirements of sacred song, while his collection of the best specimens may with safety be regarded as embracing the choicest expression of the crystallized piety of the English race.*

2.—THE PATRIOTIC AND WAR SONG.

These partake of the nature of fiery eloquence and impassioned declamation. Like the harangues of Henry V. at Harfleur and at Agincourt, they are framed to arouse the heroic in man, and nerve him to deeds of daring and endurance. Their ringing accents stir the heart like the sounds of a trumpet or the weird shrill shriek of the pibroch. Fortitude, glory, death rather than dishonour, love of home and freedom—these and such-like sentiments, clothed in stirring words, enkindle the warrior to deeds of devotion in defence of "the ashes of his fathers, the temples of his gods." The narrative element is very frequently introduced into songs of

* " The Book of Praise," selected and arranged by Lord Selborne (Macmillan & Co.)

this kind, and turns them into glowing pictures of battle and triumphant victory. And when some famous phrase is hit upon as a refrain, like " Rule Britannia, ' " Hearts of Oak," or " England expects every man this day to do his duty," the enthusiasm they arouse leaves nothing to be desired. All nations have their national songs, wedded to grand melodies; and England, the cradle of liberty, the mistress of the sea, the pioneer of progress, has reason to be proud of its own patriotic music. *God save the Queen, Rule Britannia, The Death of Nelson,* and *Scots wha hae,* &c., may be cited as typical examples.

Dibdin's Sea Songs call for special mention here. Of the twelve hundred he is said to have written, the majority are already forgotten, but many of them that remain will endure as long as our tongue is spoken. With little pretension to literary merit, they all have the genuine sniff of the briny about them, and they depict the joys and sorrows of *Poor Jack,* the hearty, simple-minded tar as we love to regard him. At a critical time in our history his songs are said to have recruited our Navy with volunteers, and to have rendered the odious press-gang unnecessary. In every forecastle over the broad ocean his "Sweet little cherub that sits up aloft," is still invoked by Jack, and even the "Gentlemen who live at home at ease" are ever hushed into appreciative silence when they hear sung the virtues of *Poor Tom Bowling.*

3.—THE LOVE SONG.

The lyric muse seems peculiarly adapted to give expression to the manifold phases of the tender flame, and the jingling of rhymes fitly harmonises with its wayward fancies. The common feelings of our nature, of which the love of the sexes is predominant, are reproduced in every son and daughter of Eve, and it is marvellous to contemplate the infinite variety of expression in which it has been clothed in all countries and in all times; and yet we are ever eager to welcome every fresh wreath that is laid upon the shrine of "all conquering Eros." In our own tongue the tenderness, the glow and grace of the love lyrics of our Elizabethan poets can never be surpassed, and it would be invidious to particularise names and examples in a slight notice of this kind. Amongst modern poets Burns, Moore, and the Brownings may, without fear of offence, be specially mentioned.*

4.—THE CONVIVIAL SONG.

The social and fraternal feelings engendered by the gregarious instinct in man, have found expression in all ages in jovial, boisterous songs, more or less Bacchanalian in character. There is a strong flavour of usquebaugh about most of them, and a

* The reader is referred to the most recent Anthologies: "Love Lyrics," edited by William Watson (Macmillan & Co.); "Seventeenth Century Lyrics," edited by George Saintsbury (Percival & Co.).

sonorous refrain seems to be an almost essential addendum. *Auld Lang Syne* may be taken as a typical example, while Burns and Moore must be considered as our joint kings of the "flowing-bowl" minstrels. We are not ashamed, however, to admit our inferiority to the Germans in this particular form of poetic expression.

5.—THE POLITICAL SONG.

The political song requires mention here, though it merits only the rank of verse as distinct from poetry. It is essentially ephemeral and partisan in character, and is devoid, for the most part, of noble and generous thoughts. Though several of the *Jacobite songs* breathe forth a spirit of devoted loyalty, they are as antiquated in sentiment to-day as the political squibs of Swift and the Tory sneers of the *Anti-Jacobin*. Moore, Elliott, and Mackay in recent times have written some political verses that deserve to live.*

In addition to the varieties of songs already enumerated, there are others that can only be classed under such a vague heading as purely *Sentimental*, of which Tennyson's "*Break, break, break,*" and Miss Proctor's "*Lost Chord*" may be cited as typical examples.

Then there is another variety in which the narrative element is more prominent than the lyrical: of such, *Song-Ballads*, "*Auld Robin Gray*," and

* See " Political Verse," edited by George Saintsbury (Percival & Co.)

Q

Kingsley's "*Three Fishers*" and "*Sands o' Dee*" are specimens.

And, lastly, there is the *Comic Song*, which, in these days of "penny dreadfuls," is rapidly becoming a popular favourite.

Before concluding this brief notice of lyric art, it seems necessary to say a few words respecting those more complex compositions of the kind that are specially designed for elaborate musical treatment, embracing solo, chorus, and recitative, viz., the librettos of the Oratorio, the Opera, and the Cantata.

The *Oratorio*, always sacred in its theme, and the *Opera*, always secular, resemble each other in nearly every other respect. Both are essentially dramatic : they have separate characters with distinct rôles, and depict changing scenes and continuous action. The latter is always acted, and embellished with all the accessories of a regular drama; the former, no doubt solely on account of its subject matter, is rendered with the picturesque effects of sound only; but no one can listen to an adequate representation of such an oratorio as Mendelssohn's *Elijah* without mentally realising the dramatic situations as though they were visibly before him.   In both, also, the lyrical element takes the form of song, duet, trio and chorus, the narrative portion being rendered in recitative.

The *Cantata* is usually devoid of the dramatic element altogether.   It gives expression to the varied emotions that arise in the contemplation of heroic deeds and lofty ideals, now pensive and mournful, now frenzied or jubilant. Several of our noblest odes which partake of this character have already been clothed in melody and harmony that at once add to their intrinsic beauty and widen the field of their appreciators.

The adaptation to our own tongue of works of this kind composed in other languages—for they are susceptible of great variety of treatment— affords excellent scope for the exercise of the purely technical side of the Art of Versification.

POETIC TRIFLES.

IN this chapter we wish to direct the student's footsteps into those by-paths of the garden of poesy where grow innumerable wild flowers with pretty blossoms and polished berries, which, for want of a more suitable name, are known as *Social* or *Occasional verses*.* It may be said that they stand in the same relation to the higher forms of poetry that a pyrotechnic display does to "the immortal Jove's dread clamours." Poets and scholars in all ages and countries have taken delight, in their leisure moments, in throwing off these metrical playthings, as momentary thought or passing incident suggested the occasion. Here, for instance, are some verses tossed off " in the ten minutes before dinner : "

> Fast falls the snow, O lady mine !
> Sprinkling the lawn with crystals fine :
> But, by the gods, we won't repine.
> While we're together
> We'll chat and rhyme, and kiss and dine,
> Defying weather.

* It would be next to sacrilege to class Pope's *Rape of the Lock* under this heading, but it is undoubtedly the most brilliant Occasional poem in the language.

So stir the fire, and pour the wine,
And let those sea-green eyes divine
Pour their love-madness into mine :
    I don't care whether
'Tis snow or sun, or rain or shine,
    If we're together.

Mortimer Collins.

These minor efforts may result in original experiments, or in translations, adaptations, or even
parodies of favourite passages from other writers.
How many scores of times have Horatian gems
been adapted to passing circumstances by busy
men of the world in their leisure moments, just to
see if they had retained their old skill in verse-
making ! And the same cultured taste leads also to
the turning of our own poetic beauties into other
tongues.

Social verse has been aptly described as "the
poetry of men who belong to society, who have a
keen sympathy with the lightsome tone and airy
jesting of fashion ; who are not disturbed by the
flippances of small talk, but, on the contrary, can
see the gracefulness of which it is capable, and
who, nevertheless, amid all the froth of society, feel
that there are depths in our nature which even in
the gaiety of drawing-rooms cannot be forgotten.
It is the poetry of bitter-sweet, of sentiment that
breaks into humour, and of thought, which, lest it
should be too solemn, breaks into laughter. When
society becomes refined, it begins to dread the exhibition of strong feeling, no matter whether real or
simulated. In such an atmosphere emotion takes

refuge in jest, and passion hides itself in scepticism of passion. We are not going to wear our hearts upon our sleeves, rather than that we shall pretend to have no heart at all; and if, perchance, a bit of it should peep out, we shall hide it again as quickly as possible, and laugh at the exposure as a good joke."* This kind of verse has rarely been produced by the professional poet of recluse habits and deep thought; men busily engaged in the affairs of the world, but with a keen zest for leisured culture, such as Suckling, Herrick, Swift, Prior, and Landor, have succeeded best. Their fancy and sense of humour have seized upon those incidents and situations of moving life most fitted for poetic treatment, while their ingenuity and wit have turned them —over their cakes and ale—into things of beauty. Perhaps it is because there is an after-dinner flavour about many of these miniature poems that coarseness occasionally disfigures their beauty, and debars their racy wit from wider appreciation. These trifles should always be refined and graceful, humorous rather than witty, the tone should not be pitched too high, nor need the treatment advance much beyond the conventional limits of social usages; their measure should run smoothly, and the rhymes ring out clearly, while a playful warmth should be perceptible throughout. Little more need be added at present, beyond reproducing a few typical specimens.

* The reader is referred to the "Lyra Elegantiarum," by Frederick Locker-Lampson.

Love is a torment of the mind,
   A tempest everlasting ;
And, Jove hath made it of a kind,
Not well, not full, nor fasting.
     Why so ?
More we enjoy it, more it dies,
If not enjoyed, it sighing cries
     Heigh ho !

Daniel.

My Love in her attire doth show her wit,
   It doth so well become her :
For every season she hath dressings fit,
   For winter, spring, and summer.
No beauty she doth miss
   When all her robes are on :
But Beauty's self she is
   When all her robes are gone.

Anon

THE HEADACHE.

My head doth ache.
O Sappho, take
   Thy fillet
And bind the pain,
Or bring some bane
   To kill it.

But less that part
Than my poor heart
   Now is sick :
One kiss from thee
Will counsel be
   And physic.

Herrick.

TO LUCASTA ON GOING TO THE WARS.

Tell me not, Sweet, I am unkind,
  That from the nunnery
Of your chaste breast and quiet mind,
  To war and arms I fly.

True, a new mistress now I chase,
  The first foe in the field,
And, with a stronger faith embrace
  A sword, a horse, a shield.

Yet this inconstancy is such
  As you too shall adore ;
I could not love thee, Dear, so much,
  Loved I not Honour more.

                      Lovelace.

Out upon it, I have loved
  Three whole days togetner,
And am like to love three more—
  If it prove fine weather.

    *   *   *   *

Had it any been but she,
  And that very face,
There had been at least, ere this,
  A dozen in her place.

                      Suckling.

False tho' she be to me and love,
  I'll not pursue revenge ;
For still the charmer I approve,
  Tho' I deplore her change.

In hours of bliss we oft have met,
  They could not always last ;
And though the present I regret,
  I'm grateful for the past.

                      Congreve.

My muse and I ere youth and spirits fled,
 Sat up together many a night, no doubt :
But now I've sent the poor old lass to bed,
 Simply because my fire is going out.
G. Colman.

ON SEEING THE SPEAKER ASLEEP.

Sleep, Mr. Speaker, 'tis only fair
If you mayn't in your bed, that you should in your chair ;
Louder and louder still they grow,
Tory and Radical, Aye and No ;
Talking by night and talking by day :
Sleep, Mr. Speaker, sleep while you may !
Praed.

As lamps burn silent with unconscious light.
So modest ease in beauty shines most bright ;
Unaiming charms with edge resistless fall,
And she who means no mischief does it all.
Aaron Hill.

Sly Beelzebub took all occasions
To try Job's constancy and patience.
He took his honour, took his health ;
He took his children, took his wealth,
His servants, horses, oxen, cows,—
But cunning Satan did *not* take his spouse.

But Heaven that brings out good from evil,
And likes to disappoint the devil,
Had predetermined to restore
Two-fold, all he had before,
His servants, camels, asses, cows,—
Short-sighted devil, *not* to take his spouse.
S. T. Coleridge.

I loved thee, beautiful and kind,
 And plighted an eternal vow ;
So altered are thy face and mind,
 'Twere perjury to love thee now.
Earl Nugent.

RICH AND POOR; OR, SAINT AND SINNER.

The poor man's sins are glaring;
In the face of ghostly warning
  He is caught in the fact
  Of an overt act—
Buying greens on Sunday morning.

The rich man's sins are hidden
In the pomp of wealth and station;
  And escape the sight
  Of the children of light,
Who are wise in their generation.

The rich man has a cellar
And a ready butler by him;
  The poor must steer
  For his pint of beer
Where the saint cannot choose but spy him

                    T. L. Peacock.

If all be true that I do think,
There are five reasons we should drink :
Good wine—a friend—or being dry—
Or lest we should be by-and-by—
Or any other reason why.

                    Dr. Aldrich.

EPITAPH ON FREDERICK PRINCE OF WALES.

Here lies Fred,
Who was alive and is dead.
Had it been his father,
I had much rather;
Had it been his brother,
Still better than another;
Had it been his sister,
No one would have missed her;

Had it been the whole generation,
Still better for the nation.
But since 'tis only Fred,
Who was alive and is dead,
There's no more to be said.
Anon.

Jenny kissed me when we met,
  Jumping from the chair she sat in;
Time, you thief, who love to get
  Secrets into your list, put that in.
Say I'm weary, say I'm sad,
  Say that health and wealth have missed me;
Say I'm growing old, but add—
                Jenny kissed me.
                Leigh Hunt.

The law locks up the man or woman
Who steals a goose from off the common;
But lets the greater villain loose,
Who steals the common from the goose.
                E. Elliott.

Thoughtless that " all that's brightest fades,"
Unmindful of the *knave of spades*,
  The sexton and his subs;
How foolishly we play our parts!
Our wives on *diamonds* set their *hearts*,
  We set our *hearts* on *clubs*.
                Sydney Smith.

God bless the King, I mean the faith's defender;
God bless—no harm in blessing—the Pretender:
But who pretender is, or who is king,—
God bless us all—that's quite another thing.
                J. Byrom.

ROSE'S BIRTHDAY.

Tell me, perverse young year!
Why is the moon so drear?
   Is there no flower to twine?
Away, thou churl, away!
'Tis Rose's natal day,
   Reserve thy frowns for mine.

W. S. Landor.

I've lost my portmanteau:
   I pity your grief.
All my sermons are in it:
   I pity the thief.

Anon.

The law allows one husband to one wife,
But wives will seldom brook this straightened life;
They must have two: besides her Jack each Jill,
In spite of law and gospel, has her Will.

R. Simpson.

THE TWO HARVEYS.

Two Harveys had a mutual wish
   To please in different stations—
The one invented "sauce for fish,"
   The other "Meditations."
Each had his pungent power applied
   To aid the dead and dying:
That gave relish to the *sole* when fried,
   This saved the *soul* from frying.

A FISHING EXPEDITION.

One morning when Spring was in her teens—
   A morn to a poet's wishing—
All tinted in delicate pinks and greens,
   Miss Bessie and I went fishing.

I in my rongh and easy clothes,
  With my face at the sunshine's mercy;
She with her hat tipped down to her nose,
  And her nose tipped *vice versâ*.

I with my rod, my reel, and my hooks,
  And a hamper for lunching recesses;
She with the bait of her comely looks
  And the sheen of her golden tresses.

So we sat down on the sunny dyke,
  Where the white pond lilies teeter;
I set to fishing like quaint old Ike,
  And she like Simon Peter.

All the morn I lay in the light of her eyes,
  And dreamily watched and waited;
But the fish were cunning and would not rise,
  And the baiter alone was baited.

And when the time for departure came,
  The bag was as flat as a flounder;
But Bessie had neatly hooked her game—
  A hundred and eighty pounder.

                    Anon.
          (Attributed to John Bright.

My temples throb, my pulses boil,
  I'm sick of Song, and Ode, and Ballad.
So, Thyrsis, take the midnight oil,
  And pour it on a lobster salad.
My brain is dull, my sight is foul,
  I cannot write a verse, or read.
Then, Pallas, take away thine Owl,
  And let us have a Lark instead.

                    Hood.

HIPPOPHAGY.

If horseflesh won't suffice to serve the masses,
The next resource will certainly be asses,
And Heaven only knows where that will end :
Some people won't have left a single friend.
Chas. Mathews.

On Easter Sunday Lucy spoke,
And said, " A saint you might provoke,
Dear Sam, each day, since Monday last ;
But now, I see, your rage is past."
Said Sam, " What Christian could be meek !
You know, my love, 'twas *Passion week ;*
And so, you see, the rage I've spent,
Was not my own—'twas only *Lent.*"
Lover.

TO MY WIFE.

To Thee, who bending o'er my table's rim
Has marked these measures flow, these pages brim ;
Who, linked for ever to a lettered life,
Hast drawn the dubious lot of student's wife ;
Kept hush around my desk, nor grudg'd me still
The long, dull, ceaseless rustling of my quill.
Content to guide the house, the child to teach,
And hail my fitful intervals of speech ;
Or bid the bald disjointed tale rehearse,
Or drink harsh numbers mellowing into verse :
Who still, mid cares sedate, in sorrows brave,
Hast for me borne the light, and with me shared the grave,
And grown from soft to strong, from fair to sage—
Flower of my youth and jewel of my age !
To Thee these lays I bring, with joy, with pride,
Sure of thy suffrage, if of none beside.
Rev. C. Merivale.
" Dedication of his Translation
of the ' Iliad.' "

IMITATION OF DRYDEN.

Three colonels in three distant counties born,
Sligo, Armagh, and Lincoln did adorn.
The first in paucity of thought surpassed,
The next in poverty, in both the last ;
The force of nature could no further go—
To make the third she shaved the other two.
D. O'Connell.

Of late years the cultivation of this species of poetic composition has greatly spread both in this country and in America ; our magazines and reviews furnish an ever-increasing crop, and much of this fugitive verse is being collected, and deservedly so, in permanent form. A fashion has also sprung up amongst the minor poets of the day and literary amateurs, for verse construction upon the models of the old Provençal poets of France; and it speaks well for the spread of culture and taste amongst us, that so much interest is taken in a refined amusement of this kind. This new fashion is certainly not much more than a quarter of a century old in this country, and already quite an imposing anthology of this kind of verse has been formed, many of the specimens being extremely beautiful.* The restrictions as to the number of lines, the number and arrangement of rhymes, and recurrence of refrains imposed by these quaint models are even greater than in the sonnet, and therefore afford ample scope for the taste, judgment, and patience of the versifier. We

---

* " Ballades and Rondeaus, &c." Selected, wirh a chapter on the various forms, by Gleeson White. The Canterbury Poets. (Walter Scott, Lond. 1887.)

proceed to explain the build, and to give specimens of the chief varieties.

1.—THE BALLADE.

The Ballade consists of three stanzas of eight or ten lines, concluding with an *envoy** of four or five lines. There must be only three rhymes in each stanza, and the same three, and in the same order, must obtain throughout; and each stanza as well as the envoy has the same refrain.

FOR ME THE BLITHE BALLADE.

Of all the songs that dwell
 Where softest speech doth flow,
Some love the sweet rondel,
 And some the bright rondeau,
 With rhymes that tripping go
In mirthful measures clad ;
 But would I choose them ?—no,
For me the blithe ballade !

O'er some, the villanelle,
 That sets the heart aglow,
Doth its enchanting spell
 With lines recurring throw ;
 Some weighed with wasting woe,
Gay triolets make them glad ;
 But would I choose them ?—no,
For me the blithe ballade !

* The *envoi* is a kind of invocation or dedication of the poem, and used to commence with the title of the person to whom it was addressed —Sire, or Princess. It forms the peroration or climax to the verses, and should more clearly express the sentiment or feeling embodied in the poem.

On chant of stately swell,
　　With measured feet and slow,
As grave as minster bell,
　　As vesper tolling low,
　　Do some their praise bestow ;
Some on sestinas sad ;
　　But would I choose them ?—no,
For me the blithe ballade !

Envoi.

Prince, to these songs a-row
　　The Muse might endless add ;
But would I choose them ?—no,
　　For me the blithe ballade !

Clinton Scollard.

BALLADE.

O Love, whom I have never seen,
　　Yet ever hope to see ;
The memory that might have been,
　　The hope that yet may be ;
The passion that persistently
　　Makes all my pulses beat
With unassuaged desire that we
　　Some day may come to meet :

This August night outspread serene,
　　The scent of flower and tree,
The fall of water that unseen
　　Moans on incessantly,
That line of fire, where breaks the sea
　　In ripples at my feet ;
What mean they all, if not that we
　　Some day may come to meet ?

About your window bowered in green
　　The night wind wanders free,
While out into the night you lean,
　　And dream, but not of me,

R

As now I dream of you who flee
　　Before my dream complete
The shadow of the day when we
　　Some day may come to meet.

　　　Envoi.

Princess, while yet on lawn and lea
　　The harvest moon is sweet,
Ere August die, who knows but we
　　Some day may come to meet.

　　　　　　　" Love in Idleness."

GRANDMOTHER.

Another new gown, as I declare !
　　How many more is it going to be ?
And your forehead all hid in a cloud of hair—
　　'Tis nothing but folly, that I can see !
　　The maidens of nowadays make too free ;
To right and to left is the money flung ;
　　We used to dress as became our degree—
But things have altered since I was young.

Stuff, in my time, was made to wear ;
　　Gowns we had never but two or three ;
Did we fancy them spoilt, if they chanced to tear ?
　　And shrink from a patch or a darn ? not we !
　　For pleasure, a gossiping dish of tea,
Or a mushroom hunt, while the dew yet hung,
　　And no need, next day, for the doctor's fee—
But things have altered since I was young.

The yellow gig, and a drive to the fair ;
　　A keepsake bought in a booth on the lea ;
A sixpence, perhaps, to break and share—
　　That's how your grandfather courted me.
　　Did your grandmother blush, do you think—not she !
When he found her, the churn and the pails among ?
　　Or your grandfather like her the less ? not he !
But things have altered since I was young.

Envoi.

Child ! you pout, and you urge your plea—
Better it were that you held your tongue !
    Maids should learn at their elders' knee—
But things have altered since I was young.

May Probyn.

2.—THE RONDEL.

The Rondel is the old form of the more popular rondeau into which it ultimately grew. It was much used as far back as the fourteenth century. It consisted originally of two four or five line stanzas, with only two rhymes, but in the hands of Charles d'Orleans (1391-1466) its form was changed, as in the specimen below.

THE WANDERER.

Love comes back to his vacant dwelling,—
    The old, old Love that we knew of yore !
    We see him stand by the open door.
With his great eyes sad, and his bosom swelling.

He makes as though in our arms repelling,
    He fain would lie as he lay before ;—
Love comes back to his vacant dwelling,—
    The old, old Love that we knew of yore !

Ah ! who shall help us from overspelling,
    That sweet forgotten, forbidden lore !
    E'en as we doubt in our hearts once more,
With a rush of tears to our eyelids welling,
Love comes back to his vacant dwelling.

Austin Dobson.

RONDEL.

How is it you and I
   Are always meeting so?
I see you passing by
   Whichever way I go.

   I cannot say I know
The spell that draws us nigh,
How is it you and I
   Are always meeting so?

Still thoughts to thoughts reply,
   And whispers ebb and flow;
I say it with a sigh
   But half confessed and low,
How is it you and I
   Are always meeting so?
              John Cameron Grant.

RONDELETS.

   " Which way he went?"
I know not—how should I go spy
   Which way he went?
I only know him gone.   " Relent?"
He never will—unless I die!
And then, what will it signify
      Which way he went?

   Say what you please,
But know, I shall not change my mind!
   Say what you please,
Even, if you wish it, on your knees—
And, when you hear me next defined
As something lighter than the wind,
     Say what you please!
           May Probyn.

3.—THE RONDEAU.

The Rondeau has gradually grown out of the older form given above, and became popularised by Voltaire, who wrote many charming specimens of it. The first example we quote is a clever adaptation of one of the great Frenchman's best. The poem consists of thirteen octosyllabic lines, arranged in three stanzas of five, three, and five verses each, with two rhymes only throughout, and a refrain recurring at the end of the second and third group.

RONDEAU.

You bid me try, Blue-eyes, to write
A Rondeau. What! forthwith ?—To-night ?
 Reflect. Some skill I have, 'tis true ;
 But thirteen lines !—and rhymed on two !—
" Refrain," as well. Ah, hapless plight !
Still there are five lines—ranged aright.
These Gallic bonds, I feared, would fright
 My easy Muse. They did, till you—
  You bid me try !

" That makes them eight.—The port's in sight :
'Tis all because your eyes are bright !
 Now just a pair to end in ' oo,'—
 When maids command, what can't we do !
Behold ! The Rondeau—tasteful, light—
  You bid me try ! "

" WITHOUT ONE KISS."

Without one kiss she's gone away,
And stol'n the brightness out of day ;
 With scornful lips and haughty brow
 She's left me melancholy now,
In spite of all that I could say.

And so, to guess as best I may
What angered her, awhile I stay
  Beneath this blown acacia bough,
    Without one kiss ;

Yet all my wildered brain can pay
My questioning, is but to pray
  Persuasion may my speech endow,
  And Love may never more allow
My injured sweet to sail away
    Without one kiss.

Charles G. D. Roberts.

CARPE DIEM.

To-day, what is there in the air
That makes December seem sweet May ?
  There are no swallows anywhere,
  Nor crocuses to crown your hair,
And hail you down my garden way.
Last night the full moon's frozen stare
  Struck me, perhaps ; or did you say
Really,—you'd come, sweet friend and fair !
                To-day ?
To-day is here :—come ! crown to-day
  With Spring's delight or Spring's despair,
Love cannot bide old Time's delay :—
Down my glad gardens light winds play,
  And my whole life shall bloom and bear
                To-day.

Theo. Marzials.

IN ROTTEN ROW.

In Rotten Row a cigarette
I sat and smoked, with no regret
  For all the tumult that had been.
  The distances were still and green,

And streaked with shadows cool and wet
Two sweethearts on a bench were set,
Two birds among the boughs were met ;
    So love and song were heard and seen
            In Rotten Row.

A horse or two there was to fret
The soundless sand ; but work and debt,
    Fair flowers and falling leaves between,
     While clocks are chiming clear and keen,
A man may very well forget
           In Rotten Row.
              W. E. Henley.

4.—THE ROUNDEL.

The Roundel is a variation of the rondeau, consisting of three stanzas of three lines each, linked together with but two rhymes, and a refrain at the end of the first and third group,

THE ROUNDEL.

A Roundel is wrought as a ring er a starbright sphere,
With craft of delight and with cunning of sound unsought,
That the heart of the hearer may smile if to pleasure his ear
    A roundel is wrought.

Its jewel of music is carven of all or of aught—
Love, laughter, or mourning—remembrance of rapture or
    fear—
That fancy may fashion to hang in the ear of thought.

As a bird's quick song runs round, and the hearts in us hear—
Pause answers to pause, and again the same strain caught,
So moves the device whence, round as a pearl or tear,
    A roundel is wrought.
        Algernon Charles Swinburne.

NOTHING SO SWEET.

Nothing so sweet in all the world there is
 Than this—to stand apart in Love's retreat
And gaze at Love. There is as that, ywis,
  Nothing so sweet.

 Yet surely God hath placed before our feet
Some sweeter sweetness and completer bliss,
 And something that shall prove more truly meet.

Soothly I know not :—when the live lips kiss
 There is no more that our prayers shall entreat,
Save only Death. Perhaps there is as this
  Nothing so sweet.
    Charles Sayle.

A RONDELAY.

Man is for woman made,
 And woman made for man :
As the spur is for the jade,
As the scabbard for the blade,
 As for liquor is the can,
So man's for woman made,
 And woman made for man.

As the sceptre to be sway'd,
As to night the serenade,
 As for pudding is the pan,
 As to cool us is the fan,
So man's for woman made,
 And woman made for man.

Be she widow, wife, or maid,
Be she wanton, be she staid,
Be she well or ill arrayed,
  * * *

So man's for woman made,
 And woman made for man.

5.—THE SESTINA.

The Sestina dates from the thirteenth century, and was in vogue in Italy as well as France, being used by Dante and Petrarch. Some writers claim for it the supreme place in poems of fixed form—above the sonnet even. It is made up of six six-line stanzas and one of three lines. There are only two rhymes throughout, and the terminal words of each stanza are the same all through, though in different order. Here is a beautiful specimen by Mr. Swinburne:

SESTINA.

I saw my soul at rest upon a day,
 As a bird sleeping in the nest of night,
Among soft leaves that give the straight way
 To touch its wings but not its eyes with light;
So that it knew, as one in visions may,
 And knew not as men waking, of delight.

This was the measure of my soul's delight;
 It had no power of joy to fly by day,
Nor part in the large lordship of the light;
 But in a secret moon-beholden way
Had all its will of dreams and pleasant night,
 And all the love and life that sleepers may.

But such life's triumph as men waking may
 It might not have to feed its faint delight
Between the stars by night and sun by day,
 Shut up with green leaves and a little light;
Because its way was as a lost star's way,
 A world's not wholly known of day or night.

All loves and dreams and sounds and gleams of night
    Made it all music that such minstrels may,
And all they had they gave it of delight ;
    But in the full face of the fire of day
What place shall be for any starry light,
    What part of heaven in all the wide sun's way ?

Yet the soul woke not, sleeping by the way,
    Watched as a nursling of the large eyed night,
And sought nor strength nor knowledge of the day
    Nor closer touch conclusive of delight,
Nor mightier joy nor truer than dreamers may,
    Nor more of song than they, nor more of light.

For who sleeps once and sees the secret light
    Whereby sleep shows the soul a fairer way
Between the rise and rest of day and night,
    Shall care no more to fare as all men may,
But be his place of pain or of delight,
    There shall he dwell, beholding night as day.

Song, have thy day and take thy fill of light
    Before the night be fallen across thy way ;
Sing while he may, man hath no long delight.
            Algernon Charles Swinburne.

6.—THE TRIOLET.

The Triolet is, indeed, a poetic morsel, with rigid rules and very little room to expand even a single thought. It is an eight-line stanza with two rhymes. The first line is repeated as the fourth and seventh, and the second and the eighth are alike :

    When first we met, we did not guess
        That Love would prove so hard a master ;
    Of more than common friendliness

When first we met we did not guess
Who could foretell the sore distress,
    The inevitable disaster,
When first we met ? we did not guess
    That Love would prove so hard a master.

R. Bridges.

I intended an Ode,
    And it turned out a Sonnet,
It began *à la mode*,
I intended an Ode ;
But Rose crossed the road
    In her latest new bonnet.
I intended an Ode,
    And it turned out a Sonnet.

Austin Dobson.

Under the sun
    There's nothing new ;
Poem or pun,
Under the sun,
Said Solomon,
    And he said true.
Under the sun
    There's nothing new.

" Love in Idleness."

7.—THE VILLANELLE.

The Villanelle consists of five three-line stanzas
and one of four, with only two rhymes throughout,
the two refrains occurring in eight of the nineteen
lines :

VILLANELLE.

The daffodils are on the lea—
    Come out, sweetheart, and bless the sun !
The birds are glad, and so are we.

This morn a throstle piped to me,
    " 'Tis time that mates were wooed and won—
The daffodils are on the lea."

Come out, sweetheart, their gold to see,
    And building of the nests begun—
The birds are glad, and so are we.

You said,—bethink you!—" It shall be
    When, yellow smocked, and winter done,
The daffodils are on the lea."

Yet, an' you will, to change be free !
    How sigh you ?—" Changes need we none—
The birds are glad—*and so are we ?* "

Come out, sweetheart ! the signs agree,
    The marriage tokens March has spun—
The daffodils are on the lea ;
The birds are glad—and so are we !

                              May Probyn.

WHEN I SAW YOU LAST, ROSE.

When I saw you last, Rose,
    You were only so high ;—
How fast the time goes !

Like a bud ere it blows,
    You just peeped at the sky,
When I saw you last, Rose !

Now your petals unclose,
    Now your May-time is nigh ;—
How fast the time goes !

And a life,—how it grows !
    You were scarcely so shy,
When I saw you last, Rose.

In your bosom it shows
    There's a guest on the sly;
How fast the time goes!

Is it Cupid? Who knows!
    Yet you used not to sigh,
When I saw you last, Rose;
How fast the time goes!

                Austin Dobson.

DEVELOPMENT OF VERSIFICATION.

THE progress of art, unlike that of science, does not present an almost unbroken triumphal march from the earliest times to the present day. The achievements of the "maker" in one age are not the starting-points of advance in the next. No poet commences his song with the accumulated knowledge and mastery of forces achieved by his predecessors, as the man of science begins his work. The discovery of nature's laws and the application of her forces to the physical needs of humanity may be regarded as practically illimitable, but it is not so with respect to the requirements and aspirations of the æsthetic side of human nature. Ideals of sensuous beauty of eye and ear, and of the loftier conceptions of our intellectual and emotional nature have already been attained and embodied in concrete forms which satisfy our finite capacities. The divinely gifted masters who have appeared in the world at rare intervals, have produced models of perfection beyond which we dare not hope to advance nor even emulate. What artist in marble, colours, or sound nowadays dreams of rivalling the beauty of a mediæval cathedral, or the Madonna of a master-hand, or a symphony by Beethoven ?

And so it is in word-composition also. Milton's sublime melody, Shakspere's mellifluous rhythmic flow, and the silvery ring of the Elizabethan lyric, remain for all times standards of excellence which succeeding songsters can only attempt to imitate and combine into new varieties. To try to analyse the methods of genius, or to frame rules for the production of a work of art like a poem, is, on the face of it, absurd; all we aim at here is to trace briefly the process of smoothing the harsh elements of our tongue, and the grafting upon it of the various embellishments necessary to the production of melodious verse.

Our mother tongue was brought over from the lowlands of North Germany by our Teutonic forefathers when they conquered and dispersed the Celts of South Britain, and settled there, from A.D. 450 to 600. They were a fierce, warlike, and heathen race, but they had within them those sterling characteristics which have enabled them to develop into the foremost nation of modern times. Their language was as rugged and harsh as their habits, but, like most semi-barbarous people, they strung together in it and sang rude verses in praise of their warriors and gods. We learn this of them as soon as history records their existence. They embraced Christianity in the seventh century, and readily began to settle down to peaceful and civilised modes of life. Their crude verses, though still full of deeds of daring and prowess, began to mellow into softness by the admission into them of the sentiment of patriotism, love of home and its surroundings, and the elevating influences of religion. Metrical versions of Biblical narratives began to take the place of descriptions of strife and bloodshed, and improvements in the form as well as in the matter of the verses gradually become perceptible.

The structure of Anglo-Saxon verse is peculiar. Each line is broken up into two short sections by a pause, and contains four accented syllables, the number of the unaccented ones not being counted at first. The two half-verses are connected together by alliteration, the same inititial sound occurring in two emphatic words of the first half, and in one in the second half. There is a marked rhythm, therefore, which rings out, as has been said, "like the sharp blows of a hammer upon an anvil." Metaphor and striking compounds are freely used, and there is a good deal of that *parallelism* which is so marked a feature in Hebrew poetry, in which the thought in the first case is repeated in the second with slight modification. Gradually we find one or two additional accented syllables introduced, and the unaccented ones arranged with greater regularity, and occasionally towards the end of the period the verses are made to rhyme together. This is the form of Anglo-Saxon and Early English verse from the sixth to the fourteenth century, and even later ; for although the influence of the French Trouvères is discernible in the poetry of the thirteenth century, all the peculiarities of the old verse are preserved in *Piers the Plowman's Vision*, written by Langlande as late as 1362. In the following extract from this poem some idea may be formed of the language and verse under consideration :—

> I was *w*eori of *w*andringe,
> And *w*ent me to reste
> Undur a *b*rod *b*anke
> Bi a *b*ourne syde ;
> And as I *l*ay and *l*eonede
> And *l*okede on the watres,
> I *s*lumberde in a *s*lepynge
> Hit *s*ownede so murie.   (ll. 13—20.)

In the first period of our literature, from A.D. 600 to 1066, which is known as Anglo-Saxon, the chief poetical compositions, all of which were upon the model described above, are as follows :—

(i) Fragments of *Gleemen's Songs*, sung by wandering minstrels, who seem to have been true Bohemians, from warnings issued to the clergy against them by King Edgar.

(ii) The *Deeds of Beowulf*, an epic of some five thousand lines. It was probably written in detached odes in the fifth century, prior to the conquest of Britain, and afterwards wrought into the form that has come down to us, with the Christian element introduced about the eighth century.

(iii) *Caedman's* metrical version of parts of the Old and New Testament history, 670. This is the first native-born poem in the language. Bede says of it, that all who heard it recited thought it was divinely given.

(iv) A fragment of the story of *Judith and Holofernes*, from the Apocrypha.

s

(v) The story of *King Lear and his Daughters*.

(vi) The *Consolations of Boethius*, attributed to King Alfred

(vii) Many sea and battle pieces.*

When the Normans subdued our forefathers at Hastings, 1066, and made themselves lords of Angle-land, amongst the many changes introduced by the new masters, there was a deliberate attempt made to supersede the old tongue of the conquered people, and to substitute Norman-French in its stead. The latter was made the language of the court, the universities, and the courts of law, while Latin was the tongue of the Church, and of all foreign intercourse; but although this effort was persisted in for two hundred years, and brought about great changes in the vocabulary and inflection of the Old English speech, it remained at the end of that time substantially as Teutonic, in all its main features, as at the beginning. The mightiest conqueror can no more change the speech of a people than can an Act of Parliament make them moral. Macaulay has pointed out that King John was probably the first monarch after the Conquest that conversed in the vernacular, and that the severance of the French possessions from the English Crown, which took place in his reign, was an unmixed blessing to the English nation, inas-

---

* Great attention has been given by scholars of late years to our early poetry. No fewer than six different versions of *Beowulf* have appeared since the one by Kemble in 1837, the last being by Professor Earle in 1892. Copious extracts from the poems mentioned above, as well as other fragments, are to be found in the works of Kemble, Turner, Thorpe, Conybeare, and Ellis. An exhaustive treatise on our early poetry, down to the accession of Alfred, by Stopford A. Brooke, was issued Dec.. 1892.

much as it greatly contributed to the blending of the two races. It may, however, with certainty be said that by the middle of the fourteenth century the various causes that had long been at work in fostering a common interest, had succeeded in amalgamating the conquerors and the conquered into one great nation, speaking that marvellous composite English tongue that is now the medium of communication in every part of the civilised world.*

During this *semi-Saxon* period, 1066—1400, a time of unrest and turmoil, there was a dearth of poetic composition, but such of it as there was is native born, and is marked by all the characteristics mentioned above; the foreign influences that were at work hardly affected it at all. The chief poems of this time are—

(i) *Layamon's "Brut,"* written about A.D. 1200. Although it is a metrical adaptation from the French of *Wace*, a Norman trouvère of the legendary history of the early British kings, it has not more than sixty non-Saxon words in all its thirty thousand short lines. It is in the old alliterative metre, with four accents and occasional rhymes.

(ii) The *Ormulum*, a metrical version of parts of the Gospels, written about 1215 in seven-accent metre, unrhymed. In the portion of it that exists,

---

* This is not the place to enter into details respecting the growth and development of the *Queen's English*. During the transition period we are now considering, our native tongue became differentiated into three clearly marked dialects, the Northern, the Southern, and the Midland, while the upper classes spoke and wrote in Latin and French. These operated in a variety of ways upon the harsh, uncouth vernacular, and when in the long run the masters were obliged to adopt the speech of their serfs, it was the *Midland* dialect that they assisted in polishing into modern English. (See Oliphant's *Standard English*.)

about twenty thousand lines, there are a few newly introduced Latin ecclesiastical terms, but not more than five French words, and the arrangement of the words is not very unlike the English of to-day.

(iii) *Piers Plowman's Vision,* 1362, alluded to above, is an allegory of deep religious feeling and sentiment, which produced a profound impression at the time, as it appeared while the country was devastated by the terrible " Black Death." There are a large number of French words in its thirty thousand lines, but it adheres to the Anglo-Saxon inflections, which had already begun to give way, and preserves the old alliterative form of verse. It is the earliest great original poem that we possess in English.

Besides these three important poems of the period, important mainly from a philological point of view, there were numerous translations from the French romantic poetry which dealt chiefly with the legends of King Arthur and Charlemagne. In these we find plainly discernible the influence of the speech of the upper classes upon the vernacular. Many of the harsh-sounding Saxon words began to drop out of use, and more euphonious Romance words took their place. Alliteration gradually gave way to the sweetness of rhyme, and as this required words with accent at the end, French words took the place of Saxon ones that bore the accent on the earlier syllables. In translating these French romances the rhyming words were ready to hand, and on this account alone, hundreds of Romance words were grafted upon the Teutonic framework of the language. In proof of the mixture of languages in use about the middle of the fourteenth century, *Gower* (1328—1408), the immediate predecessor of Chaucer, wrote his three important poems, one in French, one in Latin, and the *Confessio Amantis* in English. Our native tongue was in this transition state when *Wiclif* and *Chaucer* found it ; the former's prose *Translation of the New Testament,* 1384, did much to fix it in its present form, but it was the latter's masterly hand that polished and stamped it with the marks of permanency. By his judicious selection of conflicting grammatical forms, and the blending of foreign and native words, he moulded and stereotyped our tongue into that English which, with slight modifications, we speak and write to-day.

Chaucer (1328 or 40—1400), the prince of story-tellers in verse and the ' Father of English poetry,' was well fitted to weld the varied elements of our mediæval tongue into harmonious unity. Fully conversant with the literature of Rome, Italy, and France, he was, moreover, a typical Englishman of the middle class, and a man of the world. His matchless *Canterbury Tales* remained for two hundred years the one great poem of the language, and is still unique in portraiture of character, simple descriptive beauty, and metrical sweetness. Nearly all the tales are composed in rhymed heroics, *i.e.* in iambic pentameter arranged in continuous couplets.*

During the next hundred years, embracing the whole of the fifteenth century—the period of the

* See the opening lines of the *Prologue,* p. 113.

French wars, and the Wars of the Roses—no poet of note arose in England, though north of the Tweed several writers kept alive the roll of English verse ; the *Robin Hood* ballads, and *Chevy Chase* are the chief native productions. In the early part of the sixteenth century the revival of classical learning and the study of Italian models rekindled the poetic instincts of young England, just awakening into intellectual vigour. The Earl of Surrey enlarged the field of versification by the introduction of the *Sonnet** form, which soon became a general favourite, and by composition in *Blank verse*,† which was quickly developed into the highest form of poetic expression. Sackville at once introduced it into the drama, Marlowe improved it, while Shakspere and Milton used it with a perfection never since equalled.

By the time of Shakspere the vocabulary of our language had greatly changed and increased. About one-fifth of the old English words had become obsolete, but the eight or ten thousand words that constituted our speech at the end of the fourteenth century had grown to thirty thousand. Of these our great dramatist, to express his all-embracing thoughts, makes use of about fifteen thousand, though it should be remarked that many of these, chiefly of Latin origin, occur not more than once or twice. No succeeding poet has approached this exuberance of utterance.

The minor poets of the age of Shakspere and

---

* For a full account of the Sonnet, see p. 203.
† See p. 184.

Milton, in their lyrical efforts may be said to have rung all the changes of metrical combinations possible, and to have well-nigh exhausted the varieties of rhythm and poetic embellishment of which our language is capable, leaving to their successors little more than imitation as far as the form of verse goes. Dryden and Pope smoothed and polished the Heroic measure to the verge of monotony, and since their time but little originality has been possible in the art of versification beyond the experiments made with the classic metres.*

* See p. 264. Coleridge, in his beautiful fragment, *Christabel*, made use of what he terms a new principle, the verse consisting of lines varying in length from seven to twelve syllables, but always having four accents. There is nothing strikingly new in this beyond the carrying of it out systematically.

CLASSICAL METRES.

THE verse of the Latin and Greek poets is based upon *quantity*, and its structure is regulated by rules much more rigorous than the easy canons of English rhythm. In English verse *time* is an accessory merely, and all attempts to string together English words upon that basis only have resulted in what is neither verse nor English, for the words have to lose their proper pronunciation. Here are three lines of English words arranged on the principle of the Latin hexameter by Sir Philip Sidney:

Thāt tŏ mȳ | ādvānce | mēnt thēir | wīsdŏms | hāve mĕ ă | | bāsēd | .—
Wēll măy ă | pāstōr | plāin ; bŭt ă | lās ! hīs | plāints bĕ nŏt | | ēsteēmed | .—
Ōpprēss'd | wīth rŭĭn | oŭs cōn | cēits bȳ thĕ | aīd ŏf ăn | | oūtcrȳ | .

Spenser made similar experiments, and with like results. William Webbe, who wrote a "Discourse on English Poetry" in 1586, translated Virgil's *First Georgic* into hexameters, but with this important and necessary difference, he substituted accent for quantity. If this be done some approach to metrical effect may be attained, as will be seen later on. An hexameter verse consists of six feet, dactyls and spondees intermixed, and no others; the number of syllables varies from seventeen to thirteen, and the beats are six, though one may be weak. A Latin word may have two, three, or four consecutive long syllables, whereas English words have very rarely more than one syllable accented. It is therefore a difficult thing to construct a succession of perfect hexameter lines of English words without the skilful use of monosyllables. And when lines so constructed are read aloud all trace of quantity disappears, and the metrical accent is given to such of the long syllables as subserve the rhythmic effect, *i.e.* the spondees are turned into iambs or trochees at will.

Of our modern poets Cowper and Southey were the first to experiment with the Classic metres—of course on the basis of accent, not quantity—and Coleridge, Arnold, Whewell, and Tennyson have amused themselves by making English hexameters and pentameters. Kingsley's *Andromeda*, a poem of some five hundred lines, is in hexameters, and so are Longfellow's *Evangeline*, and *Courtship of Miles Standish*. *Evangeline* is the only really successful production of the kind. Dr. Whewell has translated some of Schiller's poems into Elegiacs, in imitation of Ovid, and Longfellow has framed original verses in the same measure. Cowper, Southey, and Canning have imitated Horace's Sapphics, while Tennyson has tried his hand upon Alcaics and Hendecasyllabics. It would be well, however, to regard all such attempts to introduce exotics like these into our verse as mere literary amusements and curiosities.

Here are the schemes of these various metres, with examples of each.

1.—HEXAMETERS.

‒ ◡ ◡ | ‒ ◡ ◡ | ‒ ◡ ◡ | ‒ ◡ ◡ | ‒ ◡ ◡ | ‒ ‒
‒ ‒ | ‒ ‒ | ‒ ‒ | ‒ ‒ | ‒ ‒ | ‒ ◡

Fair was she | to be | hold, that | maiden of | seventeen |
   | summers ;
Black were her | eyes as the | berry that | grows on the | thorn
   by the | wayside—
Black, yet how | softly they | gleamed be | neath the brown |
   | shade of her | tresses !
Sweet was her | breath as the | breath of | kine that | feed in
   the | meadows.

Evangeline.

Fasting in | sackcloth and | ashes they | came, both the | king
   and his | people,
Cametothe | mountainof | oaks,tothe | houseofthe | terrible |
   sea gods.

Andromeda.

2.—PENTAMETERS.

‒ ◡ ◡ | ‒ ◡ ◡ | ‒ ‖ ‒ ◡ ◡ | ‒ ◡ ◡ | ‒
‒ ‒ | ‒ ‒ | ‒ ‒ | ‒ ‒ | ◡ :

These lame | hexam | eters the | strong winged | music of |
   | Homer !
No—but a | most bur | lesque ‖ barbarous | experi | ment.
When was a | harsher | sound ever | heard, ye | Muses of |
   England ?
When did a | frog coarser | croak ‖ upon | our Heli | con ?

Tennyson.

Come, all ye | weary and | worn, ye | heavily | laden and |
   | sighing—
Come ye, oh, | come ye to | Christ ‖ —Saviour, | Comforter, |
   | King.

F. B. R.

3.—SAPPHICS.

Thrice repeated, followed by

Man disa | vows and | Dei | ty dis | owns me ;
Hell might | afford | my miser | ies a | shelter,
Therefore | hell keeps | her ever | hungry | mouths all
      Bolted a | gainst me.

Cowper.

Cold was the | night wind, | drifting | fast the | snow fell,
Wide were the | downs and | shelter | less and | naked,
When a poor | wand'rer | struggled | on her | journey
      Weary and | waysore.

Southey.
" The Widow."

The two following stanzas are from the *Anti-Jacobin*, in parody of Southey's matter and manner :

Needy | knife grind | er, whither | are you | going ?
Rough is | the road, | your wheel is | out of | order :
Bleak blows | the blast— | your hat has | got a | hole in't,
      So have your | breeches.

*   *   *   *   *   *   *   *

---

* The dactyl and trochee in the first and third foot respectively would
be inadmissible in classic verse. The specimens are scanned in such a
manner as to give them every chance of being considered rhythmical.

I give | thee six | pence ! I will | see thee | hanged first,—
Wretch whom | no sense | of wrongs can | rouse **to** |
    | vengeance,—
Sordid, | unfeel | ing, repro | bate, de | graded,
                Spiritless outcast !

Canning.

4.—ALCAICS.

$$\smile - \ | \smile - \ | - \ | - \smile \smile \ | - \smile \smile \ |$$

Repeated and followed by

$$- - \ | \smile - \ | - - \ | \smile - \ | \simeq$$

$$- \smile \smile \ | - \smile \smile \ | - \smile \ | - \smile$$

O might | y mouth'd | in | ventor of | harmonies,
O skilled | to sing | of | Time or E | ternity,
  God gift | ed or | gan voice | of Eng | land,
  Milton **a** | name **to re** | sound to | ages.

Tennyson

IMITATIVE HARMONY.

True ease in writing comes from art, not chance,
As those move easiest who have learned to dance.
'Tis not enough no harshness gives offence ;
The sound must seem an echo to the sense.
Soft is the strain when Zephyr gently blows,
And the smooth stream in smoother numbers flows ;
But when loud surges lash the sounding shore,
The hoarse rough verse should like the torrent roar.
When Ajax strives some rock's vast weight to throw,
The line too labours, and the words move slow ;
Not so when swift Camilla scours the plain,
Flies o'er the unbending corn, and skims along the main.

IN this oft-quoted passage from the *Essay on Criticism* Pope sounds the note of, and attempts to illustrate, what is known as "Imitative Harmony" in language, by which is meant a resemblance, real or fancied, that the sounds of words bear to the sense they convey.

The *Onomatopœtic*, or "Bow-wow" theory of the origin of language, is no longer seriously held by any philological authority, but at the same time the mimetic origin of a large number of words is undoubted. Such forms, for instance, as *coo, hiss, bump, thud, smash, pop, bang, crash, whizz, buzz, stun, tingle, chatter, squeak, murmur, scream, gurgle, howl, bubble,* and a host of others, exhibit a correspondence between sound and sense which is unmistakable. As language is made up of sounds which are more or less expressive of actions and things, we need not wonder that poets especially, whose chief concern is with the form and dress of their thoughts, should avail themselves of any such correspondence between their ideas and expressions as could enhance the impressiveness of their verses. Much has been written upon this subject both in ancient and modern times, and many fruitless attempts have been made to show that there may be an actual resemblance between the rhythm of verse and the things described; but it will be found, after a careful examination of the most noted experiments that have been made, that a general suitableness of diction, and a pleasing assistance which the similarity of sound gives to the sense, are all that have been really accomplished. This, however, is quite enough to induce writers of verse to avail themselves of such limited embellishment as this Imitative Harmony affords.

Two famous examples of this sound and sense resemblance have often been quoted, the one from Homer:

Αὖτις 'ἔπειτα πέδονδε κυλίνδετο λᾶας 'αναιδῆς—

the other from Virgil:

Quadrupedante putrem sonitu quatit ungula Campum:

the first describing a heavy stone rolling down a mountain side; the second, the hoofs of a horse galloping over a hardened plain. Now the sounds of these two movements would be, of course, quite dissimilar, yet the rhythm of the verses, which is supposed to imitate them, is exactly the same. If, then, the one is to be praised for its imitative truth-fulness, what can we say of the other? Pope's adaptation of the Greek passage describing the labour of Sisyphus is well worth quoting :

> With many a weary step, and many a groan,
> Up the high hill he heaves a huge round stone ;
> The huge round stone resulting with a bound,
> Thunders impetuous down, and smokes along the ground.

Up to the middle of the third line we have the slow laboured motion upward imitated, and then the rapid, impetuous downward roll.

In the well-known couplet from the passage at the beginning of this chapter :

> When Ajax strives some rock's vast weight to throw,
> The line too labours and the words move slow,—

we have slowness of motion expressed by a slow succession of syllables, each of the two lines having six accents, one more than the usual number; but when we come to consider the next couplet :

> Not so when swift Camilla scours the plain,
> Flies o'er the unbending corn, and skims along the main.

we are somewhat disappointed in what is intended to represent swift and rapid motion; for, in fact, we have the full number of accents and rather

more than the usual number of long syllables.
Dr. Johnson is rather severe upon this and other
instances of a similar character : he says, "The
desire of discovering frequent adaptations of the
sound to the sense has produced, in my opinion,
many wild conceits and imaginary beauties." And
then he adds, "When Pope had enjoyed for thirty
years the praise of Camilla's lightness of foot, he
tried another experiment upon sense and sound,
and produced this memorable triplet :

> ' Waller was smooth, but Dryden taught to join
> The varying verse, the full resounding line,
> The long majestic march, and energy divine.'

Here are the swiftness of the rapid pace, and the
march of slow-paced majesty exhibited by the
same poet in the same sequence of syllables, except
that the exact prosodist will find the line of *swiftness* by one time longer than that of *tardiness*."*
What he here criticises in Pope, he praises un-
grudgingly in a passage from Cowley :

> He who defers his work from day to day,
> Does on a river's bank expecting stay
> Till the whole stream that stopp'd shall be gone,
> *Which runs, and as it runs, for ever shall run on.*

He declares the last line to be "an example of
representative versification which perhaps no
other English line can equal."

Enough has perhaps been said to show that the
actual correspondence between sense and sound,

---

* Johnson's " Life of Pope."

in even the most noted examples of it, is more fanciful than real. Still there can be no question that the skilful grouping and management of sounds in poetry may greatly contribute to the sensuousness of description and the appropriateness of the rhythm. This is plainly discernible in some at least of the following examples. In *Hamlet* (v. 2), the Prince conjures his friend Horatio, who was desirous of dying with him, still to live. His words are:

> If ever thou didst hold me in thine heart,
> Absent thee from felicity awhile,
> *And in this harsh world draw thy breath in pain,*
> To tell my story.

The composition of the third line is remarkable, for it is clogged with consonants, and the aspirate, and the hissing *s*; and all the syllables but one are long, either by quantity or position; *i.e.* two consonants following the vowel. By this artificial structure, the utterance of the verse is made to resemble the sense, for it does not admit of a quick or easy pronunciation.

In *Henry IV.*, part I. iii. 1, Glendower translates his daughter's wishes to her husband Mortimer in these words:

> She bids you
> Upon the wanton rushes lay you down,
> And rest your gentle head upon her lap,
> And she will sing the song that pleaseth you,
> And on your eyelids crown the god of sleep,
> Charming your blood with pleasing heaviness,

T

Making such difference betwixt wake and sleep,
As is the difference betwixt day and night,
The hour before the heavenly-harness'd team
Begins his golden progress in the east.

The most obvious character of these lines is their monotonous flow, which, if they had been upon a different subject, would have been a fault; but in this case it was designed. They were framed to run evenly and uniformly along; that being the most proper movement to accompany and express their meaning, which is an invitation to rest and sleep. The author, to attain his purpose, has separated all the lines, except the eighth, by a stop at the end of each. This alone was enough to produce monotony; but beside this, the single pause which he has admitted into every line is generally in, or near, the middle of it: then, the feet are all such as contribute to smooth versification. There is not one foot of two accented syllables; on the contrary, some are unaccented; but by far the greatest number are regular; *i.e.* accented on the second syllable. By these means the verses have the expression which Shakspere undoubtedly designed to give them.

In Dryden's tragedy of *Edipus* there is a verse which we look upon as expressing very happily the sense by the measure: but whether so or not, the verse is eminently beautiful. The speaker announces the death of a person whose days had run on to a great length,

Till, like a clock, worn out with eating time,
The wheels of weary life at last stood still.

The first four feet of this line, being pure iambics, proceed regularly and evenly on till they are contrasted by the fifth, which is admirably composed to represent, by its consonants, short vowels, and accents, the stop and ceasing of the motion. Change the order of words thus:

> The wheels of weary life stood still at last,

and the expression is lost; so it would be if the vowels in the last foot were long.

The contrast, in Milton's description, of the opening of the gates of Heaven and of Hell is very remarkable:

> Heaven opened wide
> Her ever-during gates, harmonious sound,
> On golden hinges turning.

> On a sudden open fly,
> With impetuous recoil and jarring sound,
> The infernal doors ; and on their hinges grate
> Harsh thunder.

Keats describes the gliding motion of the clouds by the use of liquid consonants :

> And let the clouds of even and of morn
> Float in voluptuous fleeces o'er the hills.

And the soothing nature of a lullaby is expressed by Shakspere in a similar way :

> Philomel with melody
> Sing in one sweet lullaby ;
> Lulla, lulla, lullaby.

The sound of battle in the old modes of warfare is represented thus:

> Arms on armour clashing, brayed
> Horrible discord; and the maddening wheels
> Of brazen fury raged.

Unwieldy bulk and shape is depicted by Milton in these words:

> O'er all the dreary coasts
> So stretched out, huge in length, the arch-fiend lay.
> But ended foul, in many a scaly fold,
> Voluminous and vast.

Pope imitated heaven's artillery by the skilful use of two words:

> If nature *thundered* in our opening ears
> And *stunned* us with the music of the spheres.

Here are further instances of this attempted sound word-painting:

> Disparting towers,
> Tumbling all precipitate down-dashed,
> Rattling around, loud thundering to the moon.
> *Dyer.*

> Deep echoing groan the thickets brown
> Rustling, crackling, crashing, thunder down.
> *Pope.*

> The ice was here, the ice was there,
>   The ice was all around,
> It cracked and growled, and roared and howled
>   Like noises in a swound.
> *Coleridge.*

No modern poet is more conspicuously ingenious in this kind of word-painting than Tennyson. He

pictures the roaring of the seas by the reiteration
of the letter *r* :

> Those wild eyes that watch the wave,
> In roarings round the coral reef ;

the sense of chill cheerlessness by such harsh
rhythm as :

> And ghastly through the drizzling rain
> On the bald street breaks the bleak day.

The effect of varied sounds and movements is
picturesquely given in two stanzas from the *Dream
of Fair Women* :

> Her slow full words sank thro' the silence drear,
> As thunder drops fall on a sleeping sea ;
> Sudden I heard a voice that cried, " Come here,
> That I may look on thee."
> *   *   *   *   *
> She locked her lips ; she left me where I stood :
> " Glory to God," she sang, and past afar,
> Thridding the sombre boskage of the wood,
> Toward the morning star.

The description of Arthur leaving Guinevere presents a picture of such a masterly adaptation of
word and figure to the sense as cannot be surpassed
in the whole range of English poetry :

> And more and more,
> The moony vapour rolling round the king
> Who seemed the phantom of a giant in it,
> Enwound him fold by fold, and made him gray
> And grayer, till himself became a mist
> Before her, moving ghostlike to his doom.
> *Tennyson.*
> " Idylls of the King."

The subject may be fittingly closed by examples from Southey's *How the Water comes down at Lodore* and Poe's *Bells.*

And thumping and plumping, and bumping and jumping,
And dashing and flashing, and splashing and clashing,
   And so never ending,
   And always descending,
Sounds and motions for ever and ever are blending,
   All at once and all o'er
   With a mighty uproar;
And this way the water comes down at Lodore.
         Southey.

   Hear the sledges with the bells—
    Silver bells!
What a world of merriment their melody foretells!
   How they tinkle, tinkle, tinkle,
    In the icy air of night!
   While the stars that oversprinkle
   All the heavens seem to twinkle
   With a crystalline delight ;
    Keeping time, time, time,
    In a sort of Runic rhyme,
To the tintinnabulation that so musically wells
   From the bells, bells, bells, bells,
    Bells, bells, bells—
From the jingling and the tinkling of the bells.

  *   *   *   *   *

   Hear the loud alarum bells—
     Brazen bells!
What a tale of terror now their turbulency tells!
   In the startled ear of night
   How they scream out their affright!
   Too much horrified to speak,
   They can only shriek, shriek,
     Out of tune,

In a clamorous appealing to the mercy of the fire,
In a mad expostulation with the deaf and frantic fire,
    Leaping higher, higher, higher,
    With a desperate desire,
    And a resolute endeavour,
    Now—now to sit or never
By the side of the pale-faced moon.
    Oh the bells, bells, bells,
    What a tale their terror tells
        Of despair !
    How they clang, and clash, and roar !
    What a horror they outpour
On the bosom of the palpitating air.
    Yet the ear it fully knows,
        By the twanging,
        And the clanging,
    How the danger ebbs and flows ;
    Yet the ear distinctly tells,
        In the jangling,
        And the wrangling,
    How the danger sinks and swells,
By the sinking or the swelling in the anger of the bells ;
        Of the bells—
    Of the bells, bells, bells, bells,
      Bells, bells, bells, bells,
In the clamour and the clangour of the bells.
                    Poe.

BIBLIOGRAPHY.

WORKS ON VERSIFICATION:

IN this chapter the attention of the student will be directed to what has been written upon the subject of verse and poetic criticism, since the rise of the Gay Science towards the end of the sixteenth century. It does not aim at furnishing an exhaustive list of such works, but it will be found sufficiently comprehensive to guide the reader who wishes to advance beyond an elementary knowledge of the subject. And as the older works are difficult of access, more copious extracts from them are given, although many of the views there expressed have long since been abandoned.

The first English writer[*] that occurs to notice is William Webbe, who published a *Discourse of English Poetry* in 1586. It was written "to stirre up some other of meete abilitie to bestow travell on the matter." In that discourse, after treating of poetry in general, he singles out Spenser from the English poets for his especial commendation, and takes the *Shepherd's Calendar* published about

---

[*] Our King James I. published in Scotland, in 1584, "Ane schort Treatise, containing some reulis and cautelis to be observit and eschewit in Scottis Poesie."

seven years before (but which, it seems, had not
been owned by him), for the subject of his remarks
on English Versification. He says, " Of the kinds
of English verses which differ in number of syllables, there are almost infinite. To avoid therefore
tediousness, I will repeat only the different sorts of
verses out of the *Shepherd's Calendar*, which may
well serve to bear authority in this matter.

" There are in this work twelve or thirteen sundry
sorts of verses, which differ either in length, or
rhyme, or distinction of the staves." Having
quoted several passages to prove this assertion, he
adds, " I shall avoid the tedious rehearsal of all
the kinds which are used, which I think would
have been impossible, seeing they may be altered
to as many forms as the poets please : neither is
there any tune or stroke which may be sung or
played on instruments, which hath not some
poetical ditties framed according to the numbers
thereof."

But notwithstanding this abundant variety, our
author was one of those who fancied that English
poetry would be greatly improved by adopting
Greek and Latin measures, and composing in
hexameter, pentameter, sapphic, and other ancient
forms. It was a project that had already been set
on foot by some of high literary reputation ; and
he endeavoured to advance it by his advice and
example. He was aware, indeed, of the objection
"that our words are nothing resemblant in nature
to theirs, and therefore not possible to be framed
with any good grace after their use ;" but this he

proposed to surmount, by "excepting against the observance of position, and certain other of their rules." Still there remained various difficulties; and it is amusing to hear him relate his distress, when composing in the new fashion, "he found most of our monosyllables to be long," when, to serve his purpose, they should have been short : he wanted "some direction for such words as fall not within the compass of Greek or Latin rules, and thereof he had great miss." He was forced "to omit the best words, and such as would naturally become the speech best," to avoid breaking his Latin rules. Under all these discouragements, however, he translated two of Virgil's Eclogues into English hexameters, and transformed a part of the *Shepherd's Calendar* into sapphics ; and these pieces make a conspicuous portion of his book.

The next was George Gascoigne, an eminent poet of the same age. He included *Certain Notes of Instruction concerning the making of Verse or Rhyme in English* in an edition of his works published in 1575, and again in 1587. This sensible treatise, by one who was a poet himself, is certainly one of the earliest attempts in our language to establish fixed rules for the modulation of verse. It is concise ; the conclusions are neither singular nor forced, and though from the dates the whole might be expected to have acquired an obsolete character, it still retains such a just proportion of fact with the precepts forming a close alliance to the natural order of our language, that while we hesitate to recommend anything shaped like trammels for genius, the reading of these notes may be suggested as instructive, if not of advantage to poetical composition.

The more remarkable passages in Gascoigne's work are these. He speaks of no other feet, as entering into verse, than those of two syllables ; of which, says he, "the first is depressed, or short ; the second, elevate, or long." He gives rules for rhyming and for finding a rhyme. Concerning the admission of polysyllables into verse, he gives this direction—" I warn you that you thrust as few words of many syllables into your verse as may be ; and hereunto I might allege many reasons : first, the most ancient English words are of one syllable ; so that the more monosyllables you use, the truer English you shall seem, and the less you shall smell of the inkhorn. Also, words of many syllables do cloy a verse, and make it unpleasant."* Respecting the cæsura, or pause in a verse, he observes that " in lines of eight syllables it is best in the middle, as :

Amid my bale | I bathe in bliss.

In lines of ten syllables, after the fourth, as :

I smile sometimes, | although my grief be great.

In those of twelve syllables, in the middle ; and in those of fourteen, after the eighth, as :

* There are two critics of later times who have given their judgment upon the use of polysyllables in English verse, to which allusion has already been made. Of these, one is directly opposed to Gascoigne, the other agrees with him, and, upon the whole, appears to be right.

Divorce me now, good death, | from love and lingering life ;
That one hath been my concubine, | that other was my wife.*

"Lines of twelve and fourteen syllables alternate," says he (*i.e.* such as the last here quoted),
"is the commonest sort of verse which we use nowadays."

But a more celebrated work on the subject, was
a regular treatise, on the *Art of English Poesy*,
published in 1589, but written some time before,
by Puttenham. He says he writes it "to help the
courtiers and the gentlewomen of the court to
write good poetry, that the art may become vulgar
for all Englishmen's use." This author was of a
different opinion from Webbe in respect to the
introduction of Greek and Latin measures into
English poetry ; and he says, with good judgment,
thus : "Peradventure with us Englishmen it may
be somewhat too late to admit a new invention of
feet and times that our forefathers never used, nor
never observed till this day, either in their measures or their pronunciation : and perchance will
seem in us a presumptuous part to attempt ; considering also it would be hard to find many men
to like of one man's choice in the limitation of
times and quantities of words ; with which not
one, but every ear is to be pleased and made a
particular judge ; it being most truly said, that a
multitude or commonalty is hard to please, and
easy to offend." In conclusion, he condemns this
sort of versification as a frivolous and ridiculous
novelty. But, although in this particular he mani-

---

* These examples are taken from his own poems.

fested his good sense, in some other points he fell
in with the whimsical fancies of his time; such as
making poems in the shape of altars, pyramids,
and the like.

He who shall peruse Puttenham may collect
from him some information concerning the state
of poetry in his day; and may understand what
kind of verse was censured or praised, and what
degree of estimation former English poets were
then held in, but he must not expect much instruction upon the art itself. Warton* says of this
book, that it remained long as a rule of criticism.

Another work was published in 1602, with this
title, " *Observations in the Art of English Poesie*, by
Thomas Campion. Wherein it is demonstratively
proved, and by example confirmed, that the English
tongue will receive eight several kinds of numbers
proper to itself; which are all in this book set
forth, and were never before this time, by any man,
attempted." Campion was a poet and physician
during part of the reigns of Queen Elizabeth and
King James : he was also a composer of music, and
his acquaintance with the latter art appears by
some remarkable passages in his book. The eight
several kinds of numbers which he mentions are
to be understood, not of feet, nor yet altogether
of verses taken singly, but, some of them, of combinations of verses and stanzas. He has, indeed.
a chapter on " English numbers in general," by
which he means the feet admissible into English

* Warton's " History of English Poetry," vol. ii. 10.

poetry; and he reduces them to two, as being essential, and giving character and name to two different species of verse, viz. the iambic and the trochee, of which he gives this strange account, that it " is but an iambic turned over and over."

Campion might have shown, even from his own poetry, that our language can receive other numbers than he has enumerated ; but his book contains little that is new or extraordinary, except that the poetical part is all in blank verse, and that he wishes to discard entirely from our poetry what he is pleased to call " the fatness of rhyme ;" which brought forth an answer from a writer of a superior order to Campion, both in verse and prose.

This was Samuel Daniel, who, in 1603, wrote a *Defence of Rhyme,* against Campion's " Observations," " wherein is demonstratively proved, that rhyme is the fittest harmony of words that comports with our language." This is, indeed, asserted ; but in proofs and demonstration, he falls as short as his antagonist. Of him he says : " This detractor is a man of fair parts, and good reputation, and therefore the reproach forcibly cast from such a hand may throw down more at once than the labours of many shall in long time build up again. We could well have allowed of his numbers, if he had not disgraced our rhyme, which both custom and nature doth most powerfully defend ; custom that is above all law, nature that is above all art. Our rhyme is likewise number and harmony of words, consisting of an agreeing sound in the last syllables of several verses, giving both to the ear an echo of a delightful report, and to the memory a deeper impression of what is delivered therein; for as Greek and Latin verse consists of the number and quantity of syllables, so doth the English verse of measure and accent; and though it doth not strictly observe long and short syllables, yet it most religiously respects the accent; and as the short and the long make number, so the acute and grave accent yield harmony, and harmony is likewise number: so that the English verse then hath number, measure, and harmony, in the best proportion of music. But be the verse never so good, never so full, it seems not to satisfy nor breed that delight, as when it is met and combined with a like sounding accent; which seems as the jointure, without which it hangs loose, and cannot subsist, but runs wildly on, like a tedious fancy, without a close." Having thus defended the use of rhyme, he proceeds in a similar strain against the rest of Campion's book, asserting "that of all his eight several kinds of new promised numbers, we have only what was our own before;" such as have ever been familiarly used among us; and the like of his other positions. He expresses a wish, however, "that there were not that multiplicity of rhymes as is used by many in sonnets;" he acknowledges, "that to his own ear, those continual cadences of couplets used in long and continued poems are very tiresome and unpleasing;" and he confesses that his "adversary had wrought so much upon him, as to think a tragedy would best comport with a blank verse, and dispense with rhyme, saving in the chorus, or where a sentence shall require a couplet." He says too, that he thinks it wrong to mix uncertainly feminine rhymes with masculine;* which, ever since he was warned of that deformity by a kind friend, he had always so avoided, as that there are not above two couplets in that kind in all his poem of the Civil Wars; that he " held feminine rhymes to be fittest for ditties, and either to be certain, or set by themselves." The opinions of Daniel are more particularly noticed here, because his versification is equal to the best of his times.

Another poet, who valued himself upon his skill in numbers, viz. Cowley, may be joined with these authors; not indeed for any formal work upon the subject, but for certain notes made by him upon his own verses. The purport of those notes is to inform his readers that the verses are intended and framed to represent the things described by their imitative harmony. In his preface he expresses himself thus respecting the odes which he calls pindaric: " The numbers are various and irregular, and sometimes (especially some of the long ones) seem harsh and uncouth, if the just measures and cadences be not observed in the pronunciation. So that almost all their sweetness and numerosity

---

* The terms masculine and feminine, as applied to verse, are taken from the French, and signify—the first, rhymes of one syllable—the other, of two, which we now call double rhymes; and of which this character of King John, from the First Book of his Civil Wars, is an example:

> A tyrant loath'd, a homicide convented,
> Poison'd he dies, disgraced, and unlamented.

By rhymes uncertainly mixed, he means introduced irregularly; not recurring in the stanzas at set distances, which he calls certain.

(which is to be found, if I mistake not, in the roughest, if rightly repeated) lies in a manner wholly at the mercy of the reader. I have briefly described the nature of these verses in the ode entitled *The Resurrection ;* * and though the liberty of them may incline a man to believe them easy to be composed, yet the undertaker will find it otherwise.

In 1679, Samuel Woodford, D.D., published a Paraphrase on the Canticles, and Hymns; and in the preface made certain observations on the structure of English verse, which are mentioned, not so much for anything remarkable in his criticism, as for his high commendation, at the period, of Milton's *Paradise Lost ;* though he would rather " it had been composed in rhyme "!

About the same time another work came out, comprising some principles of versification, together with an assistance towards making English verse. The title was the *English Parnassus, or a Help to English Poesie ;* containing a collection of all the rhyming monosyllables, the choicest epithets and phrases, with some general forms upon all occa-

---

* The passage in the Ode on the Resurrection, to which he refers, is this:

> Stop. stop, my Muse, allay thy vigorous heat,
> Kindled at a hint so great;
> Hold thy Pindaric Pegasus closely in,
> Which does to rage begin,
> And this steep hill would gallop up with violent course:
> 'Tis an unruly and a hard-mouth'd horse,
> Fierce and unbroken yet,
> Impatient of the spur or bit:
> Now prances stately, and anon flies o'er the place:
> Disdains the servile law of any settled pace;
> Conscious and proud of his own natural force:
> 'Twill no unskilful touch endure,
> But flings writer and reader too that sits not sure.

U

sions, subjects and themes, alphabetically digested; together with a short institution to English Poesie, by way of preface. The author was Joshua Poole, M.A., of Clare Hall, Cambridge; but it was a posthumous publication. The preface is subscribed J. D.; it contains no matter worthy of particular notice; and for the book itself, it is sufficiently detailed by the title.

This work appears to have been the foundation of another, built on the same plan, but considerably enlarged. The author was Edward Bysshe, who, in 1702, published an *Art of English Poetry*. The part relating to prosody is contained in three chapters, under these heads: "Of the structure of English verses.—Of rhyme.—Of the several sorts of poems and compositions in verse." His manner of treating these topics is plain, but neither methodical nor comprehensive; it presents, however, some useful information, and though perhaps no versifier of the present day may seek from this author "Rules for making English Verse" (for so he entitles this portion of his volume), it continued for above half a century to be a popular book. It also provided a further help to verse-makers, by a plentiful magazine, or Dictionary of Rhymes. The bulk of his performance was made up of a "Collection of the most natural, agreeable, and noble Thoughts, &c. that are to be found in the best English poets"; but if the execution of this part be compared with the promise of its title, he will be found to deserve little commendation. The number of poets from whom he professes to have formed

his selection, are forty-three. Of these, more than
a third part are either men of no name, as Stone-
street, Stafford, Harvey, or of no distinguished
reputation in poetry, as Walsh, Tate, Stepney,
Dennis, and others. Then the selection is made
so unequally, that three of his number, viz. Cowley,
Butler's *Hudibras*, and Dryden, have furnished
him with at least three-fifths of the whole. Indeed
he appears to have had very little knowledge of
our poets, even of those who lived and wrote but
fourscore years before himself. Ellis, in his *Specimens of the Early English Poets*, has given extracts
from upwards of forty authors in the reigns of
Charles the First and Second, not one of whom is
mentioned in Bysshe's catalogue. Here is another
proof of the same: he affirms that "we have no
entire works composed in verses of twelve syllables;" he must therefore have been unacquainted
with Drayton.

Not long after Glover's *Leonidas* appeared, Dr.
Pemberton, a great friend of the author, published
Observations on Poetry, especially epic, occasioned
by the late poem on Leonidas, 1738. The versification of that poem is very regular: and the design
of the observations, in part, is to justify and extol
that regularity; which, in an instance or two, is
done without foundation. The sixth section of the
Observations is upon the principles of verse; and
here his singular notions, and the severe rules he
would establish, might startle and discourage a
young poet. He disallows all licence, all irregularity. He asserts that no irregular composition

of feet is by any means necessary towards that
variety which is required in the longest work.
With the same rigour he pronounces upon the last
syllables of verses : and commends Glover for
closing his lines with a firm and stable syllable,
which, he says, is necessary to support the dignity
of the verse, and which Milton designedly neglected.
The lines he means are, in Glover, such as these :

> Rehearse, O Muse, the deeds and glorious death
> Of that fam'd Spartan, who withstood the power.
> > *Leon.* b. 1.

And of the contrary sort, in Milton, such as this :

> Here swallow'd up in endless misery.
> > *Paradise Lost*, b. 1.

A close of the line, which, had he thought it
negligent, or wanting dignity, he would not have
admitted so frequently, much less three times together, as in this instance :

> And all who since, baptized or infidel,
> Jousted in Aspramont, or Montalban,
> Damasco, or Morocco, or Trebisond.
> > *Paradise Lost*, b. 1.

The foregoing censure on Milton may warrant
the mention here (though not exactly in chronological order) of Tyrwhitt's *Essay on the Versification of Chaucer*, which contains much learned research into the nature and origin of our poetical
measures ; but which, in regard to the structure of
our verse, advances some positions that are very
questionable, to say the least of them ; as in this
passage : " on the tenth or rhyming syllable, a

strong accent is in all cases indispensably required; and in order to make the line tolerably
harmonious, it seems necessary that at least two
more of the even syllables should be accented, the
fourth being (almost always) one of them. Milton,
however, has not subjected his verse even to these
rules; and particularly, either by negligence or
design, he has frequently put an unaccented syllable in the fourth place." * To make this state-
ment respecting Milton is to show very little attention to his manner of versification; and to put it
as a doubt whether he did not, through negligence,
set an unaccented syllable in the fourth place of
his line, is to doubt whether he was not grossly
negligent in that point throughout his poem; since
he has done so no less than three times within the
first seven lines:

> Of man's first disobedience, and the fruit
> Of that forbidden tree, whose mortal taste
> Brought death intŏ the world and all our woe,
> With loss of Eden, till one greater man
> Restore us, ănd regain the blissful seat,
> Sing, heavenly Muse, that on the secret top
> Of Oreb, ŏr of Sinai, &c.

Again, to affirm that " a strong accent is in all
cases indispensably required on the rhyming syllable," is to condemn the practice of our most
correct and approved authors. Pope, without
scruple, admitted an unaccented syllable to rhyme:
for instance,

* See *Paradise Lost,* book iii. 36, 586; book v. 413, 750, 874. Essay
p. 62.

Useless, unseen, as lamps in sepulchres.
"*Elegy on an Unfortunate Lady.*"

And swell the pomp of dreadful sacrifice.
"*Eloisa to Abelard.*"

That guilt is doomed to sink in infamy.
"*Essay on Satire.*"

So that, should we submit to Tyrwhitt's authority, we must renounce some of the most established and allowed licences, if they are so to be called, in English versification.

Foster, in his celebrated *Essay on Accent and Quantity*, wrote two chapters on English prosody; and the mention of them is introduced here, not for any material information which they will afford to the reader, but rather to caution him against trusting to what is there said upon the subject.

The treatise on *Painting and Poetry*, by Webbe, deserves notice, as well for some judicious remarks on our poetical measures, as for directing the public attention to Shakspere's skill and excellence in them.

To the end of the last century there still remain a few, whom it will be sufficient to specify by their names and the titles of their books. These are— Tucker (under the name of Edward Search) on *Vocal Sounds*, 1773; Walker's *Rhyming Dictionary*, 1775; Steel's *Prosodia Rationalis*, 1779; Dr. Trussler's *Dictionary of Rhymes*, 1783.

The same subject has employed the pens of certain writers in the northern part of our island,

who are by no means to be omitted; for they are
all men of high rank, and (with one exception)
would form a catalogue of Royal and Noble
Authors. They are King James the Sixth of
Scotland; the lords Kaimes and Monboddo;
Dr. Beattie; and Lord Glenbervie: not that they
challenge our notice by their rank, but by the
merit of their writings. The first, by his "Reulis
and Cautelis to be observit and eschewit in Scottis
Poesie;" the second, by his Elements of Criticism;
the third, by his volumes on the Origin and Progress of Language; Dr. Beattie by his Essays; and
lastly, Lord Glenbervie, by the Notes on his spirited
translation of the Poem of Ricciardetto.

During the present century, and especially within
the last thirty years, the study of the art of versification and of poetry generally has vastly increased, and has attracted the attention of some of
the first scholars of the day. New editions of all
our chief poets are produced year after year, and
find increasing demand. Societies have been
formed to advance the study of Chaucer, Shakspere,
Shelley and the early English writers, and at length
English poetry is a recognised subject of study and
repetition in every course of national instruction.

A list of the chief writers upon the subject
during the present century, here given, will fitly
conclude this treatise.

Mitford, "Enquiry into the Principles of Harmony in
Language and of the Mechanism of Verse" (1804); Okell,
"Essay on the Elements, Accents, and Prosody of the English
Language" (1805); Haslewood, "Art of English Poesy'

(1815); Carey, " Practical English Prosody and Versification"
(1816); Crowe, "Treatise on English Versification" (1827);
Dr. Guest, "History of English Rhythms"* (1838); A. J.
Ellis, "Essentials of Phonetics" (1847); A. J. Ellis, " Early
English Pronunciation," Part III. (1869); W. Sydney Walker,
" Versification of Shakspere" (1854); Marsh, " Lectures on
the English Language " (Murray, 1863); Bain, " English
Composition and Rhetoric " (Longmans, 1866 ; enlarged
edition, 1888); R. F. Brewer, "Manual of English Prosody "
(Longmans, 1869); E. Wadham, " English Versification "
(Longmans, 1869); Dr. Abbott, " Shaksperian Grammar "
(Macmillan) ; Abbott and Seeley, " English Lessons for
English People " (Parts II. and III.); J. J. Sylvester, F.R.S..
" The Laws of Verse, or Principles of Versification, Exem-
plified in Metrical Translations " (Longmans, 1870); Dr.
Longmuir, Preface to the Later Editions of Walker's
" Rhyming Dictionary"; Tom Hood, " Rules of Rhyme, a
Guide to Versification, with a compendious Dictionary of
Rhymes " (1877); Dowden, " Shakspere Primer " (Mac-
millan, 1877); Angus, " Handbook of English Literature
and of the English Tongue "; Gilbert Conway, " Treatise
on Versification " † (Longmans, 1878); Ruskin, "Elements
of English Prosody," for use in St. George's School (1880);
Sydney Lanier, " The Science of English Verse " (New York,
1880); Dr. Schipper, "Englische Metrik" (Bonn, 1882); Canon
Daniel, " Grammar, &c., of the English Language," Part IV.,
(1883); " Geo. H. Brown, "Notes on Shakspere's Versification " (Boston, 1884); C. Witcomb, " The Structure of
English Verse " (1884); J. B. Mayor, "Chapters on English
Metre " ‡ (1886); E. C. Stedman, " The Nature and Elements
of Poetry " (*Cent. Mag.*, Mar.-Oct., 1892).

* A work of great research and a storehouse of examples, but his
theories as to the structure of modern verse are erroneous and im-
practicable.

† A scholarly and original work, but lacking method and arrangement. The notes fill up as much space as the text.

‡ A masterly argumentative treatise on the subject of metre, in which
the *à priori* theories of Dr. Guest and Dr. Abbott are successfully
demolished, and what may be called the common-sense method of
scanning is vindicated.

A

RHYMING DICTIONARY.

INTRODUCTION.

———•———

THE lists of words comprising the Rhyming Dictionary annexed have been compiled with care and method. They are not a reprint, slightly altered, of any existing work of the same kind, but the result of a new and comprehensive overhauling of our English vocabulary, with a view to the selection of nearly all words suitable for Verse-Making at the end of the nineteenth century. The collection will be found to be more complete and varied than any that the compiler has been able to consult; while its improved arrangement will tend to facilitate reference.

Rhyme depends upon similarity of *sound* only, the *spelling* of the words being of no consequence: thus, *curl*, *pearl*, *whirl*, rhyme perfectly, as do also *laugh*, *staff*, *photograph*; whereas *bough*, *cough*, *dough*, stand in no harmonious relation to each other whatever. The words in this dictionary, therefore, are classed together as to their ending *sounds* only, and must be looked for under the letters that most plainly represent the sound: *e.g. labour* and *saviour* will be found under OR; *pious*, *harmonious*, and the like, under US; *coalesce*, *effervesce*, under ES, &c. Copious references however, are given throughout to lists that nearly correspond with each other.

Under each heading the list of words printed in *ordinary type*, which has been made as complete and suggestive as possible, rhyme perfectly, or very nearly so, with each other; and they are arranged alphabetically, and in the order of the number of their syllables. At the end of these, printed in *italics*, a few typical words are given which rhyme more or less imperfectly with the normal sound of the heading; but no attempt has been made to assist the student to find words that he ought to do his utmost to avoid. Examples of licences in rhyme taken by our standard poets are introduced here and there; but these should be regarded by the modern versifier as models to shun, for the most part, rather than to imitate. These, when given, will be found amongst the foot-notes.

Single rhymes only are given ; the inclusion of double and triple rhymes would have swelled this part of the volume out beyond due limits, without corresponding advantage. Besides, double rhymes can be easily constructed from the single ones, inasmuch as they are nearly all derivative words formed from nouns, verbs, and adjectives by the suffixes *er*, *es*, *est*, *ing*, *less*, *ness*, and *ly*. The same remark applies to most words which end in *e* mute, preceded by the liquid *l*, *i.e.* to words in *ble*, *cle*, and *dle*, and also to that numerous class of nouns ending in *ion*, very few of which find place here. Other omissions, which have been made to keep the book within reasonable limits, may be pointed out, such as the *plurals* of nouns, the *participles* and *gerunds* of verbs, and all *unemphatic monosyllables* which ought never to conclude a rhyming verse. Instead of lists of such words, their fitness is indicated by the phrase "also the preterites of verbs in *ick*," &c. No word is repeated on account of its several acceptations; but in those few cases in which a word has two different sounds as well as different meanings, as *bow*, for shooting, *bow*, a salutation, it is given in each list.

Proper names,* both of persons and places, are omitted for obvious reasons.

It has, however, been deemed desirable, in a few cases, to discriminate, with greater precision than usual, between sounds that closely assimilate; hence double lists of words in EW, OW, IVE, OVE, and Y, &c. are given.

Some few *obsolete* and *provincial* words, as well as a sprinkling of *slang* terms that are current and unobjectionable, have been inserted, as English rhymesters can ill afford to reject any material that is at all suitable to their purpose. In many such cases, however, it has been deemed fit to add short notes of explanation, or credentials of respectability. Space has been found also for a limited

---

* The vagaries of pronunciation, troublesome enough in ordinary words, become absolutely bewildering in proper names, a few instances of which are subjoined :—

Beauchamp (*beecham*).	Dillwyn (*dillon*).
Belvoir (*bever*).	Knollys (*nowls*).
Caius (*kees*).	Leveson (*lewson*).
Cholmondeley (*chumley*).	St. John (*sinjon*).
Colquhoun (*cohoon*).	Wemyss (*weems*).

It seems to be an inalienable right in every man to pronounce his name as he likes. If Mr. Smith wishes to call himself *Smythe*, there is no power on earth to prevent him. In fact, he can go much farther than this and change his name altogether with very little trouble—as a Mr. Bug did some years ago by advertising in *The Times* that henceforth he desired to be known as Mr. Norfolk-Howard! A curious instance of the uncertainty of the sound of proper names is furnished by the word Ralph. Not very long ago a lady visitor at Aldworth, Tennyson's seat, had occasion to use the word several times, and pronounced is as rhyming with *safe*. Tennyson insisted, with some vigour, that it should be sounded as *half*. "But why," a gentleman of that name might ask, "should I be done out of my *l* ?"

number of *technical* and *foreign* words with which most Englishmen are familiar.*

* Mr. W. S. Gilbert, writing some time ago in a humorous letter to the *Dramatic Review* on the paucity of rhymes in our tongue, says, "I should like to suggest that any inventor who is in need of a name for his invention would confer a boon on all rhymsters, and at the same time ensure himself many gratuitous advertisements if he were to select a word that rhymes to one of the many words in common use that have very few rhymes or none at all. A few more words rhyming to *love* are greatly wanted. *Revenge* and *avenge* have no rhyme but *Penge* and *Stonehenge*; *coif* has no rhyme at all. *Starve* has no rhyme except (O irony!) *carve*. *Scarf* has no rhyme, though I fully expect to be told that *laugh, calf* and *half* are admissible—which they certainly are not. *Scalp* has no rhyme but *Alp*; *false* has none—*valse* is near it, but the French accent disqualifies it; *waltz* is also near it, but the *t* spoils it. *Gamboge* has no rhyme but *rouge*. *Tube* would be rhymeless but for *cube* and *jujube*. *Fugue* has no rhyme at all, nor has *gulf*, unless we fall back on *Cardinal Pandulph*, and *Ulf* the minstrel. *Azimuth* has only *doth.*"

DICTIONARY OF RHYMES.

A *compare* ER, OR

asthma	aurora
comma	chimera
dogma	cupola
drama	dahlia
era	dilemma
gala	duenna
hydra	flotilla
polka	formula
sofa	fuchsia
stanza	gondola
stigma	gorilla
strata	iota
villa	madonna
vista	nebula
agenda	orchestra
algebra	regatta
area	sepia
arcana	siesta
armada	sonata
aroma	umbrella

veranda	neuralgia
ambrosia	panacea
anathema	panorama
camelia	parabola
cyclopedia	paraphernalia
dyspepsia	paranomasia
effluvia	phenomena
euthanasia	regalia
extravaganza	sciatica
fantasia	taffeta
hysteria	terracotta
inertia	walhalla
influenza	

AB

blab *	drab
cab	gab
crab	knab †
dab	scab

* This has become almost a vulgarism, but has been employed by some of our best writers.

The secret man heareth many confessions ; for who will open himself to a *blab* or babbler ?—*Bacon.*

Sorrow nor joy can be disguised by art ;
Our foreheads *blab* the secrets of our heart.—*Dryden.*

When my tongue *blabs*, then let my eyes not see.—*Shakspere.*

† An obsolete form of *nab*, to gnaw, seize with the teeth.

I had much rather lie *knabbing* crusts, without fear, than be mistress of the world with cares.—*L'Estrange.*

slab	habnab *
stab	*babe*
tab	

AC, ACK

back	rack §
black	sac
brach †	sack
brack ‡	slack
clack	smack
crack	snack ‖
hack	stack
knack	tack
lac	thwack ¶
lack	track
pack	whack
plaque	wrack
quack	arrack

attack	symposiac
lilac	aphrodisiac
nick-nack	dypsomaniac
almanac	hypocondriac
cardiac	salammoniac
celiac	*opaque*
iliac	*break*
maniac	*take*
zodiac	*neck*
demoniac	*speak*
elegiac	

ACE **

ace	chase
base	dace
brace	face
case	grace

* A vulgarism, contracted from *hap-ne-hap*, let it happen or not; at all risks; at the mercy of chance.

> Cursed be they that build their hopes on *haps.*—*Sidney.*

† A bitch hound—still current in the Eastern counties.

> Truth's a dog that must to kennel; he must be whipped out, while Lady the *brach*, may stand by the fire and stink.—*Shakspere.*

‡ Obsolete. A flaw, a crack.

> A *brack* in the stuff.—*Beaumont and Fletcher.*

§ In addition to the many ordinary meanings of this word, it is used vulgarly for *wreck*, in the phrase *rack and ruin*; and is also cognate with *reek*, vapour, mist.

> The clouds above which we call the *rack.*—*Bacon.*

> Leave not a *rack* behind.—*Shakspere.*

‖ A colloquialism from *snatch*,—a slight hasty meal; a share; to go shares, to go snacks.

¶ A vulgarism.

> With many a stiff *thwack*, many a bang,
> Hard crab-tree and old iron rang.—*Hudibras.*

> We'll *thwack* him hence with distaffs.—*Shakspere.*

** Then gladly turning sought his ancient *place*,
> And passed a life of piety and *peace.*—*Parnell.*

> By a stream side, on the *grass*:—
> On her shining hair and *face.*—*E. B. Browning.*

> All its allotted length of *days*,
> The flower ripens in its *place.*—*Tennyson.*

> From belt to belt of crimson *seas*—
> A hundred spirits whisper, " *Peace.*"—*Tennyson.*

lace
mace
pace
place
plaice
race
space
trace
abase
aggrace *
apace
birthplace
debase
deface
disgrace
displace
efface
embrace
grimace

horserace
misplace
necklace
outface
outpace
replace
retrace
solace
surface
terrace
unlace
interlace
populace
grass
cease
less
daze
scarce †

ACT

act
fact
fract
pact
tact
tract
attract
co-act
compact
contact
contract
detract
abstract
distract
enact
epact
exact
extract

impact
infract
protract
react
refract
retract
diffract
subact
subtract
transact
cataphract ‡
cataract
counteract
incompact
precontract
re-enact
bak'd
rak'd, &c.

Also the preterites of verbs in
ach, as tack'd.

ACH, ATCH

batch
catch
hatch
latch
match
patch
ratch
scratch
smatch

snatch
swatch
thatch
attach
despatch
detach
watch
wretch
botch

AD

add
bad
brad
cad §
clad
dad ‖
fad
gad
glad
had
lad
mad
pad

plaid
quod
rad
sad
shad
wad
dryad
footpad
monad
salad
fade
red
sod

ACHE (*see* AKE)

---

* Antiquated: favour, kindness.—Used by *Spenser.*

† This word has no exact rhyme.

‡ Now uncommon, but frequently employed in Feudal times; a species of armour used to defend the breast or whole body; a horseman in complete armour; one armed cap-à-pie.

    Archers and slingers, *cataphracts* and spears.—*Milton.*

§ From *cadet*, a younger son, a minor; hence a dependent, a mean fellow.

‖ A pet name for father, like *mam* for mother; both words no doubt representing the earliest articulate sounds of an infant—ma-ma, da-da.

X

ADE *

aid	abraid ¶	persuade	fusilade
bade	afraid	pervade	gasconade
blade	arcade	relaid	lemonade
braid	blockade	tirade	marmalade
cade	brigade	unlade	masquerade
dade †	brocade	upbraid	overlade
fade	cascade	accolade	palisade
glade	chamade	ambuscade	pasquinade
grade	cockade	barricade	renegade
hade ‡	crusade	bastinade	retrograde
jade	decade	cannonade	serenade
lade	degrade	cavalcade	*bad*
made	dissuade	centigrade	*bead*
maid	evade	colonnade	*head*
raid	façade	esplanade	
shade	gambade **		
slade §	grenade		
spade	invade		
trade	milkmaid		
vade ‖	parade		

Also the preterites of verbs in *ay*, *ey*, *eigh*, as prey'd, sleigh'd.

ADGE

badge	fadge ††
cadge	

* In genial spring beneath the quivering *shade*,
  Where curling vapours breathe along the *mead*.
  > *Pope.*
  Since when a boy, he plied his *trade*,
  Till on his life the sickness *weigh'd*.
  > *R. Browning.*
  Then to the still small voice I *said;*
  Let me not cast to endless *shade*,
  What is so wonderfully *made*.
  > *Tennyson.*

† Obsolete. To lead, as a child just learning to walk; to walk slowly or unsteadily, as a child just beginning to go alone.
  No sooner taught to *dade*, than from their mother trip.—*Drayton.*

‡ Obsolete. The descent of a hill.
  On the lower lees, as on the higher *hades*,
  The dainty clover grows.—*Drayton.*

§ Obsolete. A flat low piece of ground; a dale; a valley. Employed by *Drayton.*

‖ Obsolete. To vanish; to pass away; to go hastily or rapidly. Employed by *Spenser.*

¶ Obsolete. To arouse; to awake. Employed by *Spenser.*

** Obsolete. From *gambado*, a leather case attached to a stirrup; a cover for the leg worn over other clothing; a gaiter.

†† Obsolete. To be suitable; to suit; to fit.
  Clothes I must get; this fashion will not *fadge* with me.
  > *Beaumont and Fletcher.*
  To live in concord or amity; to agree.
  They shall be made, spite of antipathy, to *fadge* together.—*Milton.*
In Scotland it is still sometimes used, and is applied to a bundle of sticks; a covering of rough leather; a bannock.

AFE *

chafe	vouchsafe
naif	*leaf*
safe	*deaf*
waif	*laugh*
unsafe	

AFF, ALF

chaff †	riff-raff
draff	tipstaff
gaff	cenotaph
graff ‡	epitaph
laugh	paragraph
naff	quarter-staff
quaff	*calf*
staff	*half*
carafe	*safe*
distaff	*dwarf*
giraffe	

AFT

aft	raft
craft	shaft
daft §	waft
draft	abaft
draught	ingraft
graft	handicraft
haft	

Also the preterites of verbs in
aff, augh, as quaff'd.

AG

bag	quag
brag	rag
cag	sag
crag	scrag
dag ‖	shag
drag	slag
fag	snag ¶
flag	stag
gag	swag
hag	tag
jag	wag
knag	tag-rag
lag	zig-zag
nag	

AGE, *compare* IDGE

age	boskage ††
cage	cabbage
gage	corsage
gauge	cortege
page	courage
rage	cribbage
sage	dotage
stage	engage
suage **	enrage
swage	hostage
wage	marriage
adage	manage
assuage	menage
baggage	message

---

* And authors think their reputation *safe,*
　　Which lives as long as fools are pleased to *laugh.—Pope.*

† Note the distinction in sound between the narrow *a* of the North
and its broader sound, for the most part, in the South, as in chăff, châff.—
(chaf-charf).

‡ Obsolete. To graft.
　　Now let me *graff* my pears and prune the vine.—*Dryden.*

§ A provincialism. Silly; stupid. The Scotch meaning is playful;
frolicsome.

‖ A dagger; a slip: to form dew; drizzle.

¶ A protuberance; a knot; a shoot: also, to hew roughly; to wreck—
probably derived from snack, snatch.

** Obsolete. Now written *assuage.*
　　Nor wanting power to mitigate and *swage*
　　With solemn touches, troubled thoughts.—*Milton.*

†† A grove; foliage.
　　Thridding the sombre *boskage* of the wood.—*Tennyson*

mirage	foliage	wail	impale
mortgage	heritage	wale	prevail
passage	hermitage	whale	regale
peerage	parentage	assail	retail
potage	parsonage	avail	wassail *
presage	pasturage	blackmail	wholesale
salvage	patronage	bewail	aventail
sausage	percentage	curtail	countervail
scutage	personage	detail	farthingale
village	pilgrimage	entail	nightingale
wreckage	villanage	exhale	*seal*
appanage	concubinage	female	*sell*
appendage	*edge*		
disengage	*siege*		
equipage	*ridge*		

AID (*see* ADE)

AIL—ALE

ale	pail
bail	pale
bale	quail
brail	rail
dale	sail
fail	sale
flail	scale
frail	shale
gale	snail
grail	stale
hail	swale
hale	tail
jail	tale
mail	trail
male	vale
nail	veil

AIM—AME†

aim	acclaim
blame	became
came	declaim
claim	defame
dame	disclaim
fame	exclaim
flame	inflame
frame	misname
game	nickname
lame	proclaim
maim	reclaim
name	surname
frame	overcame
same	*ham*
shame	*hem*
tame	*dream*

AIN—ANE‡

bane	brain
blain	cane

---

* A.S., *waes hael*, health be to you; a toast, a drinking bout, a convivial song.

> Have you done your *wassail*?—*Beaumont and Fletcher.*

† Even here I sing, when Pope supplies the *theme*,
Show my own love, though not increase his *fame.—Parnell.*

‡ Thus in the scale of life and sense 'tis *plain*,
There must be somewhere such a rank as *man.—Pope.*

And black misfortune's baleful *train* !
Ah, tell them they are *men.—Gray.*

chain	amain	quaint	constraint
crane	arraign	saint	distraint
deign	attain	taint	restraint
drain	campaign	acquaint	*rant*
fain	champagne	attaint	*rent*
fane	complain	complaint	
feign	constrain		
gain	contain		**AIR—ARE †**
grain	curtain		
lain	detain	air	tear (verb)
lane	disdain	bare	there
main	distrain	bear	ware
mane	domain	care	wear
pain	enchain	chair	where
pane	explain	dare	yare
plain	henbane	e'er	affair
plane	maintain	ere	armchair
rain	murrain	fair	aware
reign	obtain	fare	beware
rein	ordain	flare	coheir
sane	pertain	gare	compare
skein	profane	glair	declare
slain	refrain	glare	despair
sprain	regain	hair	elsewhere
stain	remain	hare	ensnare
strain	restrain	heir	forbear
swain	retain	lair	forswear
thane	sustain	mare	howe'er
train	appertain	ne'er	impair
twain	entertain	pair	prepare
vain	hurricane	pare	repair
vane	*mean*	pear	whate'er
vein	*scene*	scare	whene'er
wain	*pan*	share	where'er
wane	*pen*	snare	debonnair
abstain		spare	howsoe'er
		square	millionaire
	AINT *	stair	*car*
		stare	*her*
faint	mayn't	swear	*were*
feint	plaint	tare	*hear*

* When in the sultry glebe I *faint*,
Or on the thirsty mountain *pant.—Addison.*

† To sing those honours you deserve to *wear*,
And add new lustre to her silver *star.—Pope.*
There was no motion in the dumb dead *air*,
Gross darkness of the inner *sepulchre.—Tennyson.*

AIRS—ARES

theirs　　　　　　unawares

And the plurals of nouns and the third persons singular of verbs in *are, air, eir* ; as mares, repairs.

AISE—AZE

blaze	raise
craze	raze
daze	amaze
gaze	cross-ways
glaze	paraphrase
graze	*ease*
maze	*seize*
phrase	*keys*
praise	*has*

Also the plurals of nouns and third person singular of verbs in *ay, ey, eigh* ; as lays, obeys, weighs.

AIT—ATE *

bait	slate
bate	straight
date	strait
eight	wait
fate	abate
gait	await
gate	belate
grate	collate
great	create
hate	cremate
late	debate
mate	dilate
pate	elate
plate	estate
prate	frustrate
rate	ingrate
sate	innate

irate	desolate
migrate	desperate
narrate	dislocate
prostrate	dissipate
rebate	educate
relate	elevate
sedate	emigrate
translate	emulate
abdicate	estimate
abrogate	extricate
accurate	formulate
adequate	fornicate
advocate	fortunate
aggravate	generate
agitate	hesitate
alienate	hibernate
animate	imitate
annotate	immolate
antedate	impetrate
apostate	imprecate
arbitrate	innovate
arrogate	instigate
aspirate	intimate
cachinate	intricate
calculate	irritate
candidate	inundate
captivate	magistrate
castigate	meditate
celebrate	micturate
celibate	mitigate
circulate	moderate
congregate	nominate
consecrate	obstinate
contemplate	oscillate
cultivate	passionate
dedicate	penetrate
delegate	perforate
delicate	perpetrate
deprecate	personate
derogate	potentate

---

* Beauty is seldom fortunate when *great*,
A vast estate, but overcharged with *debt*.
　　　　　　　　　　　　Dryden.

If thirst of knowledge shall not then *abate*—
—Then like one who with the *weight*, *&c.*
　　　　　　　　　　　　Shelley.

predicate
profligate
propagate
regulate
reprobate
ruminate
rusticate
separate
stipulate
subjugate
suffocate
syndicate
terminate
tête-à-tête
titivate
tolerate
triturate
vindicate
violate
abominate
accelerate
accentuate
accommodate
accumulate
adulterate
affectionate
annihilate
anticipate
articulate
assassinate
capacitate
capitulate
chalybeate
coagulate
commemorate
commiserate
communicate
compassionate

confederate
congratulate
considerate
contaminate
co-operate
corroborate
debilitate
degenerate
deliberate
denominate
depopulate
disconsolate
discriminate
effeminate
elaborate
emancipate
emasculate
equivocate
eradicate
evaporate
exaggerate
exasperate
expectorate
expostulate
exterminate
facilitate
illiterate
illuminate
immoderate
importunate
inanimate
initiate
insatiate
intemperate
intimidate
intoxicate
invalidate
investigate

inveterate
inviolate
legitimate
matriculate
necessitate
participate
precipitate
predestinate
predominate
premeditate
prevaricate
procrastinate

prognosticate
recriminate
regenerate
reiterate
reverberate
subordinate
unfortunate
weight
height
heat
bet

AITH, ATH (*see* EATH)

AKE * *compare* EAK

ache
bake
brake
break
cake
drake
fake
flake
hake
lake
make
quake
rake
sake
shake
snake
spake
stake
steak

take
wake
awake
bespake
betake
corn-crake
forsake
keepsake
mandrake
mistake
namesake
partake
overtake
snowflake
undertake
rack
neck
weak
check

---

* Sparkle in Jenny's e'e, and flush her *cheek ;*
Wi' heart-struck anxious care, enquires his name,
While Jenny hafflins is afraid to *speak ;*
Weel pleased the mother hears, it's nae wild worthless *rake*
                                                    Burns.

There in two sable ringlets taught to *break*.
One gave new beauties to the snowy *neck.*
                                    Pope.

AL *

mall †	capital
pal	cardinal
shall	carnival
cabal	comical
canal	conjugal
cymbal	cordial
dismal	corporal
dual	criminal
equal	critical
feudal	decimal
final	festival
formal	funeral
legal	general
loyal	genial
martial	hospital
medal	inimical
metal	initial
mettle	interval
mortal	liberal
naval	literal
partial	littoral
pedal	madrigal
portal	magical
rival	medical
regal	mineral
royal	municipal
rural	musical
total	mystical
trivial	natural
admiral	nocturnal
animal	octagonal
annual	pastoral
arsenal	pedestal
autumnal	personal
cannibal	physical

principal	imperial
prodigal	intellectual
rational	original
seneschal	poetical
several	political
sepulchral	problematical
temporal	prophetical
terminal	reciprocal
tragical	rhetorical
whimsical	satirical
colloquial	sempiternal
dogmatical	schismatical
equinoctial	tyrannical
equivocal	*all*
hymeneal	*ale*

ALD

bald	piebald
scald	emerald

Also the preterites of verbs in *all, awl;* as call'd, bawl'd.

ALE (*see* AIL)

ALF (*see* AFF)

ALK—AUK *compare* ORK

auk	stalk
balk	talk
baulk	walk
calk	tomahawk
chalk	*soak*
hawk	*catafalque*
mawk	

* Unfinished things one knows not what to *call,*
 Their generations so *equivocal.*
 Pope.

† A wooden hammer, a mallet; also the blow struck by one.
 And give that reverend head a *mall,*
 Or two or three, against a *wall.*
 Butler.

 Note that the walk in St. James's Park is pronounced The Mâll, whereas
the neighbouring street Pall-Mall is sounded pĕll-mĕll,

ALL

awl	small
ball	sprawl
bawl	squall
brawl	stall
call	tall
caul	thrall
crawl	trawl
drawl	wall
fall	appal
gall	enthral
hall	football
haul	install
mall	waterfall
pall	windfall
scrawl	*cabal*
shawl	

ALM (*see* ARM)

ALT

fault	assault
halt	default
malt	exalt
salt	*dolt*
vault	*thought*
asphalt	

ALVE

calve	salve
halve	*valve*

AM

cam	bedlam
clam	beldam
cram	madam
dam	quondam
damn	wigwam
dram	anagram §
flam *	amalgam
ham	diagram
jamb	diaphragm
kam †	epigram
lamb	monogram
pam ‡	oriflamb
ram	telegram
sham	parallelogram
swam	*dame*

AME (*see* AIM)

AMP

camp	stamp
champ	swamp
clamp	vamp
cramp	decamp
damp	encamp
lamp	*pomp*
scamp	

---

* Obsolete. A freak, whim, illusion, deceit.

Cant and cheat, *flam* and delusion.—*South.*

† Obsolete. Crooked, awry.

This is clean *kam.*—*Shakspere.*

‡ Pam from palm, as trump from triumph.—*Johnson.* Used by Pope for the knave of clubs.

§ Anagram, a word or sentence formed by transposing the letters or another word or sentence : e.g. *William Noy* (attorney-general to Charles I.) —*I moyl in law ; Horatio Nelson—Honor est a Nilo.*

Live, vile, and *evil* have the selfsame letters ;
They *live* but *vile* whom *evil* holds in fetters.

AN *

ban	trepan
bran	unman
can	artisan
clan	barracan
fan	caravan
man	charlatan
pan	christian
plan	courtesan
ran	musician
scan	oppidan
span	ortolan
swan	ottoman
tan	partisan
van	pelican
wan	publican
began	cosmopolitan
divan	attitudinarian
foreran	latitudinarian
organ	platitudinarian
orphan	*on*
pagan	*won*
sedan	*pain*

ANCE

chance	expanse
dance	intrance
glance	mischance
lance	romance
prance	séance
trance	ambulance
advance	arrogance
askance	circumstance
balance	complaisance
enhance	concordance

consonance	temperance
countenance	utterance
defiance	vigilance
dissonance	deliverance
ignorance	exorbitance
importance	extravagance
maintenance	exuberance
ordinance	inheritance
purveyance	intemperance
sufferance	*hence*
sustenance	*pretence*

ANCH

blanch	paunch
branch	ranche
ganch	stanch
haunch	carte-blanche
launch	

AND

band	command
bland	demand
brand	disband
gland	expand
grand	withstand
hand	contraband
land	countermand
rand †	deodand
sand	reprimand
stand	understand
strand	*stain'd*
wand	*send*

ANE (*see* AIN)

---

* To give my counsels all in *one*,
 The tuneful flame still careful *fan ;*
Preserve the dignity of *man.*
     Burns.

† Obsolete. A border, seam, shred.
   To cut me into *rands.—Beaumont and Fletcher*
 Also, with cordwainers, a thin inner sole, as of cork.

ANG

bang	slang
clang	stang *
fang	swang
gang	tang †
hang	twang
pang	harangue
rang	*long*
sang	

ANGE

change	estrange
grange	exchange
range	interchange
strange	*revenge*
arrange	

ANK

bank	brank ‡
blank	clank

crank	rank
dank §	shank
drank	slank
frank	spank
hank	stank
lank ‖	thank
plank	disrank
prank	mountebank

ANSE (*see* ANCE)

ANT ¶

ant	aslant
aunt	displant
cant	enchant
chant	gallant
grant	implant
pant	merchant
plant	mordant
rant	rampant
slant	recant

---

* Obsolete. A measure of land, a perch, a long pole, shaft.

Riding the stang was a rude outcome of popular indignation against wife beaters and such-like offenders, which was prevalent in Yorkshire some forty or fifty years ago. The youth of a neighbourhood would assemble, and mount one of their number upon a pole borne upon the shoulders of others. Gathering a noisy crowd they would go round the district denouncing the evil-doer in a strange rigmarole of imprecations, which they brought to a climax in front of the offender's house.

† Probably from sting : a strong flavour, a piercing sound, a twang.

The least *tang* of misery.—*Scott.*

She had a tongue with a *tang*,
Would cry to a sailor, go hang.—*Shakspere.*

‡ Obsolete. A bridle, an instrument formerly used for punishing scolds
—*(Halliwell).*

§ Damp, wet, moisture.

Folds his *dank* wing beneath the ivy shade.—*Heber.*

The *dank* of winter.—*Marston.*

‖ Thin, empty, languid.

My body *lank* and lean.—*Gascoigne.*

A *lank* purse.—*Barrow.*

He, piteous of her woes, reared her *lank* head.—*Milton.*

¶ No nightingale did ever *chant*,
More welcome notes to weary bands
Of travellers, in some shady *haunt*.
Wordsworth.

remnant	miscreant	enwrap	*top*
servant	petulant	mishap	*heap*
supplant	poignant	*tape*	
tenant	protestant		
transplant	recreant		
adamant	recusant		**APE**
arrogant	ruminant	ape	scape
combatant	termagant	cape	scrape
complaisant	vigilant	chape	shape
consonant	visitant	crape	tape
conversant	exorbitant	drape	trape §
cormorant	extravagant	grape	escape
covenant	inhabitant	jape	*heap*
disputant	predominant	nape	*sleep*
dissonant	significant	rape	
dominant	*want*		
elegant	*font*		
elephant	*can't*	**APH** (*see* **AFF**)
ignorant	*upon't*		
jubilant	*faint*		
lieutenant	*tent*	**APSE**
militant	*haunt*		
		lapse	*capes*
		elapse	*trapse*
		perhaps	*heaps*
		relapse	

Also the plurals of nouns, and the third person singular of verbs in *ap*; as maps, raps.

AP

cap	pap
chap	rap
clap	sap
dap	scrap
fap *	slap
flap	snap
gap	strap
hap	tap
knap†	trap
lap	wrap
map	affrap ‡
nap	entrap

APT

apt	*ap'd*
adapt	*escap'd*

Also the preterites of verbs in *ap*; as rapp'd.

AQUE (*see* **ACK**)

* Obsolete. Fuddled, drunk; used by *Shakspere.*
† To break short, to gnash. *Knapped ginger.—Shakspere.*
‡ Obsolete. To strike down.

    Affrap the warlike rider.—*Spenser.*

§ Obsolete. To loiter, to trapse: used by *Swift.*

AR *

are	hookah
bar	hussar
car	liar
char	mortar
far	nectar
jar	unbar
mar	angular
pa	avatar
par	calendar
scar	caviare
spar	cinnabar
star	popular
tar	regular
war	secular
afar	scimitar
bazaar	singular
briar	titular
cellar	vinegar
catarrh	particular
cigar	perpendicular
collar	*bare*
debar	*wear*
durbar	*ear*
felspar	*sailor*
friar	*saviour*
guitar	

ARB

barb	rhubarb
garb	*herb*

ARCE—ARSE

farce	sarse †
parse	sparse

ARCH *compare* ARK & ARSH

arch	starch
larch	countermarch
march	*church*
parch	*search*

ARD

bard	dastard
card	discard
guard	dotard
hard	drunkard
lard	leopard
nard	niggard
pard ‡	petard
shard	regard
sward	renard
ward	retard
yard	vineyard
bastard	wizard
blackguard	disregard
blizzard	interlard
bombard	*reward*
charade	*lord*
costard §	*aboard*
coward	*restored*
custard	

Also the preterites of verbs in
ar ; as barr'd,

---

* Late as I ranged the crystal fields of *air*,
In the clear mirror of thy ruling *star*.

Pope.

When tempests *war*—
And the pale dalesmen watch with eager *ear*.

Shelley.

† Obsolete. A sieve, to sift.
‡ Leopard or panther in poetry.

Bearded like a *pard.—Shakspere.*

§ A kind of apple, the head.

Take him over the *costard* with the hilt of thy sword.

Shakspere.

ARF (*see* AFF)

ARGE

barge	o'ercharge
charge	surcharge
large	*verge*
marge	*urge*
discharge	*forge*
enlarge	

ARK

arc	spark
ark	stark
bark	embark
cark	monarch
clerk	remark
dark	hierarch
lark	heresiarch
mark	*fork*
park	*lurk*
shark	

ARL

carl	snarl
gnarl	*curl*
marl	*girl*
parle	

ARM

arm	calm
balm	charm
barm	farm

harm	disarm
palm	gendarme
psalm	salaam
qualm	*swarm*
alarm	*storm*
becalm	

ARN

barn	*warn*
darn	*horn*
tarn	*pawn*
yarn	*earn*

ARP

carp	counterscarp
harp	*warp*
sharp	*thorp***

ARSH (*see also* ARCH)

harsh	*march*
marsh	

ART †

art	braggart
cart	depart
dart	dispart
hart	impart
heart	counterpart
mart	*quart*
part	*port*
smart	*dirt*
start	*hurt*
tart	*court*
apart	

* A hamlet.
> By thirty hills to hurry down,
> By twenty *thorps*, a little town.
> > *Tennyson.*

† The Power, incens'd the pageant will *desert*,
But haply, in some cottage far *apart*.
> > *Burns.*

Thou friend whose presence on my wintry *heart*,
How beautiful and calm and free thou *wert*.
> > *Shelley.*

ARTH (*see* EARTH)

ARVE

carve	*nerve*
starve	

AS *

ass	morass
brass	repass
class	surpass
crass	coup de grace
grass	embarrass
lass	erysipelas
mass	*has*
pass	*mace*
alas	*base*
amass	*toss*
cuirass	*was*
harass	

ASE (*see* ACE)

ASH

ash	pash
bash	plash
brash	rash
cash	sash
clash	slash
crash	smash
dash	thrash
flash	trash
gash	abash
gnash	*wash*
hash	*bosh*
lash	*quash*
mash	

ASK

ask	flask
bask	hask
cask	mask

ASM

chasm	cataplasm
spasm	enthusiasm
miasm	protoplasm
phantasm	*theism*
sarcasm	*euphemism*

ASP

asp	hasp
clasp	rasp
gasp	*wasp*
grasp	*wisp*

ASS (*see* AS)

AST †

blast	bombast
cast	forecast
caste	repast
fast	outcast
mast	overcast
last	enthusiast
past	iconoclast
vast	*cost*
aghast	*taste*
avast	*plac'd*

Also the preterites of verbs in *ass*; as mass'd.

ASTE

baste	haste
chaste	paste

* Let them *pass.*—
Is not so much more glorious than it *was.*
> *Shelley.*

§ And lay thy glories *waste*,
Unconscious of the *blast.*
> *Beattie.*

taste	*past*
waist	*rest*
waste	*dress'd*
distaste	

Also the preterites of verbs in *ace, ase;* as lac'd, chas'd.

AT

bat	spot
brat	sprat
cat	tat
chat	that
fat	vat
flat	cravat
gnat	cushat
hat	polecat
mat	acrobat
pat	*what*
rat	*not*
sat	*hate*

ATCH (*see* ACH)

ATE (*see* AIT)

ATH (*see* EATH)

ATHE (*see* EATHE)

AUB (*see* OB)

AUD

bawd	applaud
broad	defraud
fraud	*ode*
laud	*load*
abroad	*old*

And the preterites of verbs in *aw;* as caw'd.

AUGH (*see* AFF)

AUGHT (*see* AFT—ORT)

AUK (*see* ALK)

AUN (*see* AWN)

AUNT *compare* ANT

daunt	vaunt
gaunt	avaunt
haunt	*ant*
jaunt	*can't*
taunt	

AUSE—AUZE

cause	applause
clause	because
gauze	*was*
pause	

Also the plurals of nouns and the third person singular of verbs in *aw;* as laws, caws.

AVE

brave	slave
cave	stave
crave	wave
gave	behave
grave	deprave
knave	engrave
lave	forgave
nave	margrave
pave	outbrave
rave	architrave
save	*have*
shave	

AW

chaw	saw
claw	squaw
craw	straw
daw	thaw
draw	foresaw
flaw	cat's-paw
gnaw	guffaw
haw	hawhaw
jaw	jackdaw
law	withdraw
maw	overawe
paw	usquebaugh
raw	

AWL (*see* ALL)

AWN *compare* ORN

awn	pawn
brawn	prawn
dawn	spawn
drawn	yawn
fawn	withdrawn
lawn	

AX

axe	poll-tax
flax	nicknacks
lax	relax
tax	thorax
wax	parallax
borax	*cakes*
climax	*takes*
gimcracks	

Also the plurals of nouns, and the third person singular of verbs in *ak;* as backs, lacks.

AY *

aye †	away
bray	ballet
clay	belay
day	betray
dray	bewray
eh ?	convey
fay	decay
flay	defray
fray	delay
gay	denay
grey	dismay
hay	display
jay	essay
lay	gainsay
may	horseplay
nay	hurrah
neigh	inlay
pay	inveigh
play	levée
pray	obey
prey	portray
ray	purvey
say	relay
slay	repay
spray	soirée
stay	subway
stray	survey
sway	tramway
they	déjeuner
tray	disarray
tway	disobey
way	matinée
weigh	roundelay
whey	stowaway
affray	runaway
allay	cabriolet
array	*tea*
astray	*fee*

---

* Th' ethereal coursers bounding from the *sea*,
From out their flaming nostrils breath'd the *day.—Dryden.*

† Aye **ever,** is pronounced as *ay* in day. Ay, aye, the affirmative, as the word *eye,* as in " The ayes have it."

Y

AZE (*see* AISE)

CRE, CHRE (*see* ER)

E, EA (*see* EE)

EACE, EASE*

cease	decease
geese	decrease
grease	increase
fleece	release
lease	surcease
niece	frontispiece
peace	*less*
piece	*lace*
apiece	*miss*
caprice	*lees*

EACH

beach	reach
bleach	teach
breach	impeach
each	*beech*
peach	*etch*
preach	

EAD (*see* EDE *and* EED)

EAF (*see* IEF)

EAGUE

league	renege
teague	*vague*
fatigue	*beg*
intrigue	

EAK † *compare* AKE

Words in *eek* may be allowed to pass as almost perfect rhymes with *beak*.

beak	sneak
bleak	speak
cheek	squeak
clique	streak
creak	teak
creek	tweak ‡
eke	weak
freak	week
leak	wreak
leek	antique
meek	bezique
peak	bespeak
pique	critique
reek	oblique
seek	*break*
sheik	*brake*
shriek	*thick*
sleek	

EAL, EEL§

deal	heal
deil	heel
eel	keel
feel	kneel

---

* 　　　　Lest we rust in *ease*,
We all are changed by still *degrees.*
　　　　　　　　　　Tennyson.

† The wreathed serpent who did ever *seek*
Upon his enemy's heart a mortal wound to *wreak.*
　　　　　　　　　　Shelley.

‡ To pull rudely, pinch.
　　　Who calls me villain, breaks my pate across,
　　Tweaks me by the nose.
　　　　　　　　　　Shakspere.

§ Or, as Ixion fix'd, the wretch shall *feel*
The giddy motion of the whirling *mill.*
　　　　　　　　　　Pope.

leal	wheal
meal	wheel
peal	zeal
peel	anneal
reel	appeal
seal	conceal
squeal	congeal
steal	repeal
steel	reveal
teal	*tell*
veal	*tale*
weal	*till*

EALM—ELM

elm	whelm
helm	overwhelm
realm	*film*

EALTH

health	wealth
stealth	commonwealth

EAM—EEM

beam	ream
bream	scheme
cream	scream
deem	seam
dream	seem
gleam	stream

team	extreme
teem	misdeem
theme	redeem
beseem	supreme
beteem *	*him*
blaspheme	*ethm*
esteem	*name*

EAMT—EMPT

dreamt	contempt
tempt	exempt
attempt	

EAN †—EEN

Words in *een* may be allowed to pass as almost perfect rhymes to *bean*.

bean	sheen
clean	seen
dean	skein
e'en	spleen
glean	teen
green	wean
keen	ween
lean	yean §
mean	between
mien	canteen
quean ‡	careen
queen	convene
screen	demean

* Obsolete : to bestow, permit, suffer.

> So loving to my mother,
> That he might not *beteem* the winds of heaven
> Visit her face too roughly.
> *Shakspere.*

† A sordid god, down from his hoary *chin*
> A length of beard descends, uncomb'd, *unclean.*
> *Dryden.*

‡ A worthless woman, a strumpet.
> A witch, a *quean*, an old cozening *quean.*
> *Shakspere.*

In Scotland the word is used not in a bad sense :—

> O, she was a dainty *quean.—Old Song.*

§ To bring forth young, to lamb. Used by *Dryden.*

demesne	margarine	deer	cohere
foreseen	nicotine	ear	compeer
machine	quarantine	fear	endear
obscene	submarine	fleer	revere
routine	tambourine	gear	severe
serene	vaseline	hear	sincere
terrene *	velveteen	here	veneer
unclean	*bane*	jeer	auctioneer
aniline	*ban*	leer	bandolier
crinoline	*been*	mere	buccaneer
guillotine	*bin*	near	chandelier
intervene		peer	chanticleer
		queer	chiffonier
		rear	disappear
EANT (*see* **ENT**)		sear	domineer
		seer	engineer
		sheer	gondolier
EAP		smear	hemisphere
cheap	sleep	sneer	interfere
creep	steep	spear	mountaineer
deep	sweep	sphere	muleteer
heap	weep	steer	musketeer
keep	asleep	tier	mutineer
neap	beweep	veer	persevere
peep	*ship*	year	pioneer
sheep	*shape*	adhere	privateer
		appear	charioteer
		austere	*dare*
EAR †		besmear	*fair*
beer	clear	career	*her*
cheer	dear		

* An adjective from *terra*, the earth.
  Advanced in honour and *terrene* power.
  Hooker.

Milton uses it as a noun :—
  The length of this *terrene.*

† Where I may oft outwatch the *Bear*
With thrice-great Hermes, or *unsphere*
The spirit of Plato.
  Milton.

Of man what see we but his station *here*,
From which to reason, or to which *refer.*
  Pope.

Think, ye may buy the joys o'er *dear :*
Remember Tam O'Shanter's *mare.*
  Burns.

EARCH (*see* ERCH)

EARD (*see* ERD)

EARL (*see* URL)

EARN (*see* ERN)

EART (*see* ART)

EARTH—ERTH *

berth	*worth*
birth	*swarth*
dearth	*hearth*
earth	*breath*
mirth	*north*

EAST †

beast	priest
east	*best*
feast	*list*
least	*hiss'd*

Also the preterites of verbs in *ease;* as ceas'd.

EAT, EET ‡

Words in *eet* may be allowed to pass as almost perfect rhymes to *beat.*

beat	complete
bleat	conceit
cheat	concrete
eat	deceit
feat	defeat
feet	discreet
fleet	discrete
greet	entreat
greit §	escheat
heat	estreat
meat	replete
meet	retreat
mete	obsolete
neat	plebiscite
seat	*bate*
sheet	*gait*
sleet	*great*
street	*bet*
sweet	*sweat*
treat	*hit*
wheat	

EATH, ETH ‖

baith	death
breath	faith

---

* Far from all resort of *mirth*
Save the cricket on the *hearth.*
Milton.

The holly round the Christmas *hearth*,
A rainy cloud possessed the *earth.*
Tennyson.

† And sometimes casts an eye upon the *east*,
And sometimes looks on the forbidden *west.*
Addison.

‡ With his morning-winged *feet*,
Whose bright print is gleaming *yet.*
Shelley.

§ Provincial : generally spelt *greet*, to weep
What gars thee *greit ?—Spenser.*

‖ Greet her with applausive *breath*
In her rignt a civic *wreath.*
Tennyson

heath	*hath*
neath	*wrath*
wraith	*rath* *
wreath	*teeth*
underneath	*cometh*
bath	

And the archaic third person singular of verbs.

EATHE

breathe	*bathe*
seethe	*scathe*
sheathe	*swathe*
wreathe	*wreath*
bequeathe	

EAVE

cleave	conceive
eave	deceive
eve	unweave
grieve	perceive
heave	receive
leave	relieve
sleeve	reprieve
thieve	disbelieve
weave	interleave
achieve	interweave
aggrieve	*live*
believe	*lave*
bereave	

EB, EBB

bleb	web
ebb	*babe*
neb †	*glebe*

ECK

beck	reck ‡
check	spec
deck	speck
fleck	wreck
geck	*bake*
neck	*beak*
peck	

ECT

sect	project
affect	protect
aspect	reflect
collect	reject
correct	respect
deject	select
direct	subject
dissect	suspect
detect	architect
effect	circumspect
eject	disaffect
elect	disrespect
erect	indirect
expect	intellect
infect	incorrect
inspect	recollect
neglect	retrospect
object	*leak'd*

Also the preterites of verbs in *ech;* as henpeck'd.

ED

bed	bred
bled	dead
bread	dread

---

* Or *rathe,* early, before the time. The adverb *rather* is the regularly formed comparative of it.

The *rath* primrose that forsaken dies.—*Milton.*

† Nose, beak: also a euphonic contraction for Ebenezer.

‡ To regard, take care of.

I *reck* as little what betideth me.—*Shakspere.*

Recks not his own rede.—*Shakspere.*

Little he'll *reck.*—*Wolfe.*

fed	tread
fled	wed
head	abed
lead	behead
read	homestead
red	instead
said	misled
shed	o'erspread
shred	*plead*
sped	*blade*
spread	*maid*
stead	*obey'd*
thread	

EDE (*see* EED)

EDGE *compare* AGE, IDGE

edge	wedge
fledge	allege
hedge	knowledge
kedge	*age*
ledge	*privilege*
pledge	*porridge*
sedge	

EE * (*see* Y, *second list*)

bee	key
dree †	knee
flea	lea
flee	lee
free	me
glee	ne
gree	plea
he	sea

see	devotee
she	disagree
spree	filigree
tea	jubilee
thee	jeu d'esprit
three	mortgagee
tree	nominee
agree	peccavi
bawbee	pedigree
decree	recipe
degree	referee
foresee	repartee
fusee	simile
grandee	vis-a-vis
houri	animalculæ
lessee	con amore
on dit	extempore
rupee	felo de se
trustee	fac simile
calipee	hyperbole
cap-a-pie	lapsus linguæ
committee	sotto voce
coterie	agapemone

Words ending in *y* short; as merry, symmetry.

EECE (*see* EACE)

EECH (*see* EACH)

EED, EDE ‡

bead	creed
bleed	deed
breed	feed

---

* Poets, a race long unconfin'd and free,
 Still fond and proud of savage *liberty*.
  Pope.

† Cognate with dry—long, tedious.

‡ In genial spring beneath the quiv'ring *shade*,
 Where cooling vapours breathe along the *mead*.
  Pope.

heed	exceed
knead	impede
lead	indeed
mead	linseed
meed	precede
need	proceed
plead	recede
read	succeed
rede*	stampede
seed	intercede
speed	supersede
steed	velocipede
weed	*made*
concede	*bed*
decreed	*bid*

EEF (*see* IEF)

EEK (*see* EAK)

EEL (*see* EAL)

EEM (*see* EAM)

EEN (*see* EAN)

EESE, EEZE

breeze	these
cheese	wheeze
ease	appease
freeze	disease
please	displease
seize	dives
sneeze	*images*
squeeze	*soliloquies*
tease	*place*

Also the plurals of nouns in *ee,*
ea ; as fees, seas.

EET (*see* EAT)

EF (*see* IEF)

EFT

cleft	bereft
left	*lift*
theft	*whiff`d*
weft	*laugh'd*

EG

beg	seg
egg	philabeg
leg	*league*
keg	*vague*
peg	

EGM (*see* EM)

EIGN (*see* AIN)

EIN (*see* AIN)

EINT (*see* AINT)

EIT (*see* EAT)

EL

bell	hell
belle	knell
cell	mell
dwell	quell
ell	sell
fell	shell

---

* Provincial.   Advice, to advise
     Recks not his own *rede.—Shakspere.*
     I *rede* you tent it.—*Burns.*

smell
spell
swell
tell
well
yell
befell
compel
dispel
excel
expel
foretell
gazelle
hotel
hovel
impel
laurel
libel
mongrel

petrel
rebel
repel
sorrel
towel
vowel
yokel
asphodel
calomel
citadel
doggerel
infidel
muscatel
parallel
sentinel
pole
peal
peel

ELD

eld
geld
held
beheld

upheld
withheld
heal'd
hail'd

Also the preterites of verbs in
ell; as swell'd.

ELF

delf
elf
pelf

self
shelf
himself

ELK

elk
kelk

whelk
milk

ELM (*see* EALM)

ELP

help
kelp

whelp
yelp

ELT

belt
dealt
dwelt
felt
gelt

melt
pelt
smelt
welt
hilt

ELVE

delve
helve

shelve
twelve

EM

gem
hem
kemb
phlegm
stem
them
anthem
condemn
contemn

anadem
apothegm
diadem
requiem
stratagem
tame
team
theme

EME (*see* EAM)

EMPT

dreamt
tempt
attempt
contempt

exempt
unkempt
prompt

EN

den
fen
hen
ken
men
pen
ten
then
wren
amen

cozen
dozen
foemen
frozen
hyphen
omen
open
oxen
seamen
semen

sharpen	denizen
syren	oxygen
vixen	*bane*
warden	*bean*
acumen	*been*
citizen	

ENCE, ENSE *

cense	silence
dense	suspense
fence	abstinence
hence	conference
pence	confidence
sense	consequence
thence	continence
whence	difference
commence	diffidence
condense	diligence
defence	eloquence
dispense	eminence
expense	evidence
immense	excellence
incense	frankincense
intense	inference
nonsense	impotence
offence	impudence
pretence	indigence
prepense	indolence
prudence	innocence

negligence	indifference
penitence	intelligence
preference	incontinence
providence	impenitence
recompense	impertinence
reference	improvidence
residence	magnificence
reverence	munificence
vehemence	omnipotence
violence	*dance*
benevolence	*cleanse*
circumference	*dens*
concupiscence	*scent*

ENCH

bench	tench
blench †	trench
clench	wench ‡
drench	wrench
quench	intrench
stench	retrench

END

bend	lend
blend	mend
end	rend
fend §	send
friend	spend

---

* Can ye listen in your *silence?*
Can your mystic voices tell us
Where ye hide? In floating *islands.*
                    E. B. Browning.

† Or *blanch*, to grow white, to flinch.

        I'll observe his looks;
I'll tent him to the quick : if he but *blench*
I know my course.

                    Shakspere.

‡ A maid, a girl, a strumpet.

A royal *wench.—Shakspere.*
A *wench* went and told them.—*II. Samuel xvii.* **17.**
I am a gentlewoman and no *wench.—Chaucer.*
Now, the word is provincial and vulgar.

§ To keep off, exclude, to fold.

    To *fend* the bitter cold.—*Dryden.*
    He *fends* his flock.—*Phillips.*

tend	offend	brent †	lament
vend	obtend	hent ‡	misspent
amend	portend	lent	o'erspent
ascend	pretend	pent	ostent
attend	protend	meant	present
befriend	suspend	rent	prevent
commend	transcend	scent	relent
contend	unbend	sent	repent
defend	apprehend	shent §	resent
depend	comprehend	spent	rodent
descend	condescend	tent	sergeant
distend	dividend	vent	solvent
expend	recommend	went	strident
extend	reprehend	absent	student
forefend	reverend	ascent	tangent
impend	*wean'd*	assent	torment
misspend	*fiend*	attent ‖	torrent

Also the preterites of verbs in *n;* as kenn'd.

ENE (see EAN)

ENGE

avenge	revenge

ENGTH

length	strength

ENT

bent	blent *

augment	unbent
cement	abasement
consent	accident
content	aliment
crescent	argument
descent	banishment
dissent	battlement
extent	blandishment
ferment	chastisement
foment	circumvent
frequent	concurrent
indent	competent
intent	complement
invent	compliment

Blended.

'Tis beauty truly *blent*, whose red and white
Nature's own sweet and cunning hand laid on.
Shakspere.

† Obsolete. From *bren* to burn. Used by *Spenser*
‡ Obsolete. From *hend* to lay hold of. Used by *Shakspere.*
§ Obsolete. From *shend*, to blame, injure.

I am *shent* for speaking to you.—*Shakspere.*

That knight should knighthood ever so have *shent.—Spenser.*

‖ Obsolete. Intent, attentive.

Season your admiration for a while
With an *attent* ear.
Shakspere.

Spenser uses the word as a noun.

condiment	nourishment	arbitrament	indifferent
confident	nutriment	armipotent	incandescent
continent	occident	astonishment	incompetent
corpulent	opulent	belligerent	incontinent
detriment	ornament	bellipotent	intelligent
different	parliament	benevolent	irreverent
diligent	penitent	disparagement	lineament
discontent	permanent	embellishment	magnificent
document	pertinent	establishment	malevolent
element	precedent	equivalent	mendicament
eloquent	president	experiment	omnipotent
eminent	prevalent	impenitent	temperament
evident	provident	imprisonment	*paint*
excellent	punishment	improvident	*pant*
excrement	ravishment		
exigent	redolent		
facculent	regiment	ENTS (*see* ENCE)	
firmanent	represent		
flatulent	resident	EP	
fraudulent	reticent		
fundament	reverent	nep	demirep
government	rudiment	rep	*reap*
imminent	sacrament	step	*rape*
impertinent	sediment	skep	
implement	sentiment		
impotent	settlement	EPT	
impudent	subsequent		
incident	succulent	crept	adept
indictment	supplement	kept	except
indigent	tenement	sept	intercept
indolent	testament	slept	*reap'd*
innocent	tournament	wept	*peep'd*
insolent	turbulent	accept	
instrument	underwent		
languishment	vehement	ER,* ERR *compare* OR, UR	
ligament	violent		
malcontent	virulent	blur	fir
management	accomplishment	burr	fur
monument	acknowledgment	cur	her
negligent	admonishment	err	myrrh

* The vulgar thus by imitation *err*,
  As oft the learn'd by being *singular*.
Pope.

   It was no reason then for *her*
To wanton with the sun, her lusty *paramour*.
Milton.

purr
sir
slur
spur
stir
whirr
aver
barber
blister
brother
cadger
caper
cipher
cloister
clover
codger
coster
cruiser
dapper
daughter
dempster
deter
differ
douceur
foster
ginger
heifer
hunger
inter
lawyer
leather
ledger
leper
lobster
lover
lubber
martyr
master
miller
miser
mitre
murmur
nadir
ogre
oyster
pauper

pepper
pilfer
prefer
plunger
rambler
robber
rooster
rover
scatter
simper
singer
sinner
sister
skipper
sloper
smatter
smuggler
soldier
sombre
spinster
stammer
steamer
stopper
stutter
summer
temper
toper
trapper
transfer
trooper
whisper
arbiter
armiger
barrister
bespatter
canister
character
chorister
conjurer
cottager
cucumber
cylinder
dowager
flatterer
forager
foreigner

forerunner
gardener
grasshopper
harbinger
islander
lavender
lawgiver
loiterer
lucifer
mariner
massacre
messenger
minister
murderer
officer
passenger
pillager
presbyter
prisoner
provender
register
reveller
sepulchre
slanderer
sophister

sorcerer
terrier
theatre
thunderer
traveller
usurer
villager
victualler
voyager
waggoner
wanderer
administer
adulterer
artificer
astronomer
astrologer
filibuster
idolater
interpreter
philosopher
amphitheatre
precentor
sugar
fear

Also the comparative of adjectives, and nouns formed from verbs in *y* as higher, buyer.

ERCE (*see* ERSE)

ERCH

church
lurch
perch
search

smirch
research
preach
parch

ERD

bird
heard
herd
sherd

bard
fear'd
weird

Also the preterites of verbs in *er, ur ;* as err'd, purr'd.

ERF

scurf	turf
serf	*half*
surf	

ERGE

dirge	urge
gurge*	verge
merge	diverge
purge	emerge
scourge	immerge
serge	*barge*
surge	*forge*

ERM

firm	affirm
term	confirm
worm	*harm*

ERN †

burn	learn
churn	quern
dern	spurn
earn	stern
fern	tern
hern	turn
kerne	urn

yearn	sojourn
adjourn	overturn
concern	*yarn*
discern	*mourn*
return	*born*

ERSE ‡

curse	commerce
hearse	disperse
nurse	immerse
purse	perverse
terse	rehearse
verse	reverse
worse	traverse
accurse	intersperse
adverse	reimburse
amerce	universe
asperse	*fierce*
averse	*farce*
coerce	*course*
converse	

ERT

blurt	pert
curt	shirt
dirt	skirt
flirt	spurt
hurt	squirt

---

* A whirlpool, abyss.
    A black bituminous *gurge.—Milton.*

† ———Ye twinkling sentries bright,
        My Matthew *mourn ;*
For through your orbs he's ta'en his flight
        Never to *return.*

                                                                        Burns.

                    In its palaces
Sits lust alone, while o'er the land is *borne*
Her voice, whose awful sweetness doth repress
All evil, and her foes relenting *turn*
And cast the voice of love in hope's abandoned *urn.*
                                                                Shelley.

‡ Married to immortal *verse*
    Such as the melting soul may *pierce.*
                                                                Milton.

vert	divert
wert	exert
wort	expert
advert	inert
assert	insert
avert	invert
concert	pervert
convert	subvert
culvert	controvert
desert	*part*
dessert	*port*

ERTH (see EARTH)

ERVE

curve	disserve
nerve	observe
serve	preserve
swerve	reserve
conserve	subserve
deserve	*carve*

ES, ESS

bless	actress
cess	address
chess	artless
cress	assess
dress	caress
guess	compress
less	confess
mess	congress
press	countess
stress	countless
tress	depress
yes	digress
abbess	distress
abscess	duchess
access	

duress	repress
express	sadness
excess	seamstress
fortress	sickness
fruitless	spotless
gladness	success
guileless	tigress
guiltless	transgress
hopeless	acquiesce
impress	adultress
largess	bashfulness
madness	coalesce
oppress	effervesce
possess	pennyless
princess	foolhardiness
profess	*pass*
recess	*place*
redress	

And numerous compounds in *less* and *ness*.

ESE (see EESE)

ESH

flesh	thresh
fresh	afresh
mesh	refresh
nesh*	*mash*

ESK

desk	arabesque
burlesque	picturesque
grotesque	*ask*
moresque	*risk*

EST †

best	chest
breast	crest

* Provincialism : soft, tender, delicate, easily hurt.

†   Rosy is the *west*,
     Rosy is the south,
    Roses are her *cheeks*,
     And a rose her mouth.—*Tennyson.*

guest	divest	regret	coronet
jest	infest	rosette	epaulette
lest	inquest	roulette	epithet
nest	invest	sestet	etiquette
pest	molest	serviette	floweret
quest	obtest	signet	marionette
rest	protest	streamlet	martinet
test	request	target	mignonette
vest	suggest	ticket	minaret
west	unrest	toilet	minuet
abreast	interest	triplet	minuet
arrest	manifest	upset	novelette
attest	overdrest	vignette	omelette
bequest	palimpsest	al habet	parapet
contest	*past*	amulet	parroquet
detest	*paste*	anchoret	pirouette
digest	*beast*	basinet	rivulet
		bayonet	violet
		castinet	wagonette
		cigarette	*bate*
			beat

Also the preterites of verbs in *ess;* as express'd.

ET, ETTE

bet	cadet
debt	carpet
fret	coquet
get	coquette
jet	corset
let	couplet
met	cricket
net	cygnet
set	diet
sweat	dulcet
threat	fidget
wet	forget
whet	gazette
yet	hamlet
abet	leaflet
banquet	magnet
basket	pamphlet
beget	picket
beset	piquette
blanket	quiet
bracelet	quartet
brunette	quintet

ETCH

fetch	wretch
sketch	*patch*
stretch	*peach*

ETH (*see* EATH)

ETE (*see* EAT)

EVE (*see* EAVE)

EUD (*see* UDE)

EUM (*see* UME)

EW * *compare* OO

cue	few
dew	hew
due	hue

* As a virtue golden through and *through,*
And prove its worth at a moment's *view.*
                    R. Browning.

Jew	mildew
knew	nephew
mew	perdue
new	purlieu
pew	pursue
sue	renew
view	review
yew	statue
adieu	subdue
anew	avenue
askew	impromptu
bedew	interview
bellevue	parvenu
curfew	residue
emew	retinue
endue	revenue
ensue	*flew*
eschew	*coo*
imbue	

EX

sex	perplex
vex	reflex
annex	vortex
apex	circumflex
codex	*wax*
complex	*takes*
convex	*likes*
index	

Also the plurals of nouns and the preterites of verbs in *eck;* as decks, recks.

EY (*see* AY)

I (*see* Y *first list*)

IB

bib	nib
crib	rib
drib *	squib
glib	*bribe*

IBE

bribe	inscribe
kibe †	prescribe
scribe	proscribe
tribe	subscribe
ascribe	transcribe
describe	diatribe
imbibe	superscribe

IC (*see* ICK)

ICE ‡ *compare* ISE

dice	spice
ice	splice
mice	rice
nice	thrice
price	trice §
slice	

* Cognate with *dribble, drip, drop.*

    With daily lies she *dribs* thee into cost.—*Dryden.*

    Rhymes retailed in *dribs.*—*Swift.*

† A chap, chilblain.

    If a man's brains were in his heels, were't not in danger of *kibes*
                                Shakspere.

‡   The critics of less judgment than *caprice*,
      Curious, not knowing, not exact, but *nice.*—*Pope.*

      A wretched fall :—uplift thy charmed voice,
      Pour on those evil men the love that *lies,* &c.—*Shelley.*

      Ye to yourselves *suffice*
      Without its *flatteries.*—*E. B. Browning.*

§ A small portion, an instant, a trifle.

      In this *trice* of time.—*Shakspere.*

      He could raise scruples dark and nice
      And after solve them in a *trice.*—*Butler.*

vice
advice
concise
device
entice
precise
suffice
paradise

sacrifice
jaundice
edifice
kiss
demise
size
fleece

ICH (*see* ITCH)

ICK

brick
chick
kick
lick
nick
pick
quick
sick
stick
thick
tick
trick
attic
arctic
antic
caustic
chronic
colic
comic
critic
cynic
drastic
hectic
physic
picnic
plastic
rustic
acrostic
agnostic
aquatic
artistic
bucolic

catholic
choleric
didactic
dogmatic
domestic
dramatic
electric
emetic
emphatic
erratic
euphonic
exotic
forensic
heretic
iambic
fantastic
lunatic
lymphatic
magnetic
majestic
mechanic
mimetic
memphitic
narcotic
nomadic
pacific
pathetic
phlegmatic
plethoric
poetic
politic
prophetic

prognostic
quixotic
realistic
rhetoric
romantic
schismatic
splenetic
antiseptic
antagonistic
arithmetic
beatific
cabalistic

dyspeptic
eccentric
epidemic
hieroglyphic
idiomatic
morganatic
paleocrystic
panegyric
peripatetic
prognostic
like
leak

ICT

strict
addict
afflict
convict
conflict

inflict
relict
contradict
lik'd
leak'd

Also the preterites of verbs in *ick ;* as kick'd.

ID

bid
chid
grid
hid
kid
lid
quid
rid
slid
squid
acid
amid
arid
bestrid
eyelid
florid

fœtid
forbid
frigid
hybrid
morbid
orchid
placid
rabid
solid
sordid
torpid
turgid
bide
bead
free'd

Also the preterites of verbs in *ry ;* as married, buried.

IDE

bide	beside
bride	bestride
chide	collide
glide	confide
gride *	decide
guide	deride
hide	divide
nide †	misguide
pied ‡	preside
pride	provide
ride	reside
side	subside
slide	parricide
stride	regicide
tide	subdivide
wide	suicide
abide	infanticide
aside	*bead*
astride	*bid*
betide	

Also the preterites of verbs in *ie, y;* as died, defied, and sigh'd.

IDES

Ides	*beads*
besides	*bids*

Also the plurals of nouns and the preterites of verbs in *ide;* as tides, rides.

IDGE *compare* AGE

bridge	steerage
fidge	privilege
midge	sacrilege
ridge	*age*
abridge	*edge*
college	

IDST

didst	*rid'st*
midst	*read'st*
amidst	

Also the second person singular of verbs in *id;* as bidd'st.

IE (*see* Y)

IEF

beef	thief
brief	belief
chief	relief
fief	*deaf*
grief	*clef*
lief	*chef*
sheaf	*leaf*
reef	*cliff*

IEGE

liege	assiege
siege	besiege

IELD

field	afield
shield	*heal'd*
weald	*weald*
wield	*gild*
yield	

Also the preterites of verbs in *eel;* as wheel'd.

IEN (*see* EAN)

IEND (*see* END)

---

* Obsolete. To smite, pierce.

    Through his thigh the mortal steel did *gride.—Spenser.*

† Nest, or brood. A *nide* of pheasants.—*Johnson.*

‡ Of different colours, variegated.

    Meadows trim, with daisies *pied.—Milton.*

IERCE (*see* SREE)

IES (*see* IS, ISE)

IEST (*see* EAST)

IEVE (*see* EAVE)

IF, IFF

cliff	caliph
skiff	dandriff
sniff	midwife
stiff	plaintiff
tiff	sheriff
whiff	hieroglyph
caitiff	*fife*

IFE *

fife	strife
knife	wife
life	*cliff*
rife	*leaf*

IFT

drift	rift
gift	shift
lift	shrift †

sift	adrift
thrift	snowdrift
tiff'd	spendthrift
whiff't	

IG

big	snig
dig	sprig
fig	swig
gig	twig
grig	whig
jig	wig
pig	whirligig
prig	*league*
rig	*fatigue*

IGE

oblige	*siege*
(no rhyme)	

IGH (*see* Y, *first list*)

IGHT (*see* ITE)

IGN (*see* INE)

IGUE (*see* EAGUE)

IKE ‡

dike	like
glike	pike

---

* The memories of an ante-natal *life*
  Made this, where now he dwelt, a penal hell ;
  And others said that such mysterious *grief*, &c.
                    Shelley.

† Confession ; from *shrive.* Compare *Shrove* Tuesday.

‡ If straight thy track, or if *oblique.*
  Thou knowest not. Shadows thou dost *strike.*
  Embracing cloud, Ixion-*like.*
                    Tennyson.

shrike	dislike
spike	*leak*
strike	*antique*
alike	*lick*

ILD

child	*gild*
mild	*build*
wild	*fill'd*

Also the preterites of verbs in *ile;* as smil'd, revil'd.

ILE

Words terminating in *ile* with the accent on the penultimate have the final *i* short generally; as *hostile* (*hostīl*,. The following are exceptions : *edile, exile, gentile, pensile, profile.* When the accent is on the antepenultimate the same rule generally holds good ; as in *juvenile, puerile :* exceptions—*camomile, reconcile.* Both sounds, however, form passable rhymes. In reading poetry, it is advisable to give the long sound to *i* in all such words, except when rhyme demands the short one ; *e.g.* " fertile vales," wīnd for wĭnd.

aisle	tile
bile	vile
chyle	while
file	awhile
guile	beguile
isle	compile
mile	defile
pile	edile
smile	erewhile
stile	exile
style	gentile

pensile	bibliophile
revile	*bill*
crocodile	*boil*
reconcile	

ILL * *compare* ILE

bill	thrill
chill	till
drill	trill
fill	will
frill	distil
gill	fulfil
grill	idyll
hill	instil
ill	missile
kill	pencil
mill	peril
pill	Sibyl
quill	codicil
rill	daffodil
shrill	deshabille
skill	utensil
spill	*file*
still	*feel*
swill	*peal*

Also many words in *ile* accented on the penultimate or antepenulti. mate syllable ; as fertile, juvenile- (See note under ILE.)

ILK

bilk †	silk
milk	

ILT

built	hilt
gilt	jilt
guilt	milt

---

* Thy stone, O Sisyphus, stands *still ;*
  Ixion rests upon his *wheel.*
  Dryden.

† Vulgar, to cheat, deceive.
  But be sure, says he, you don't *bilk* me.—*Addison.*

quilt
spilt

stilt
tilt

ILTH

filth
tilth

spilth *

IM

brim	skim
dim	slim
glim †	trim
grim	whim
him	pilgrim
hymn	pseudonym
limb	synonym
limn	*time*
prim	*team*
rim	

IME

chime	rhyme
climb	slime
clime	time
crime	thyme
grime	sublime
lime	maritime
mime ‡	overtime
prime	*him*

IMES

betimes
sometimes

beams
swims

Also the plurals of nouns, and the third person singular of verbs in *ime* ; as times, rhymes.

IMP

gimp	limp
imp	pimp
jimp	

IMPSE

glimpse   limps

IN § *compare* INE

bin	griffin
chin	margin
din	maudlin
fin	muffin
gin	raisin
grin	ruin
inn	sanguine
kin	satin
lin	tiffin
pin	tocsin
shin	virgin
sin	urchin
skin	welkin
spin	cannakin
thin	javelin
tin	kilderkin
twin	mandolin
whin	manikin
win	origin
akin	palanquin
begin	violin
buskin	*dine*
chagrin	*dean*
codlin	*machine*

* Nearly obsolete. From *spill*, used by *Shakspere* and *Browning*.

† Nautical. A light. " Dowse the glim."

‡ One who mimics, a buffoon, a farce. " Scaliger defines a *mime* to be a poem imitating any action to stir up laughter."—*Milton.*

§ Death forerunneth love, to *win*
Sweetest eyes were ever *seen.*
E. B. *Browning.*

|| And let me the *canakin* clink
A soldier's a man,
A life's but a span,
Why then, let the soldier drink.
Shakspere.

INCE

mince	since
prince	wince
quince	convince
rinse	evince

INCH

clinch	pinch
finch	winch
inch	

INCT

link'd	instinct
tinct	precinct
distinct	succinct
extinct	

IND *

bind	wind
blind	behind
find	remind
grind	unkind
kind	*rescind*
mind	*join'd*
rind	

Also the preterites of verbs in *ine*; as twin'd.

INE *compare* EAN

There is no certain rule as to the letter *i* in the suffix *ine* being long or short, but in either case words so ending form passable rhymes. It is long in *feline, confine, crystalline, turpentine*, &c.; short in *genuine, heroine, jessamine, medicine*, &c.; in such words as *alkaline, uterine*, custom is unsettled.

brine	dine
chine	eyne †

fine	entwine
kine	incline
linee	indign
min	opine
nine	recline
pine	refine
shine	repine
sign	saline
sine	supine
shrine	alkaline
syne	brigantine
thine	columbine
trine	concubine
twine	countermine
vine	crystalline
whine	incarnadine
wine	interline
assign	leonine
combine	porcupine
condign	superfine
confine	turpentine
consign	undermine
decline	*tin*
define	*genuine*
design	*heroine*
divine	*adamantine*
enshrine	*loin*

ING

bring	string
cling	swing
ging	thing
fling	wing
king	wring
ring	darling
sing	foundling
sling	starling
spring	sterling
sting	stripling

---

* Best seemed the thing he was, and *joined*—
And native growth of noble *mind*.
　　　　　　　　　Tennyson.

† This archaic plural of *eye* is formed regularly by the old suffix *en*; as in *oxen, eyen, eyne*.

suckling   underling
yearling

Also the present participles of verbs, and participial adjectives in *ing ;* as drinking, laughing.

INGE

cringe	tinge
dinge	twinge
fringe	lozenge
hinge	infringe
singe	orange
springe	syringe
swinge	

INK

blink	sink
brink	skink
chink	slink
clink	stink
drink	swink
ink	think
link	wink
pink	zinc
rink	bethink
shrink	forethink

INT

dint	quint
flint	squint
hint	tint
lint	asquint
mint	imprint
print	

INTH

absinthe	hyacinth
plinth	labyrinth

INX

jinks	sphinx
minx	

IP

chip	whip
clip	courtship
dip	cowslip
drip	equip
hip	friendship
lip	gossip
nip	hardship
rip	horsewhip
pip	landslip
scrip	township
ship	tulip
sip	turnip
skip	worship
slip	fellowship
snip	workmanship
strip	*wipe*
tip	*weep*
trip	

IPE

gripe	wipe
pipe	archetype
ripe	prototype
snipe	stereotype
stripe	*tip*
type	*weep*

IPSE

Eclipse—rhymes with the plurals of nouns, and the third person singular of verbs in *ip ;* as nips, clips.

pipes   *wipes*

IQUE (*see* EAK)

IR (*see* ER)

IRCH (*see* URCH)

IRD (*see* URD)

IRE *compare* AR, ER

dire	aspire
fire	attire
gyre	conspire
hire	desire
ire	entire
lyre	expire
mire	inspire
pyre	inquire
quire	require
sire	retire
spire	satire
squire	transpire
tire	umpire
wire	*friar*
acquire	*prior*
admire	*satyr*

IRGE (see ERGE)

IRK

burke	murk
dirk	perk *
firk	quirk †
jerk	smirk
kirk	stirk
lurk	work

IRL (see URL)

IRM

chirm	affirm
firm	confirm
term	infirm
worm	

IRST (see URST)

IRT (see ERT)

IRTH ‡

birth	mirth
dearth	worth
earth	*north*

IS, IZ §

his	whiz
fizz	breeches
phiz	*rise*

Also the plurals of many nouns in *cy, sy ;* as mercies.

* From *perch*, to set up, pert, proud.
>> To be *perked* up in glistering grief.—*Shakespere.*

>> *Pert* as a peacock.—*Spenser.*

† A jerk, twist, quick stroke, quibble, retort.
>> Iv'e felt so many *quirks* of joy and grief.—*Shakspere.*

I may chance have some odd *quirks* and remnants of wit broken on me.
>> *Shakspere.*

>> Like *quirks* of music, broken and uneven.—*Pope*

‡ Or when the deep green-mantled *Earth*
Warm-cherish'd every flow'ret's *birth*,
And joy and music pouring *forth*
>>> In every grove.
>>> *Burns.*

§ Dissolve me into *ecstasies*,
And bring all heaven before mine *eyes*.
>>> *Milton.*

ISS *

bliss	service
hiss	thesis
kiss	analysis
miss	antithesis
spiss	artifice
this	chrysalis
wis	emphasis
abyss	paralysis
amis	prejudice
axis	prolapsis
chalice	synthesis
crisis	verdigris
dais	amanuensis
dismiss	aposiopesis
gratis	diagnosis
jaundice	metamorphosis
lattice	metempsychosis
lettuce	metropolis
notice	necropolis
novice	parenthesis
phthisis	*nice*
remiss	*lease*

ISE † *compare* ICE

guise	advise
prize	assize
rise	chastise
size	comprise
wise	despise

devise	exercise
disguise	idolise
excise	pulverise
premise	realise
revise	improvise
supplies	sacrifise
surmise	signalise
surprise	solemnise
agonise	summarise
authorise	sympathise
canonise	tyrannise
catechise	immortalise
circumcise	systematise
civilise	*ice*
criticise	*hiss*
enterprise	

Also the third person singular of verbs in *y;* as cries, tries.

ISH

cuish ‡	parish
dish	perish
fish	radish
pish	relish
banish	squeamish
cherish	rubbish
finish	astonish
flourish	demolish
nourish	

* When beneath the palace *lattice,*
　　You ride slow as you have done,
　　And you see a face there—*that is*
　　Not the old familiar one.

E. B. Browning.

† If all was good and fair we met,
　　This earth had been the *Paradise*
　　It never looked to human *eyes*
　　Since our first sun arose and set.

Tennyson.

‡ Or *cuisse* : the armour for the thigh.

　　I saw young Harry with his bearer on,
　　His *cuishes* on his thigh, gallantly armed,
　　Rise from the ground like feathered Mercury.

Shakspere.

ISK

brisk	basilisk
disc	obelisk
frisk	odalisque
risk	tamarisk
whisk	

ISM

chrism	nepotism
prism	organism
schism	occultism
abysm	optimism
altruism	pantheism
baptism	pessimism
deism	plagiarism
theism	radicalism
truism	realism
aphorism	socialism
barbarism	solecism
cataclysm	stoicism
criticism	syllogism
egotism	vandalism
euphemism	vulgarism
euphuism	witticism
heroism	anachronism
hypnotism	malthusianism
mesmerism	*chasm*
mysticism	

ISP

crisp	wisp
lisp	

IST

fist	chemist
list	consist
mist	desist
twist	dentist
whist	exist
wrist	insist
assist	linguist
artist	papist

persist	pessimist
resist	pianist
sophist	pugilist
subsist	rhapsodist
alchemist	ritualist
amethyst	satirist
annalist	socialist
analyst	vocalist
bigamist	anatomist
dogmatist	antagonist
eucharist	diplomatist
exorcist	evangelist
herbalist	rationalist
humourist	*ic'd*
oculist	*slic'd*
optimist	*lac'd*
organist	

Also the preterites of verbs in *iss* ; as hiss'd.

IT

bit	commit
cit	emit
chit	forfeit
fit	hermit
flit	minute
grit	omit
hit	outwit
knit	orbit
pit	permit
quit	pewit
sit	rabbit
split	refit
twit	remit
whit	submit
wit	transmit
writ	benefit
acquit	jesuit
admit	perquisite
biscuit	*beat*
bowsprit	*bite*

ITCH

bitch	fitch
ditch	flitch

hitch	which
itch	witch
niche	bewitch
stitch	enrich
switch	*etch*
pitch	*hatch*
rich	*botch*
twitch	

ITE *

In the suffix *ite* the *i* is long in the great majority of words, as it is in all proper adjectives, like *Puseyite.* In the following it is short: respite, granite, favourite, infinite, hypocrite, apposite, requisite, &c.

bite	slight
blight	smite
bright	spite
cite	sprite
dight †	tight
fight	trite
flight	white
fright	wight
height	write
kite	accite
knight	affright
light	alight
mite	aright
night	bedight
pight	benight
plight	contrite
quite	delight
right	despite
rite	excite
sight	foresight

incite	disunite
indict	appetite
indite	cœnobite
invite	dynamite
midnight	expedite
moonlight	oversight
polite	parasite
recite	proselyte
requite	reunite
twilight	satellite
unite	stalactite
upright	sybarite
zoophyte	archimandrite
aconite	*wit*
acolyte	*favourite*
anchorite	*eight*

ITH ‡

frith	sith
kith	smith
pith	zenith
	with

(this word has no perfect rhyme)

ITHE

blithe	tithe
hithe	writhe
lithe	*with*
scythe	

IVE *(as in dive)*

dive	five
drive	gyve

* Nor lose for that malignant dull *delight,*
   The generous pleasure to be charmed with *wit.*
   Pope.

† Obsolete: to dress, deck.
   Storied windows richly *dight,*
   Casting a dim, religious light.
   Milton.

‡ From the noontide *zenith;*
   Named as fancy *weeneth.*
   E. B. Browning.

hive	connive
rive	contrive
shrive	deprive
strive	derive
thrive	revive
alive	survive
arrive	

IVE * *(as in give)*

give	perspective
live	positive
sieve	punitive
active	purgative
forgive	relative
furtive	sensitive
massive	subjective
motive	talkative
native	affirmative
outlive	contemplative
passive	demonstrative
pensive	diminutive
restive	distributive
suasive	imaginative
votive	inquisitive
fugitive	prerogative
laxative	submissive
narrative	restorative
objective	

IX

fix	onyx
six	prefix
mix	statics
nix	transfix
affix	crucifix
matrix	intermix

mechanics	mathematics
hydrostatics	rheumatics

Also the plurals of nouns in *icks ;* as bricks.

IZE *(see* ISE)

O

ago	photo
beau	plateau
dough	polo
foe	quarto
fro	rondeau
go	solo
hoe	stingo
lo	zero
mo	apropos
no	calico
oh	cameo
roe	comme il faut
sloe	domino
though	de novo
throe	embryo
woe	falsetto
ago	fandango
banjo	folio
bureau	indigo
chapeau	in petto
chateau	libretto
cocoa	mistletoe
dado	mulatto
depot	octavo
echo	piano
grotto	portmanteau
gusto	sirocco
negro	soprano

---

* We lived a day as we were wont to *live,*
  But Nature had a robe of glory on,
  And the bright air o'er every shape did *weave*
      Intenser hues.
                Shelley.

  Wasps in a bottle, frogs in a *sieve,*
  Worms in a carcase, fleas in a *sleeve.*
                R. Browning.

stiletto
tobacco
tomato
tornado
torpedo
virago
volcano
adagio
duodecimo

braggadocio
imbroglio
magnifico
innuendo
oratorio
peccadillo
seraglio
generalissimo
quid pro quo

OACH

broach
brooch
coach
loach
poach
abroach
approach

encroach
reproach
porch
notch
much
church

OAD (*see* ODE)

OAF (*see* OFF)

OAK (*see* OKE)

OAL (*see* OLE)

OAM (*see* OME)

OAN (*see* ONE)

OAP (*see* OPE)

OAR (*see* ORE)

OARD (*see* ORD)

OAST (*see* OST)

OAT (*see* OTE)

OATH (*see* OTH)

OB

bob
cob
fob
hob
lob
knob
mob
nob
rob

sob
squab
swab
throb
cabob
hobnob
nabob
orb
globe

OBE

globe
lobe
probe
robe

conglobe
rob
rub

OCE (*see* OSE)

OCK

block
brock
cock
clock
crock
dock
flock
frock
hough
knock
lock
lough
mock
shock
sock

stock
toque
rock
bannock
bullock
havoc
haycock
hillock
padlock
peacock
pibroch
shamrock
oak
look
buck

OCT

| decoct | *cook'd* |
| concoct | *yok'd* |

Also the preterites of verbs in *ock;* as shock'd.

OD *

cod	rod
clod	shod
God	sod
hod	tod
nod	trod
odd	wad
plod	*ode*
pod	*ow'd*
quad	*blood*
quod	

ODE †

bode	commode
code	corrode
goad	explode
load	forebode
mode	à-la-mode
node	episode
ode	incommode
road	*ow'd*
rode	*hood*
toad	*hod*
woad	*fraud*
abode	

ODGE

| bodge | lodge |
| dodge | podge |

OFF

cough	trough
doff	*loaf*
off	*roof*
scoff	*rough*

OFT

croft	soft
cough'd	scoff'd
oft	aloft

OG, OGUE

bog	shog
clog	agog
cog	prologue
dog	catalogue
grog‡	demagogue
hog	dialogue
fog	epilogue
frog	pedagogue
jog	synagogue
log	*rogue*
prog	*prorogue*

* " An honest man's the nobl'st work of *God* ";
And certes in fair virtue's heavenly *road*
   The cottage leaves the palace far behind :
What is a lordling's pomp ? a cumbrous *load*.

Burns.

Eight times emerging from the *flood*,
She mew'd to every watery *God*.

Cowper.

† In vain the barns expect their promis'd *load*,
Nor barns at home, nor ricks are heaped *abroad*.

Dryden.

‡ " Old Grog " was a nickname for Admiral Vernon of the seventeenth century, on account of remarkable *gogram* overalls he wore in bad weather. It was then applied to a mixture of hot spirits, which he was the first to introduce.

OICE * compare OISE

choice	*vice*
voice	*wise*
rejoice	*toys*

OID

void	amyloid
avoid	cycloid
devoid	spheroid
asteroid	*bide*
alkaloid	

Also the preterites of verbs in *oy*; as buoy'd.

OIL †

boil	dsepoil
coil	embroil
foil	recoil
moil	turmoil
oil	*mile*
soil	*cole*
spoil	*while*
toil	

OIN

coin	proin
foin	quoin
groin	adjoin
join	disjoin
loin	enjo

purloin	*fine*
rejoin	*thine*
subjoin	*sign*
sirloin	

OINT

joint	aroynt ‡
oint	disjoint
point	counterpoint
anoint	disappoint
appoint	*pint*

OISE § compare OICE

noise	*wise*
poise	*sighs*
counterpoise	*tries*
equipoise	*voice*

Also the plurals of nouns, and the preterite of verbs in *oy*; as toys, employs.

OIST

foist	rejoic'd
hoist	*splic'd*
moist	

OIT

coit	adroit
doit ‖	exploit
quoit	dacoit

* And sits among his *boys*;
  He hears the parson pray and preach;
  He hears his daughter's *voice.—Longfellow.*

† Some soothe the lab'rer's weary *toil*
  For humble gains,
  And make his cottage scenes *beguile*
  His cares and pains.—*Burns.*

‡ Plague on you! Begone!
  Aroynt thee, witch, *aroynt* thee!—*Shakspere.*

§ When ripen'd fields and azure *skies*,
  Call'd forth the reaper's rustling *noise.—Burns.*

‖ Through the French *doigt*, finger. "As much brass as can be covered with the tip of the finger"; a small Dutch and Scotch coin; any small piece.
When they will not give a *doit* to relieve a lame beggar, they will lay out ten to see a dead Indian.—*Shakspere.*
He slept, poor dog! and lost it (purse of gold) to a *doit.—Pope.*

OKE *

broke	yoke
cloak	yolk
croak	awoke
folk	bespoke
joke	invoke
oak	revoke
poke	artichoke
smoke	*rook*
soak	*work*
spoke	*walk*
stroke	

OL

doll	alcohol
loll	capitol
poll	*droll*
carol	*hole*
extol	*all*
	awl

OLD

bold	behold
cold	cuckold
fold	enfold
gold	foretold
hold	freehold
mould	unfold
old	uphold
scold	withhold
sold	manifold
told	marigold
wold	*pull'd*

Also the preterites of verbs in *oll, ole, owl*; as roll'd, bowl'd.

OLE † *compare* OWL

bole	whole
coal	cajole
dole	condole
droll	console
foal	creole
goal	parole
hole	pistole
jole	aureole
mole	girandole
pole	girasole
role	*bowl*
shoal	*owl*
sole	*full*
stole	*fool*

OLN

stol'n	swol'n

OLT

bolt	moult
colt	thunderbolt
dolt	*fault*
holt	*malt*

OLVE

solve	dissolve
absolve	involve
convolve	resolve
devolve	revolve

OM *see* UM

* So strong they *struck*,
There seemed less force required to fell an *oak*.
Dryden.

† The lightnings flash from pole to *pole*,
Near and more near the thunders *roll*.
Bruce.

This foot once planted on the *goal*,
This glory-garland round my *soul*.
R. Browning.

AA

OMB *see* OOM

OME *compare* OOM

dome	tome
foam	*hum*
home	*come*
loam	*dumb*
mome	*tomb*
roam	

OMP

pomp	swamp
romp	

ON • *compare* UN

con	pardon
don	parson
gone	poison
swan	prison
anon	reason
arson	season
bonbon	squadron
canon	tendon
cannon	amazon
colon	battalion
felon	cinnamon
iron	clarion
lemon	dies non
jargon	environ
mammon	halcyon

horizon	criterion
lexicon	diapason
million	phenomenon
myrmidon	sine qua non
orison	*run*
pro et con	*won*
simpleton	*own*
automaton	

ONCE (*see* UNCE)

OND

bond	despond
conn'd	second
donn'd	correspond
fond	diamond
pond	vagabond
abscond	*stunn'd*
almond	*moan'd*
beyond	

ONE† *compare* OWN

bone	moan
cone	prone
drone	stone
groan	tone
hone	throne
loan	zone
lone	alone

°
See ! the lightnings *yawn*
Deluging heaven with fire, and the lash'd deeps
Glitter and boil beneath : it rages *on*,
One mighty stream, whirlwind and waves *upthrown*.
Shelley.

Like whirlpools of fire-flowing *iron*,
With splendour and terror the black ship *environ*
Shelley

That low man goes on adding one to *one* ;
That high man aiming at a *million.*
R. Browning.

†
I heard, *alone,*
The pity and the love of *every tone* :
But to the snake those accents sweet were *known—*
—— but winding *on.*
Shelley.

atone	undertone
dethrone	*own*
enthrone	*dawn*
postpone	*moon*
monotone	*dun*
telephone	

ONG *

long	among
prong	belong
song	ding-dong
strong	prolong
thong	bon-vivant
throng	*hung*
wrong	*tongue*
along	

ONK (*see* UNK)

ONSE (*see* UNCE)

ONT *compare* UNT

ont	*don't*
want	*wont*
front	

OO *compare* EW

blew	crew
blue	drew
brew	glue
chew	grew
clue	coup
coo	fou
loo	canoe

rue	cuckoo
screw	debut
shrew	imbrue
slew	shampoo
threw	taboo
through	tattoo
too	undo
true	withdrew
two	yahoo
who	billet-doux
woo	entre nous
you	cockatoo
accrue	kangaroo
ado	*knew*
bamboo	*hue*
bas-blue	*go*
canoe	

OOD † *compare* UD, UDE

brood	woo'd
brew'd	*feud*
coo'd	*attitude*
food	*good*
mood	*cud*
rude	

OOF

hoof	behoof
oof ‡	disproof
proof	reproof
roof	*ruff*
woof	*enough*
aloof	*off*

* When youthful love, warm-blushing, *strong*,
Keen-shiv'ring shot thy nerves *along*,
Those accents grateful to thy *tongue*, &c.
Burns.

† When mankind doth strive
With its oppressors in a strife of *blood*,
Or when free thoughts, like lightnings, are alive ;
And in each bosom of the *multitude*
Justice and truth, with Custom's hydra *brood*,
Wuge silent war.
Shelley.

‡ Slang ; coin, " the needful."

OOK *compare* UCK *

book	shook
brook	took
cook	betook
crook	forsook
fluke	mistook
hook	undertook
look	*buck*
rook	*broke*

OOL *compare* ULE

buhl	tool
cool	befool
fool	cesspool
pool	*pule*
rule	*pull*
school	*pole*
spool	*role*
stool	

OOM *compare* UME †

bloom	tomb
doom	whom
gloom	womb
groom	entomb
loom	*spume*
plume	*home*
rheum	*comb*
room	*thumb*
spoom	

OON *compare* UNE

boon	noon
croon	prune
moon	shoon ‡

soon	poltroon
spoon	pontoon
swoon	quadroon
balloon	shalloon
basoon	simoon
buffoon	typhoon
cartoon	honeymoon
cocoon	octoroon
dragoon	pantaloon
festoon	*tune*
lagoon	*hewn*
lampoon	*dun*
monsoon	*moan*

OOP

coop	stoop
droop	stoup
group	troop
hoop	whoop
loop	nincompoop
poop	*dupe*
scoop	*hope*
sloop	*hop*
soup	

OOR *compare* ORE, URE

boor	detour
moor	paramour
poor	*bore*
sure	*door*
tour	*pure*
your	*power*
amour	*tower*
contour	

OOSE (*see* UCE)

---

* The mother cow must wear a low'ring *look*,
Sour-headed, strongly neck'd, to bear the *yoke*.
                    Dryden.

† Alas! regardless of their *doom*,
    The little victims play!
No sense have they of ills to *come*.—*Gray.*

‡ Provincialism. Plural of *shoe*

OOT *compare* UTE

boot	soot *
coot	cheroot
flute	uproot
hoot	*vote*
loot	*coat*
moot	*foot*
root	*got*
shoot	

OOTH †

booth	*youth*
smooth	*truth*
soothe	*uncouth*
tooth	*both*

OOVE (*see* OVE)

OOZE (*see* USE)

OP

chop	prop
crop	shop
drop	slop
flop	strop
fop	sop
hop	stop
mop	swop
pop	top

bishop	develop
collop	envelop
gallop	*cope*
scallop	*cup*
trollop	*coop*

OPE

cope	elope
hope	antelope
grope	envelope
mope	heliotrope
ope	horoscope
pope	interlope
rope	kaleidoscope
soap	microscope
scope	misanthrope
slope	telescope
trope	*hoop*
aslope	*hop*

OR ‡ *compare* ER, ORE

corps	flavour
tor	horror
war	honour
abhor	labour
anchor	mirror
author	motor
doctor	parlour
donor	prior
hector	sailor

---

* This word may rhyme with *boot* or *but*.

† Betray sweet Jenny's unsuspecting *youth* ?
Curse on his perjured arts ! dissembling *smooth.*—*Burns*

And all hearts pray, " God love her ! "
Ay, and certes, in good *sooth,*
We may all be sure He *doth.*"
                    E. B. Browning.

‡ Would I had been some maiden coarse and *poor !*
O me, that I should ever see the light !
Those dragon eyes of anger'd *Eleanor*
Do haunt me day and night.—*Tennyson.*

I will look out to his *future,*
Should he ever be a *suitor.*—*E. B. Browning.*

sculptor	metaphor	floor	adore
stupor	orator	four	afore
suitor	saviour	gore	ashore
tailor	senator	lore	claymore
tenor	warrior	more	deplore
traitor	alligator	oar	encore
tutor	ambassador	o'er	explore
vendor	competitor	ore	forebore
victor	conspirator	pore	foreswore
ancestor	excelsior	pour	implore
auditor	progenitor	roar	restore
bachelor	solicitor	score	albicore
chancellor	*awe*	shore	hellebore
conqueror	*caw*	snore	heretofore
creator	*bore*	soar	sycamore
creditor	*hoar*	sore	troubadour
counsellor	*pour*	store	*poor*
emperor	*err*	swore	*tour*
governor	*sir*	tore	*hour*
		whore	*power*
		wore	*tower*
		yore	

ORCE (*see* ORSE)

ORCH

porch	*march*
scorch	*lurch*
torch	*birch*

ORGE

forge	regorge
gorge	*urge*
disgorge	*dirge*

ORD

board	aboard
cord	accord
ford	afford
hoard	implor'd
horde	record
lord	*word*
roar'd	*bird*
sword	*stirr'd*
abhorr'd	*code*

ORK *compare* ALK

cork	stork
fork	*walk*
ork	*work*
pork	*coke*

ORE *compare* OOR

ORM

form	transform
storm	misinform
conform	multiform
deform	uniform
inform	*arm*
perform	*worm*
reform	

ORE

boar	core
bore	door

ORN compare AWN

born	foresworn
borne	forlorn
corn	lovelorn
horn	suborn
lorn	capricorn
morn	chloroform
scorn	multiform
shorn	overborne
sorn	thunderstorm
sworn	unicorn
thorn	uniform
torn	*bourn*
worn	*mourn*
adorn	*urn*
foreborne	*concern*

ORSE, ORCE

coarse	endorse
corse	remorse
course	unhorse
force	*worse*
horse	*hearse*
morse	*purse*
torse	

ORT compare OUGHT

court	wart
fort	cohort
mort	consort
port	distort
short	exhort
snort	extort
sort	report
tort	resort

retort	*taut* *
ought	hurt
caught	shirt

ORTH

forth	*worth*
fourth	*earth*
north	*mirth*
wrath	

OS (*see* OSS)

OSE, OZE †

chose	expose
close (verb)	foreclose
doze	impose
foes	oppose
froze	propose
goes	repose
glose ‡	suppose
hose	transpose
nose	discompose
pose	interpose
prose	presuppose
rose	recompose
those	*gross*
toes	*dose*
arose	*jocose*
compose	*morose*
depose	*bellicose*
disclose	*choose*
dispose	*lose*
enclose	*glows*

OSS

boss	doss
cross	dross

* Nautical term : tight (Dana).

† Yet all beneath the unrivall'd *rose*
 The lovely daisy sweetly *blows.—Burns.*

‡ To flatter, wheedle, gloss over.
  So *glosed* the tempter.—*Milton.*

loss	albatross
moss	asbestos
across	*close*
bathos	*dose*
chaos	*us*
emboss	

OST *

cost	exhaust
frost	*ghost*
lost	*post*
toss'd	*toast*
accost	*must*
holocaust	*roost*

OT †

blot	not
clot	plot
cot	pot
got	quat
grot	rot
hot	shot
jot	sot
knot	spot
lot	squat

trot	counterplot
yacht	idiot
allot	melilot
ballot	polyglot
bigot	*vote*
boycot	*quote*
complot	*but*
forgot	*ought*
apricot	

OTCH

blotch	notch
botch	watch
crotch	*such*

OTE

bloat	mote
boat	note
coat	quote
dote ‡	rote
float	smote
goat	throat
gloat	tote
groat	vote
lote	wrote
moat	

*   As silent as a *ghost*—
With solemn speed, and stunning music *cross'd.*
Shelley.

I feel it when I sorrow *most* :
  'Tis better to have loved and *lost*,
Than never to have loved at all.
Tennyson.

† For many a beast to dead she *shot*,
  And perish'd mony a bonnie *boat.*
Burns.

And mercy, encouraging *thought !*
Gives even affliction a grace,
And reconciles man to his *lot.*
Cowper.

Still moving after truth long *sought,*
Will learn new things when I am *not.*
Tennyson.

‡ To rave, to drivel, be overfond.
  I never knew a woman, so *dote* upon a man.
Shakspere.

afloat
denote
devote
lifeboat
misquote
promote
remote
anecdote

antidote
asymptote
petticoat
table d'hôte
flout
cot
boot

OUGH

This much abused combination of letters—the terror of foreigners who try to speak our tongue—has no fewer than nine different sounds, as enumerated below.

cough	*as in*	off
chough ⎱		
rough ⎰		
slough ⎬	,,	stuff
sough ⎰		
tough ⎰		
bough ⎱	,,	cow
plough ⎰		
hough ⎱	,,	lock
lough ⎰		
hiccough	,,	cup
slough	,,	slow
through	,,	too
dough ⎱	,,	toe
though ⎰		
ought ⎱	,,	awe
thought ⎰		

OTH

broth
cloth
froth
moth
sloth

troth
wrath
oath
growth
doth

OTHE (*see* OOTH)

clothe
loathe

sooth
smooth

OU (*see* OO *and* OW)

OUGHT *compare* ORT

aught
bough
brought
caught
fought
fraught
naught
nought
ought
sought

taught
thought
wrought
besought
bethought
forethought
methought
knot
yacht
note

OUCH

couch
crouch
ouch
pouch
slouch

vouch
avouch
barouche
coach
such

OUL (*see* OLE, OWL)

OULD (*see* OLD, UD)

OUD

cloud
crowd
loud
proud
shroud
aloud

enshroud
o'ercloud
o'ershroud
flow'd
flood
mud

Also the preterites of some verbs in *ow;* as bow'd.

OUNCE

bounce
flounce

ounce
pounce

denounce   renounce
pronounce

OUND *

bound	around
found	compound
frown'd	confound
ground	expound
hound	profound
mound	propound
pound	rebound
round	resound
sound	surround
wound (to wind)	*wound* (woond)
abound	*moan'd*
aground	

OUNT

count	miscount
fount	remount
mount	surmount
account	*want*
amount	*punt*
discount	*don't*
dismount	

OUP (see OOP)

OUR *compare* OOR, ORE

bower	tower
dower	deflower
cower	devour
flour	*mower*
hour	*pour*
lour	*poor*
power	*pure*
scour	*her*
sour	

OURN (see ORN, URN)

OURS

ours	*ores*
moors	*stirs*
cures	

The plurals of nouns and the third person singular of verbs in *our, ower ;* as hours, towers, devours.

OURSE (see ORSE)

OUS (see US)

OUSE *compare* OWSE

chouse	nous †
dowse	*rouse*
grouse	*spouse*
house	*use*
louse	*noose*
mouse	

OUT ‡

bout	stout
clout	tout
doubt	trout
drought	about
gout	devout
grout	misdoubt
out	redoubt
pout	throughout
rout	without
scout	*boat*
shout	*vote*
snout	*lute*
spout	*boot*
sprout	

---

* Hope that blessed me, bliss that *crowned*,
  Love, that left me with a *wound*,
  Life itself, that turneth *round.—E. B. Browning.*

† The Greek word for *mind, understanding* ; expressively used to imply common sense, tact, *gumption.*

‡ ——His ears alone pricked *out :*—
  Each one pointing to his *throat.—E. B. Browning.*

OUTH *

drouth	*truth*
mouth	*youth*
south	*smooth*
	mouth

(the verb, which has no rhyme)

OVE †

As in LOVE

dove	shove
glove	above
love	

As in PROVE

move	disprove
groove	disapprove
prove	improve
approve	reprove

As in WOVE

clove	strove
drove	throve
grove	wove
hove	alcove
rove	behove
stove	interwove

OW ‡ *compare* OO

As in LOW

blow	trow
bow	below
crow	bestow
flow	billow
glow	callow
grow	fallow
know	foreknow
low	pillow
mow	sallow
owe	shallow
row	swallow
sew	wallow
sow	willow
show	window
slough	winnow
slow	yellow
snow	outgrow
stow	overflow
strow	overthrow
throw	

As in NOW

bough	brow
bow	

---

* The low cares of the *mouth*,
  The trouble *uncouth*.
  R. Browning.

† And such is Nature's law divine, that those
    Who grow together cannot choose but *love*,
  If faith or custom do not interpose,
    Or common slavery mar what else might *move*
  All gentlest thoughts, as in the sacred *grove*, &c.
  Shelley.

‡ That mocks the tear it forced to *flow*
    Amid severest *woe*.
  Gray.

  To paint with Thomson's landscape *glow*,
  Or wake thy bosom-melting *throe*
    With Shenstone's art.
  Burns.

  I know not yet was it a dream or *no*,—
  In hues which, when through memory's waste they *flow*,
  Make their divided streams more bright and rapid *now*.
  Shelley.

  The shadows flicker to and fro,
  The cricket chirps, the light burns *low*.
  Tennyson.

cow	sow
frau	thou
how	vow
now	allow
plough	avow
prow	endow
row	disallow

OWL *compare* OLE

The sounds of *owl* in *bowl* and *howl*, and of *ole* in *hole* are so similar as to be allowed to pass as almost perfect rhymes.

bowl	scowl
cowl	soul
fowl	toll
ghoul	troll
growl	control
howl	enrol
owl	patrol
poll	*hole*
prowl	*dull*
roll	*fool*

OWN * *compare* ONE

The sounds of *own* in *blown* and *frown*, and of *one* in *stone* are so similar as to be allowed to pass as almost perfect rhymes.

blown	shown
brown	strewn
clown	thrown
crown	town
down	adown
drown	embrown
frown	renown
gown	*tone*
mown	*dawn*
noun	*noon*
own	

OWSE

blowze †	trouse
browse	carouse
house (verb)	espouse
rouse	*hose*
spouse	*those*
touse	

* Also the plurals of some nouns, and the 3rd person singular of verbs in *ow*; as, brows, allows.

OX

box	paradox
fox	heterodox
ox	*oaks*
equinox	*sucks*
orthodox	

Also the plurals of nouns, and the 3rd person singular of verbs in *ock*; as, cocks, mocks.

OY

boy	annoy
buoy	convoy
cloy	decoy
coy	destroy
joy	employ
toy	enjoy
alloy	sepoy

OZE (*see* OSE)

U (*see* EW)

Perhaps no one of our vowels is so frequently mispronounced as the *u*, especially in the north of England. The rapid repetition of such a short list of words as *put, but, pulpit, sugar, understood*, will be found to be almost an invariable *shibboleth* for the detection of York-shire and Lancashire men.

---

* When I contemplate all *alone*
To which thy crescent would have *grown.—Tennyson.*

† Cognate with *blush*: a ruddy, fat-faced wench.

Sweet *blowze*, you are a beauteous blossom, sure.—*Shakspere.*

UB

chub	shrub
club	slub
cub	snub
drub	tub
dub	hubbub*
grub	beelzebub
hub	*tube*
rub	*rob*

UBE

cube	jujube
tube	*tub*

UCE

deuce	induce
goose	misuse
juice	obtuse
moose	produce
puce	propose
sluice	recluse
spruce	reduce
truce	seduce
use (noun)	traduce
abuse	introduce
obstruse	*noose*
conduce	*news*
deduce	*dose*
disuse (noun)	*rose*
excuse	

UCH

crutch	touch
much	retouch
hutch	*pitch*
such	

UCK

buck	suck
duck	truck
luck	tuck
muck	*book*
pluck	*duke*
struck	

UCT

suck'd	obstruct
conduct	aqueduct
duck'd	viaduct
deduct	*hook'd*
instruct	*puk'd*

UD †

blood	rud
bud	wood
could	would
cud	brotherhood
flood	likelihood
good	neighbourhood
hood	understood
mud	widowhood
scud	*rood*
should	*rude*
stood	*ode*
stud	

UDE *compare* UD ‡

brood	prude
crude	nude
feud	rood
lewd	rude

* A universal hubbub wild.—*Milton.*

† 'Tis winter cold and *rude*,
Heap, heap the warming *wood.*—*Cowper.*

Enjoying each the other's *good*:
What vaster dream can hit the *mood*
Of love on earth?—*Tennyson.*

‡   Then the *multitude,*
And I among them, went in joy—a nation
Made free by love,—a mighty *brotherhood.*—*Shelley.*

snood	lassitude
allude	latitude
conclude	longitude
delude	magnitude
elude	multitude
exclude	platitude
exude	plenitude
include	promptitude
intrude	servitude
obtrude	solitude
protrude	beatitude
seclude	ingratitude
altitude	inaptitude
aptitude	similitude
attitude	solicitude
fortitude	vicissitude
gratitude	*hood*
habitude	*bud*
interlude	*could*

Also the preterites of some verbs in *ew* ; as view'd.

UDGE

budge	sludge
drudge	smudge
fudge	trudge
grudge	adjudge
judge	prejudge
nudge	

UE (*see* EW, OO)

UFF

bluff	rough
buff	ruff
chough	slough
chuff	snuff
cuff	stuff
gruff	tough
huff	enough
luff	rebuff
muff *	counterbuff
puff	*loaf*

UG

bug †	rug
drug	shrug
dug	slug
hug	smug §
jug	snug
lug ‡	tug
mug	humbug
pug	*rogue*

UICE *see* OOSE

* Humorously defined in its double sense as "a thing that holds a lady's hands without squeezing them."

† This word is of Celtic origin, and signifies a ghost, a hobgoblin, as we still have it in *bugbear.*

Tush, tush, fright boys with *bugs.—Shakspere.*

In Matthew's Bible, published 1539, Psalm xci. is rendered, "Thou shalt not be afraid for any *bugs* by night." In the Authorised Version the word *terror* is substituted. This word was not applied to the troublesome house pest till late in the seventeenth century.

‡ The ear (North dialect), to drag or pull by the ear.

I'm as melancholy as a *lugg'd* bear.—*Shakspere.*

But let me whisper i' your *lug,*
Ye're aiblins nae temptation.
Burns.

§ Smart, spruce, trim.

A *smug* bridegroom.

A beggar that used to come so *smug* upon the mart.—*Shakspere.*

UISE (see ISE, OOZE)

UIT (see UTE)

UKE

duke	rebuke
fluke	*cook*
puke	*hook*
chibouque	

IJL, ULL *

bull	brimful
cull	careful
dull	dreadful
full	faithful
gull	grateful
hull	thoughtful
lull	beautiful
mull	bountiful
null	dutiful
pull	fanciful
skull	merciful
trull	sorrowful
wool	wonderful
annul	worshipful
awful	*tool*
bashful	*rule*

ULE compare OOL

mule	ridicule
pule	vestibule
yule	*fool*
ferule	*rule*
reticule	*full*

ULGE

bulge	indulge
divulge	

ULK

bulk	skulk
hulk	sulk

ULP

gulp	sculp
pulp	

ULSE

pulse	impulse
convulse	insulse †
expulse	repulse

ULT

cult	occult
adult	result
consult	catapult
exult	difficult
indult	*bolt*
insult	*vault*

UM ‡

chum	glum
come	gum
crum	hum
crumb	mum
drum	mumm §
dumb	numb

* Fear most to tax an honourable *fool*,
  Whose right it is uncensured to be *dull.—Pope.*

† Obsolete. Dull, stupid.
  Insulse and frigid affection.—*Milton.*

‡   The *doom*
  Is this, which has, or may, or must *become*
  Thine, and all mankind's. Ye are the spoil
  Which time thus makes for the devouring *tomb.—Shelley.*

§ *Mumm*, to mask, to act or sport in disguise; hence, *mummer, mummery*
  Mum, silent, and silence. "*Mum's* the word."
      The citizens are *mum.—Shakspere.*

plum	millennium
scum	minimum
slum	opium
sum	overcome
swum	pendulum
thrum	quarrelsome
thumb	solatium
become	troublesome
gruesome	auditorium
gypsum	crematorium
handsome	delirium
hansom	gymnasium
humdrum	encomium
laudanum	interregnum
phantom	memorandum
succumb	opprobrium
winsome	palladium
asylum	pandemonium
burdensome	residuum
cumbersome	symposium
frolicsome	*fume*
humoursome	*rheum*
mausoleum	*tomb*
maximum	*hecatomb*

UME *compare* OOM

fume	resume
plume	volume
assume	*doom*
consume	*tomb*
deplume	*comb*
perfume	*come*
presume	

UMP

bump	frump
clump	jump

lump	stump
plump	thump
pump	trump
rump	

UN *compare* ON *

done	tun
dun	won
gun	begun
none	boatswain
nun	coxswain
one	undone
pun	comparison
run	garrison
shun	onion
son	skeleton
spun	union
stun	*don*
sun	*tune*
ton	*tone*

UNCE

unce	*sconce*
once	

UNCH

bunch	munch
crunch	punch
hunch	scrunch
lunch	

UND

fund	refund
shunn d	moribund
stunn'd	*hound*

---

* When thus, not rising from his lofty *throne*,
In state unmov'd, the king of men *begun*.
                    Dryden.

But no power to seek or *shun*,
He is ever drifted *on*.
                    Shelley.

UNE *compare* OON

hewn	importune
tune	*soon*
jejune	*sun*
untune	

UNG

bung	stung
clung	sung
dung	swung
flung	tongue
hung	wrung
rung	young
slung	among
sprung	unsung
strung	*song*

UNGE

lunge	sponge
plunge	expunge

UNK

bunk	shrunk
chunk	skunk
drunk	slunk
funk *	spunk †
hunk	stunk
junk	sunk
monk	trunk
punk	

UNT

blunt	hunt
brunt	runt ‡
front	wont
grunt	

UP

cup	stirrup
dup §	syrup
pup	*soap*
sup	*group*
hiccough	*dupe*

UPT

abrupt	supp'd
corrupt	interrupt

UR (*see* ER)

URB

curb	disturb
herb	suburb
verb	*orb*

URCH (*see* ERCH)

URD

bird	referr'd
curd	*broad*
gird	*cord*
stirr'd	*cur'd*
word	*injur'd*
absurd	

URE

cure	skewer
dure	abjure
ewer	adjure
lure	allure
pure	azure

---

* Stench, to emit a stink. Also, as slang, to turn coward.

† Rotten wood, tinder. Also spirit, mettle, pluck (vulgar).

‡ A small or stunted bullock or other animal. In Scotland, a little old woman.

§ *Dup.* to do up ; as *don.* to do on; *doff,* to do off; to open, used by *Shakspere.*

brochure
conjure
demure
endure
immure
inure
manure
mature
obscure
ordure
procure
secure
calenture
coverture
cynosure *

epicure
forfeiture
immature
miniature
overture
portraiture
sinecure
investiture
temperature
primogeniture
poor
sure
cur
furniture

URF

scurf
serf

surf
turf

URGE (*see* ERGE)

URK (*see* IRK)

URL

churl
curl

earl
furl

girl
hurl
pearl
purl †

twirl
uncurl
unfurl

URLD

world

The preterites of verbs in *url* as, furl'd, hurl'd.

URN (*see* ERN)

URP

chirp
discerp

extirp
usurp

URSE (*see* ERSE)

URST

burst
curst
durst
first
thirst

worst
accurst
vers'd
dispers'd
immers'd

* Literally, a dog's tail. A name of the constellation *Ursa minor*, which contains, in the tail, the *Pole star*, hence a centre of attraction.

As seamen that are run
Far northward find long winters to be light,
And in the *cynosure* adore the sun.
Davenant.

Where perhaps some beauty lies,
The *cynosure* of neighbouring eyes.
Milton.

† Contracted from *purfle*: an embroidered, puckered border; a drink made of hot beer, gin, &c Als to flow, to murmur, to ripple.
A *purling* stream.—*Pope.*

From his lips did fly
Thin winding breath, which *purled* up to the sky,
Shakspere

URT (*see* ERT)

US, OUS

buss	glutinous
hus	gluttonous
thus	hazardous
truss	hideous
us	humorous
bulbous	impetuous
bumptious	incubus
callous	infamous
caucus	lecherous
cautious	libellous
circus	litigious
crocus	luminous
discuss	marvellous
focus	mischievous
gracious	mountainous
grievous	mutinous
heinous	numerous
litmus	odious
mucus	odorous
nervous	ominous
nimbus	omnibus
pious	overplus
porous	perilous
rebus	poisonous
vicious	ponderous
amorous	populous
arquebuse	prosperous
bibulous	pugnacious
blasphemous	ravenous
boisterous	rigorous
clamorous	riotous
credulous	ruinous
curious	scandalous
dangerous	scrupulous
delicious	sedulous
dolorous	serious
emulous	slanderous
fabulous	sonorous
frivolous	stimulus
garrulous	timorous
generous	traitorous
glorious	treacherous

tyrannous	indigenous
valorous	libidinous
venomous	oleaginous
vigorous	magnanimous
villainous	miraculous
adventurous	necessitous
adulteress	obstreperous
ambiguous	odoriferous
calamitous	omnivorous
cadaverous	pachydermatous
calcareous	ridiculous
cantankerous	solicitous
diaphanous	somniferous
fortuitous	thaumaturgus
gratuitous	victorious
harmonious	viviparous
hilarious	vociferous
hocus-pocus	ubiquitous
idolatrous	unanimous
ignis fatuus	ungenerous
impecunious	*use*
impetuous	*loose*
ignoramus	*dose*
incredulous	*house*

USE

booze	diffuse
bruise	disuse (verb)
choose	excuse
lose	infuse
muse	misuse
noose	peruse
ooze	refuse
ruse	suffuse
shoes	transfuse
use (verb)	*dose*
abuse	*does*
accuse	*buzz*
amuse	*foes*

Also the plurals of nouns and the third person singular of verbs in *ew* and *ue ;* as dews, sues

USH

blush	hush
brush	lush
bush	push
crush	rush
flush	thrush
frush	tush
gush	

USK

brusque	musk
lusk	tusk
husk	

UST

bust	discuss'd
crust	disgust
dust	distrust
just	focuss'd
lust	locust
must	intrust
rust	mistrust
thrust	robust
trust	unjust
adjust	

UT

butt	soot	
cut	strut	
glut	abut	
gut	gamut	
hut	catgut	
jut	englut	
nut	rebut	
rut	walnut	
scut	*foot*	
shut	*boot*	
slut	*lute*	
smut		

UTCH

clutch	such
crutch	touch
hutch	retouch
much	

UTE* compare OOT

bruit	refute
brute	repute
cute	salute
flute	absolute
fruit	attribute
lute	constitute
mute	contribute
newt	destitute
suit	dissolute
acute	execute
compute	institute
confute	parachute
depute	persecute
dilute	prosecute
dispute	resolute
impute	substitute
minute	*boot*
pollute	*boat*
recruit	*but*

UX

crux	reflux
dux	*oaks*
flux	*jokes*
lux	*cooks*

Also the plurals of nouns and the third person singular of verbs in *uch*; as trucks, sucks.

She glanced upwardly *mute* :
" My own wife ! " he said. and fell stark at her *foot*.
E. B. *Browning*

Y .

As an end letter **y** has two sounds, the long *ī*, **as in** *mile*, and the short *ĭ*, as in *mill*, the former rhyming perfectly with such words as *die*, *sigh*, the latter allowably with *he*, *see*, &c. Both, however, are used indiscriminately by all our poets; but for convenience' sake, lists of words of the two sounds are given separately.

Y long, as in *eye*.

ay	sigh	defy
buy	sky	deny
cry	sly	descry
die	spy	imply
dry	sty	espy
eye	thigh	outvie
fie	tie	outfly
fry	try	rely
hie	vie	reply
high	why	supply
lie	ally	untie
nigh	apply	amplify
pie	awry	beautify
ply	belie	certify
pry	comply	crucify
rye	decry	deify
		dignify
		edify
		falsify
		fortify
		fructify
		gratify
		glorify
		horrify
		justify
		magnify
		modify
		mollify

mortify
multiply
pacify
petrify
prophesy
purify
putrefy
qualify
ramify
rarefy
ratify
rectify
sanctify
satisfy
scarify
signify
simplify
specify
stupefy
terrify
testify
verify
villify
vivify
indemnify
intensify
lullaby
solidify

Here shall he *see*
No *enemy*,
But winter and rough weather.

Shakspere.

And in thy right hand lead with *thee*,
The mountain nymph, sweet *Liberty*.

Milton.

Suddenly
She would arise, and like the secret bird,
Whom sunset wakens, fill the shore and *sky*
With her sweet accents—a wild *melody !*

Shelley.

Dissolved the *mystery*
Of folded sleep.   The captain of my dreams
Ruled in the eastern *sky*.

Tennyson.

And thou, perchance, art more than *I*,
And yet I spare them sympa*thy*.

Tennyson.

Y short, as *ty* in *duty*

beauty	kindly	ruddy	canopy
bonnie	kingly	rudely	cavalry
brandy	knightly	saintly	charity
busy	lady	saucy	chastity
comely	lastly	scurvy	chemistry
cosy	lonely	singly	chivalry
crazy	lordly	simply	clemency
crusty	lovely	sleepy	colony
curly	manly	snappy	comedy
daily	marry	sorry	company
dainty	meanly	sunny	constancy
dally	merry	steady	cosily
dandy	misty	strophe	contrary
doubly	mouldy	study	courtesy
dreamy	nasty	sweetly	cruelty
duly	neatly	tally	daintily
dusky	nearly	tardy	dairy
duty	nobly	thirsty	decency
empty	noisy	trophy	destiny
filly	orgie	truly	diary
gaily	palmy	trusty	dignity
gaudy	palfrey	twenty	drapery
ghastly	paltry	ugly	drollery
glory	party	vainly	drudgery
gory	parsley	vary	ecstasy
greedy	pastry	wary	elegy
grumpy	petty	weary	embassy
guilty	pigmy	wealthy	enemy
happy	poorly	whisky	energy
haughty	portly	worthy	equity
hearty	posy	academy	eulogy
heavy	pretty	agony	euphony
homely	princely	amity	factory
honey	proudly	anarchy	family
hourly	pulley	apathy	fallacy
humbly	purely	artery	fealty
hungry	queenly	augury	fecundity
hurry	quickly	battery	finery
jaunty	racy	beggary	flattery
jetty	rally	bigamy	foolery
jerky	rarely	bigotry	foolishly
jockey	rosy	blasphemy	gaiety
jury	rocky	botany	gallantry
justly	roughly	bravery	gallery
lily	ruby	bribery	galaxy
		brevity	granary
		calumny	gravity

haughtily	poesy	victory	democracy
history	poetry	villainy	discovery
honesty	policy	votary	dishonesty
idolatry	potency	watery	dexterity
industry	poverty	wearily	disparity
injury	primary	wantonly	diversity
infamy	privacy	womanly	divinity
infancy	prodigy	worthily	dormitory
infantry	progeny	absurdity	doxology
jollity	prosody	activity	duplicity
knavery	purity	adversity	electricity
laity	quality	affability	emergency
laxity	quantity	affinity	enormity
legacy	raillery	agility	equanimity
leprosy	rectory	alacrity	eternity
lethargy	regency	allegory	etymology
levity	remedy	ambiguity	extempore
liberty	ribaldry	anatomy	extraordinary
library	rivalry	animosity	extremity
livery	robbery	antiquity	familiarity
lottery	royalty	anxiety	fatality
loyalty	salary	apostasy	fecundity
lunacy	sanctity	apostrophe	felicity
majesty	secrecy	aristocracy	ferocity
malady	simony	astronomy	fertility
melody	slavery	austerity	fidelity
memory	sorcery	authority	freemasonry
misery	strawberry	auxiliary	frivolity
modesty	subsidy	aviary	frugality
monarchy	surgery	brevity	futurity
mummery	symmetry	calamity	generosity
mutiny	sympathy	capacity	geography
mystery	symphony	captivity	geometry
nicety	tapestry	catastrophe	genealogy
noisily	tragedy	complexity	gravity
novelty	treachery	concavity	gratuity
nunnery	treasury	confederacy	hostility
nursery	trinity	conformity	hospitality
penalty	trumpery	congruity	humanity
penury	tyranny	conspiracy	humility
perfidy	urgency	cosmography	hypocrisy
perjury	unity	credulity	idiosyncrasy
piety	usury	curiosity	imaginary
pillory	vacancy	customary	immensity
piracy	vanity	declivity	immorality
pleurisy	verily	deformity	immortality

immaturity
immutability
impartiality
impecuniosity
impetuosity
impiety
impossibility
importunity
impurity
inability
inaccuracy
incapacity
incivility
inclemency
incongruity
inconsistency
inconstancy
indemnity
inequality
infidelity
infinity
infirmary
inflexibility
insanity
instability
integrity
intensity
liberality
loquacity
luminosity

magnanimity
malignity
maturity
mediocrity
mendacity
minatory
minority
monastery
mortality
municipality
mutability
nationality
namby-pamby *
nativity
necessary
necromancy
neutrality
nobility
nonconformity
obesity
obscurity
opportunity
partiality
perfunctory
perpetuity
perplexity
philosophy
polyandry
polygamy
pomposity

preliminary
priority
probability
prodigality
profanity
profundity
propensity
prosperity
radically
rapidly
rascality
reality
reciprocity
rotundity
rudimentary
satiety
security
seniority
sensibility
sensuality
severity
simplicity
sincerity
sobriety
society
solemnity
solidity
soliloquy
sovereignty
sublimity

supremacy
stupidity
shilly-shally
tautology
tenacity
temerity
temporary
theology
theosophy
timidity
tranquillity
transparency
trigonometry
unanimity
ubiquity
uncertainty
uniformity
university
unparliamentary
vacuity
validity
variety
veracity
verbosity
vicinity
virginity
visibility
vivacity
volubility

* Affected, finical.

Another of Addison's favourite companions was Ambrose Phillips, a good Whig and a middling poet, who had the honour of bringing into fashion a species of composition which has been called, after his name, *namby-pamby.—Macaulay.*

STIRLING